Aspects of Schenkerian Theory

ASPECTS
OF
SCHENKERIAN THEORY

Edited
by
David Beach

New Haven and London
YALE UNIVERSITY PRESS

Published with assistance from the Eastman School of Music, University of Rochester.

Designed by Stephen Reynolds
and set in Baskerville type. Printed in the United States of America by
The Alpine Press, Stoughton, Massachusetts.

Library of Congress Cataloging in Publication Data
Main entry under title:

Aspects of Schenkerian theory.

Contents: Schenker's theories, a pedagogical view /
David Beach — Thematic content, a Schenkerian view /
John Rothgeb — Motive and text in four Schubert songs /
Carl Schachter — [etc.]
1. Schenkerian analysis. I. Beach, David, 1938–
MT6.A766 1983 781 82–13498
ISBN 0–300–02800–8
ISBN 0–300–02803–2 (pbk.)

10 9 8 7 6 5 4 3 2

Contents

Preface

Aspects of Schenkerian Theory is a collection of ten essays, each of which deals in some way with a specific area of Schenkerian research. Some of the contributions focus on aspects of Schenker's own work, while others are concerned with extensions of his ideas beyond the boundaries of traditional tonality. Those that are primarily explanatory in nature are complemented by others that are mostly analytical. And those that extend existing areas of investigation are balanced by those that open up new areas or explore topics that are all but ignored in the existing literature. All of these—the traditional and the innovative alike—are valuable contributions to the growing field of Schenkerian studies.

This work is intended for all those interested in Schenkerian theory, though quite obviously it would be most appropriate for those with some background in Schenkerian analysis. It is my firm conviction—and I think my colleagues would agree—that the only way to understand Schenker's theories is through directed studies in harmony, counterpoint, and analysis, and that such studies should precede the reading of articles such as those printed here. Thus this collection of essays is most appropriate for upperclassmen, graduate students, and beyond, possibly as the basis for a reading course or research seminar. Those who dig a little beyond the surface will soon realize that each of the essays is the door to an almost limitless area of musical research and understanding.

One area that has not been addressed in the existing literature is the teaching of Schenkerian theory. This topic is more appropriate than ever before, now that instruction in Schenkerian analysis is offered at so many institutions of higher learning. A preliminary study of many of the pertinent issues is offered in the opening article, "Schenker's Theories: A Pedagogical View." The opinions expressed reflect my own teaching experiences and are intended as a stimulus for additional study and future dialogue. The paper is divided into three sections, the first of which deals with the teaching of strict counterpoint and harmony as prerequisites to the study of Schenkerian analysis.[1] Suggestions are made regarding how such studies might be incorporated into the undergraduate theory curriculum. The second section is concerned with the teaching of analysis and the corresponding principles of graphic notation, beginning with introductory studies and progressing to more advanced topics. The final section deals with readings and related studies, including extensions of Schenker's theories to the analysis of pre-Baroque and post-tonal music, topics covered in depth in this collection by Saul Novack and James Baker, respectively.

Several articles in this collection, including the next three, deal either directly or indirectly with Schenker's important concept of motivic connection. Fundamental to this concept is the notion that any two statements of a given melodic pattern can occur at different levels, one thus being an enlargement or contraction of the other.[2] In "Thematic Content: A Schenkerian View," John Rothgeb discusses and provides numerous illustrations of the various types of concealed repetitions described by Schenker. The crucial word here is "concealed." The notion that relationships exist between different levels and thus are often obscured or concealed by the more easily perceived characteristics of the musical surface is at the core of Schenker's thought. In the subsequent article, "Motive and Text in Four Schubert Songs," Carl Schachter explores the relationship between motivic design and poetic imagery. Schachter begins with rather simple and direct relationships and progresses to those created by less direct or concealed repetitions. The most extensive analysis is of "Nacht und Traüme," Op. 43, No. 2, one of Schubert's most famous songs. Finally, the idea of "progressive motivic enlargement" is discussed by Roger Kamien in his analysis of a single work, the opening movement of Haydn's Piano Sonata in C♯ minor (Hob. XVI:36).[3]

---

1. A slightly altered version of this section, titled "Prerequisites to the Study of Schenker Analysis," was read at the national meeting of the Society for Music Theory in Denver, Colorado (November 8, 1980). Other papers on this session ("Workshop in Teaching Schenker Analysis") were: "Schenkerian Theory and the Undergraduate Curriculum" by John Rothgeb and "Schenkerian Concepts and Notational Procedures" by Steven Gilbert.
2. See Charles Burkhart, "Schenker's 'Motivic Parallelisms,' "*Journal of Music Theory* **22** (1978), pp. 145–175.
3. This study is an expanded and revised version of a paper delivered at the joint meetings of the American Musicological Society, College Music Society, and Society for Music Theory in Denver, Colorado (November 1980).

In the following article, "Schenker's Theory of Levels and Musical Performance," Charles Burkhart addresses a feature of Schenker's work that is often mentioned but rarely discussed—the relationship between theory and performance-related issues. In addition to Schenker's carefully researched editions of music, some of which are accompanied by extensive commentary, there are numerous analytical studies that include directions on performance.[4] Burkhart presents several examples from Schenker's and his own work and in this way demonstrates how details of performance are often related to larger-scale compositional associations. This is an important contribution, one that, hopefully, will stimulate additional research and publication in this rather elusive, though obviously vital, area.

Another area that is of interest to many is the application of Schenkerian concepts to the analysis of music beyond the boundaries set by Schenker himself. In his article, "The Analysis of Pre-Baroque Music," Saul Novack reinforces the position he and others have taken in modifying and applying Schenker's ideas to earlier music.[5] Novack not only summarizes the main arguments for this position, but answers the main objections to it. This is an excellent introduction to a controversial topic, and thus most appropriate for those who are interested but have not yet read widely in the area. Novack's article is nicely complemented by Felix Salzer's contribution to this collection, a structural analysis of Monteverdi's *Oimè, se tanto amate,* from the fourth book of madrigals (1603).

James Baker's article, "Schenkerian Analysis and Post-Tonal Music," is divided into two main sections. The first is a survey and critique of the various attempts to apply Schenkerian concepts to music of the twentieth century. In the second he proposes an analytic approach to works that lie on the borderline between tonality and atonality, and demonstrates this approach by applying it to an analysis of Scriabin's *Enigme,* Op. 52, No. 2. A unique feature of this approach is the simultaneous use of two analytic systems, one borrowed from Schenker and the other from Allen Forte,[6] to demonstrate the work's tonal and atonal properties, respectively.

---

4. See, for example, the monographs on Beethoven's Fifth and Ninth symphonies, and the essays in *Der Tonwille* and *Das Meisterwerk in der Musik.*
5. See, for example, the articles by Bergquist, Mitchell, Novack, Salzer, and Schachter in the first two issues of *The Music Forum.*
6. Allen Forte, *The Structure of Atonal Music,* New Haven: Yale University Press, 1973; second printing, 1977.

   Forte combines his own ideas about atonal structure with ideas derived from Schenker in "Schoenberg's Creative Evolution: The Path to Atonality," *The Musical Quarterly* **64** (1978), pp. 133–176.

In the Appendix to this collection I have included two articles by the late Ernst Oster, both of which were published previously in *Musicology,* a short-lived journal of the late 1940s. Unfortunately copies of this journal were not widely circulated, and thus these excellent articles have not been generally available until now.[7] Both are outstanding examples of the depth that can be achieved in applying Schenker's ideas. In "The *Fantaisie-Impromptu:* A Tribute to Beethoven,"[8] Oster poses the interesting question of why Chopin should want to have suppressed publication of his *Fantaisie-Impromptu.* (It was published posthumously, along with other compositions, by his friend Jules Fontana.) The answer, says Oster, is that Chopin's work was consciously patterned after certain features of a work by Beethoven that he greatly admired, the *Sonata quasi una Fantasia,* Op. 27, No. 2. Thus Chopin knew that his work was not totally original but based in part on Beethoven's, particularly the finale. To prove his thesis Oster points out a number of close relationships between the two works. Some of the similarities are quite apparent, while others (e.g., larger-scale motivic relationships) are less obvious. Of all the evidence provided, possibly the most convincing is the almost literal quotation in mm.7-8 of a passage from the coda of Beethoven's sonata. The second article, "The Dramatic Character of the *Egmont Overture,*"[9] utilizes Schenker's concept of motivic connection. In this remarkable study Oster not only traces the motivic relationships in Beethoven's overture, but relates their use to the drama of Goethe's play.

Those who already know these two articles by Oster may note that certain editorial changes have been made. These changes were incorporated into the present versions only after careful consideration. They were necessitated by the large number of mistakes, both misprints and grammatical errors, contained in the original versions. To my knowledge these were the first two articles that Ernst Oster wrote in English, so it is not surprising that he had some difficulty with details of grammar and punctuation. It is unfortunate that these types of mistakes were never corrected before publication. Thus I hope to do a service by making these corrections, especially since I am convinced that Ernst Oster would have wanted his ideas, not just his words, conveyed in the clearest possible manner.

---

7. I would like to thank my colleague, Bruce Campbell, for suggesting that these articles be included in this collection.
8. *Musicology* **1,** No. 4 (1947), pp. 407-429.
9. *Musicology* **2,** No. 3 (1949), pp. 269-285.

The idea for this collection of essays grew out of a workshop, "Perspectives on Schenker's Theories," held at the Eastman School of Music in the summer of 1976. Shortly thereafter I contacted several individuals requesting contributions. Unfortunately, two of these, Oswald Jonas and Ernst Oster, were never able to complete their work. Others responded in record time, and to those individuals I offer my apologies, since I am sure they expected to see their work in print long before now. Their promptness and, in fact, all the contributions are greatly appreciated.

I would like to take this opportunity to thank several individuals who were involved either directly or indirectly in the publication of this collection of essays. First I would like to thank Robert Freeman, Director of the Eastman School of Music, who provided a generous grant to support publication. I am also most grateful to Walter Biddle Saul II for his careful autography of the musical examples. (Examples 1 and 4 in Charles Burkhart's article are reprinted by kind permission of European American Music Distributors, sole U.S. agent for Universal Edition.) And finally I would like to express my appreciation to the staff of the Publications Unit, Department of Communications, of the University of Rochester—particularly Ceil Goldman, Marsha Kontje, Sean McCormack, Martha McNeill, and Stephen Reynolds—for their thoughtful advice and assistance in preparing the camera-ready copy.

David Beach
Rochester, New York

Schenker's Theories: A Pedagogical View

DAVID BEACH

In the preface to his recently published translation of *Der freie Satz,* Ernst Oster makes the following statement regarding the recent increase of interest in Schenker's theories:

> Interest in Schenker has been growing at an ever-increasing pace in the United States. More and more colleges and universities are offering courses devoted to Schenker's theories, his name appears almost regularly in the programs of musical conventions, and, especially during the past decade, the number of "Schenker-oriented" or more or less "Schenker-influenced" books has increased to a remarkable degree.[1]

This growth of activity indicates the degree to which Schenker's ideas about music and musical structure have begun to influence our thinking. For those like Oster who strove for years to convince us of the value of Schenker's ideas, gradual, even partial, acceptance must have been particularly satisfying. At the same time the tone of Oster's comments indicates that the taste of "success" was bittersweet. He, for one, was well aware of the pitfalls that accompanied the new-found popularity of Schenkerian theory. Unfortunately it is a fact that much of the published material that has grown out of this wave of interest does not represent Schenker's ideas accurately, and in some cases actually misrepresents them. This causes more vexation than difficulty for those who understand Schenker's work, but poses a serious problem for those who lack the background to determine what is or is not "authentic." No doubt this situation will be alleviated in part by the long-awaited translation of *Der freie Satz.* But one does not learn Schenkerian theory simply by reading a book, even *this* book; rather it takes years of serious study and practice. An additional concern is the difference between what might be considered the *ideal* pedagogical situation, namely how Schenkerian theory should be introduced, and the situation as it too often exists. Though I do not intend to dwell on negative matters here, this "conflict," if I may use that term, is worthy of additional comment, since it relates directly to the topic at hand. I shall return to this point in a moment.

---

1. Ernst Oster, "Preface to the English Edition" of Heinrich Schenker's *Free Composition* (*Der freie Satz*), New York: Longman, 1979, p. xi.

Schenker himself has provided us with a clear outline of what we must study in order to understand his concept of musical coherence and thus the music of the great masters.

> The following instructional plan provides a truly practical understanding of this concept [of organic coherence]. It is the only plan which corresponds exactly to the history and development of the masterworks, and so is the only feasible sequence: instruction in strict counterpoint (according to Fux-Schenker), in thoroughbass (according to J. S. and C. P. E. Bach), and in free composition (Schenker). Free composition, finally, combines all the others, placing them in the service of the law of organic coherence as it is revealed in the fundamental structure (fundamental line and bass arpeggiation) in the background, the voice-leading transformations in the middleground, and ultimately in the appearance of the foreground.[2]

What Schenker outlined corresponds very closely with the contents of his major work, *Neue musikalische Theorien und Phantasien (New Musical Theories and Phantasies)*.[3] The first volume of this work, though in some ways a traditional study of harmony, contains several important ideas that were developed in later publications. It is interesting that in the passage just cited, which was written almost thirty years after the *Harmonielehre*, Schenker does not recommend the study of harmony (according to Schenker), but of thoroughbass (according to J. S. and C. P. E. Bach).[4] No doubt Schenker was thinking historically here, but the passage may also suggest that over a period of years the study of thoroughbass had become synonymous for him with the study of harmony. The second volume, which was published in two parts, is an

---

2. Heinrich Schenker, Introduction to *Free Composition*, p. xxi.
3. *Neue musikalische Theorien und Phantasien.*
   - I: *Harmonielehre*, Vienna: Universal, 1906; reprinted, with a foreword by Rudolf Frisius, 1978. *Harmony*, edited and annotated by Oswald Jonas, translated by Elisabeth Mann Borgese, Chicago and London: The University of Chicago Press, 1954; paperback edition, Cambridge: M.I.T. Press, 1973.
   - II: *Kontrapunkt*
     Part I: *Cantus firmus und zweistimmiger Satz*, Vienna: Universal, 1910.
     Part II: *Drei-und mehrstimmiger Satz*, Vienna: Universal, 1922.
   - III: *Der freie Satz,* Vienna: Universal, 1935; second edition, edited and revised by Oswald Jonas, Vienna: Universal, 1956; English edition, translated by Ernst Oster, New York: Longman, 1979.
4. Throughout his career Schenker made repeated reference to C. P. E. Bach's *Versuch über die wahre Art das Clavier zu spielen*, part 2, Berlin, 1762. It is clear that of the older theorists C. P. E. Bach was the one for whom he had the utmost respect. The work of J. S. Bach to which he refers is a short manuscript that was originally owned by Johann Peter Kellner. See Philipp Spitta, *Johann Sebastian Bach*, vol. 2, appendix 12, Leipzig, 1880.

adaptation of species counterpoint (according to Fux). A particularly important part of this work is the section on combined species, which is published at the end of the second part. In this section, which is called "Transition to Free Composition," Schenker reveals his conception of the relationship between strict composition (species counterpoint) and "free" composition. It is crucial to understand Schenker's conception of this relationship in order to appreciate much of what he says in the third and final volume, *Free Composition*.

From these comments it seems perfectly clear what we must study to understand Schenker's work: (1) strict (species) counterpoint, (2) harmony (including traditional thoroughbass), and finally (3) the music of the masters. It is also clear that a superficial knowledge of the first two, counterpoint and harmony, is insufficient for a true understanding of the music. It may be possible to learn about Schenker in a relatively short period of time by reading some of his works as well as selected secondary sources, but there is an important distinction between learning about Schenker—treating him as an historical figure—and learning his theories. As noted above, the latter, which includes developing a skill for graphic notation of musical structure, requires years of diligent study and practice. The conflict, as I have called it, results from the difference between the time needed to develop these skills and the time pressures at institutions of higher education in this country, where these skills are now taught.[5] Because we have an obligation to teach our students many things about many different types of music, we are often forced by time and curricular restraints to make choices of omission rather than admission. As far as theory curricula are concerned, one finds that the emphasis is placed too often on minimal requirements rather than on quality education. Such a situation does not lead to an understanding of music, nor of Schenker's concept of musical structure, since his is a very sophisticated view of very sophisticated music. It is my feeling that *thorough* training in harmony and counterpoint is the only path to understanding Schenker's work. Furthermore, I would say that lack of proper training in these areas is at the root of much of the misunderstanding and misinterpretation of his theories.

By this point I may have offended some people, which is not my intention. Nor is it my intention, despite my concerns, to suggest a large-scale revision of our educational system. Rather, I seek to suggest various

5. For a brief description of the history of instruction in Schenker's theory in this country see Allen Forte, "Introduction to the English Edition" of *Free Composition*, p. xvii.

ways by which I feel Schenkerian theory can be incorporated into the present educational structure. For the most part my comments are not directed at those who already have expertise in this area, but rather to those who, for one reason or another, would like to include some of Schenker's ideas into their own teaching. I do not mean to suggest that I will be offering some easy solution or shortcut to learning and teaching Schenker's theories, because there simply isn't one. But I do feel, rather I know from experience, that many of these ideas can be included with success in the traditional theory curricula.

The following thoughts are divided into three main sections: (1) Instruction in Counterpoint and Harmony, (2) The Teaching of Schenker Analysis, and (3) Readings and Related Studies. Discussion of graphic notation is included in the second section, while in the last consideration is given to extensions of Schenker's theories to the analysis of pre-Baroque music, twentieth-century music, and rhythmic structure in tonal music.

I. INSTRUCTION IN COUNTERPOINT AND HARMONY

It has already been noted that Schenker recommends the study of species counterpoint, more specifically the study of species counterpoint according to Fux-Schenker. This raises two important questions. First, what are the advantages of the species as opposed to some other approach to teaching counterpoint? And second, how does Schenker's approach differ from that of Fux? The answer to the first question is rather obvious. From a pedagogical point of view, species counterpoint has the distinct advantage that it begins with simple musical relationships and progresses through various stages to more complex ones. That is, in the first species one is concerned solely with consonance and its treatment, while in the successive species, dissonant elements—first the passing tone, then the neighbor-notes, cambiata, suspensions, and their combination—are gradually introduced. This approach stresses the role of dissonance as an elaboration of consonant relationships, a most important concept to the understanding of tonal structure. As traditionally taught, species counterpoint normally progresses from exercises in two parts to those in three and then more parts and culminates with combined species, which, as has been noted, were regarded by Schenker as the bridge between elementary counterpoint and free composition.

With regard to the second question, it is important to keep in mind that it was Fux's intention that his *Gradus ad Parnassum*[6] offer instruction in the contrapuntal style of Palestrina. Whether or not he was successful in this attempt is another matter. But what is important is that Fux did provide a concise method of presenting the basic materials of music, a method that is more pedagogically sound than those of his predecessors. Many years later Schenker revived the Fux method, not just for its pedagogical advantages and historical significance, but because he recognized that the principles it presents are basic to all tonal music. This is one of Schenker's greatest achievements—his recognition that the principles of strict counterpoint underlie the music of many composers and styles. His adaptation of Fux was simply the removal of the matter of stylistic consideration from the study of elementary counterpoint. This does not imply that the teaching of stylistic counterpoint—the compositional imitation of a Palestrina motet or a Bach fugue, for example—has no place in the education of a musician. But is does mean that we must first study the underlying principles, the principles of strict counterpoint and voice leading that apply to a Mozart piano sonata or a Beethoven string quartet just as much as they do to a work of Palestrina or Bach.

The ultimate purpose of studying strict counterpoint is to understand its relationship to free composition. This requires that the study of counterpoint be coupled at some point with that of harmony. When this should be done depends on many factors but primarily on the length and orientation of the particular program in question. In an integrated program, one that incorporates the study of harmony and counterpoint with the analysis of tonal music, it would seem most logical to introduce harmony concurrently with or immediately after the study of elementary counterpoint. The latter course is taken by Felix Salzer and Carl Schachter in their book, *Counterpoint in Composition*, the one current text on counterpoint that attempts to present the topic from a Schenkerian point of view.[7] Immediately after the section on species

6. Johann Joseph Fux, *Gradus ad Parnassum*, Vienna, 1725.
Steps to Parnassus: The Study of Counterpoint, translated and edited by Alfred Mann with the collaboration of John Edmunds, New York: W. W. Norton, 1943; revised edition, *The Study of Counterpoint*, 1965.

7. Felix Salzer and Carl Schachter, *Counterpoint in Composition: The Study of Voice Leading*, New York: McGraw-Hill, 1969.
The first book to present a reorganization (as well as a modification and expansion) of Schenker's writings from a pedagogical standpoint is Felix Salzer's *Structural Hearing: Tonal Coherence in Music*, New York: Charles Boni, 1952; reprinted by Dover Publications, 1962. Though Salzer's book does contain some exercises, it is not easily adaptable as a textbook on harmony or counterpoint.

counterpoint—before the final chapters on the chorale, combined species, and the analysis of voice leading in various compositions—the authors insert two lengthy chapters that show the relationship of elementary counterpoint to composition. These two important chapters fulfill a dual purpose. On the one hand they show how the principles of species counterpoint underlie tonal composition; however, viewed from a different perspective, free composition can be seen as an elaboration of the underlying voice-leading structure. In a way this process of elaboration is inherent in species counterpoint itself but at a more abstract level. That is, the contents of the second and third species, for example, can be understood as successive elaborations of the consonant structures of the first species. Similarly we can understand surface characteristics of music as elaborations or *diminutions*, if you will, of the underlying contrapuntal structure. Without an understanding of both levels—the underlying structure and its surface manifestations—proper interpretation of passages such as those given in examples 1 and 2 would be most difficult.

The opening measures of the Menuet from Bach's French Suite in C minor (BWV 813) are given at (a) in example 1. As shown at (b), which is a metric reduction of this material, the eighth-note motive that is transferred from the treble in m.1 to the bass in m.2 can be interpreted as an elaboration of a simpler pattern composed of three quarter notes spanning a descending third. In m.1 this idea moves in contrary motion to the bass, resulting in a voice exchange between the two parts. In m.2 to the downbeat of m.3 it forms a simple contrapuntal pattern with the treble, a series of parallel tenths spanning a fourth. Recognition of this underlying pattern and its continuation is crucial to our interpretation of the phrase beginning in m.17, which will be discussed in a moment. Here it is internal to a larger-scale prolongation of the tonic harmony and $e\flat^2$ ($\hat{3}$), as shown in the graph at (c). This larger-scale connection of phrase 1 to the beginning of phrase 2 is accomplished by the filling in of the octave c to c^1 in the bass, as indicated by the brackets under the disjunct tetrachords in (b). What remains to be discussed is the interpretation of the treble part in mm.3-4. First, it should be noted that though the two measures are related motivically the harmony requires that they be interpreted differently. This is an important point, since it emphasizes the role harmony plays in the interpretation of tonal structure. Second, it is important to note that the combined melodic motion of these measures unfolds the interval of a sixth from $e^{\flat 2}$ down to g^1, a filling in of the opening melodic interval, as indicated by the dotted brackets in (b). This motion connects an outer to an inner voice, and interpretation of its meaning in relation to the harmony suggests that the descent to $b^{\natural 1}$ and beyond is a substitution for an implied d^2, as shown in the graph at (c). The significance of this interpretation will become apparent in the following discussion of mm.17–28 of the same piece.

Example 1: Bach, French Suite 2 (BWV 813); Menuet 1–4.

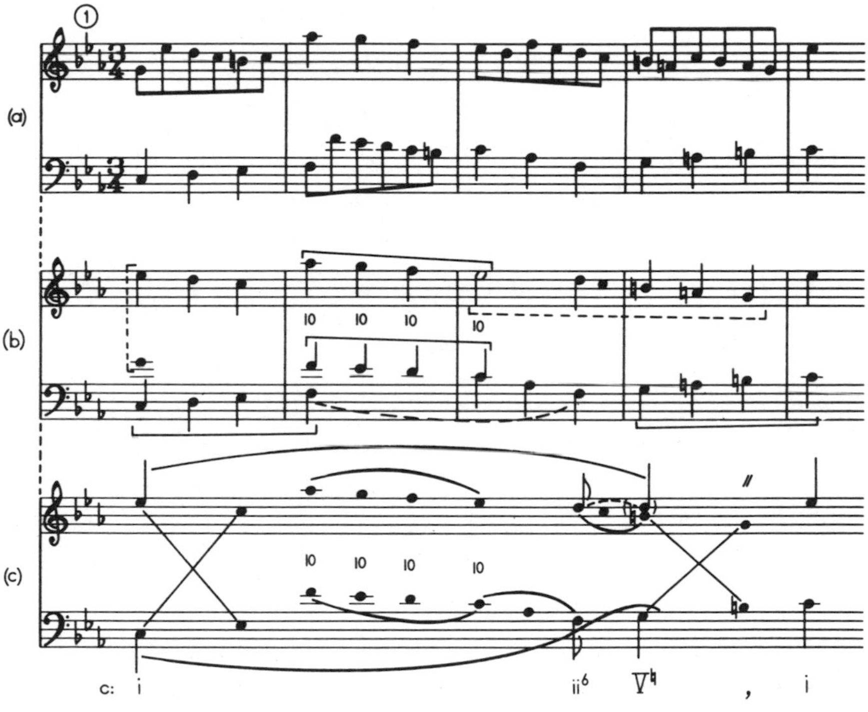

The sequential pattern beginning in m.17 is an expansion of the underlying motion in tenths of mm.2–3. Here each of the steps of the original pattern is extended over two measures by means of a motivic elaboration of the voice-leading pattern 10–7, as indicated in example 2. The parallel between these two passages becomes clear when comparing their continuations. Measures 23–24 correspond almost exactly to mm.3–4. Here, however, the dominant harmony is extended for an additional four measures before returning to the tonic harmony and $e^{\flat 2}$ ($\hat{3}$). As shown in part (b) of example 2, the stepwise descent from $a^{\flat 2}$ begun in m.17 is continued in the bass until its completion in m.29. This shift from treble to bass in m.25, which is articulated by a return to the opening motivic idea, picks up the implied d^2 of the preceding measure, adding support to the interpretation of m.4 given above. The function of this descending sixth from $a^{\flat 2}$ (m.17) to c (m.29, bass) in the larger context of the piece is also indicated in part (b) of example 2.

Example 2

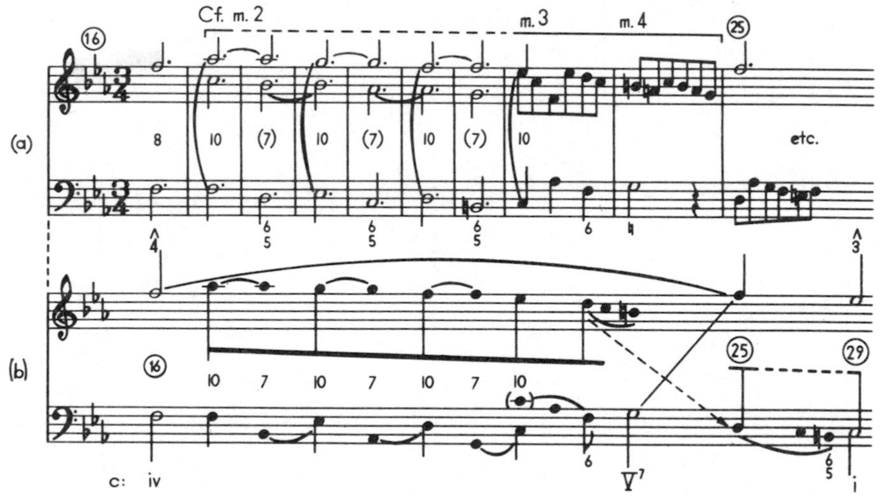

My main purpose in discussing these passages from the Bach Menuet is to demonstrate the necessity of understanding the relationship between strict counterpoint, the principle that underlies composition, and its elaborations at various levels. In this example we have seen the elaboration of an underlying structure, i.e., the motion in parallel tenths, at two levels, first through diminution and later through expansion.

Now I would like to return to two important issues raised earlier, namely what should be taught as a prerequisite to analysis of this sort and how much time should be allotted to this study. From an idealistic point of view it seems clear that a four-year program for all undergraduates would be warranted in order to cover the areas of harmony, counterpoint, and analysis adequately. In this respect it is worth noting the recommendation made by Felix Salzer and Carl Schachter regarding the use of their book, *Counterpoint in Composition*.

> In ideal circumstances a period of three years would be devoted to this book (together, of course, with work in other aspects of music theory). Such ideal circumstances very seldom exist in our colleges and universities. However, if some analytical illustrations are omitted, a period of two years will suffice.[8]

It must be kept in mind that the use of this text is predicated on prior knowledge of the fundamentals of music, including chord grammar and figured bass, as well as elementary ear-training; furthermore, it is intended to be used with supplementary studies in harmony and traditional analysis. All this adds up to more time than suggested, a luxury not available to many teachers. The core program in music theory, the minimum required of all undergraduate music majors regardless of degree program, is two, sometimes three, years at most institutions. Such a program normally includes fundamentals, studies in harmony, counterpoint, and analysis, as well as an introduction to twentieth-century music. The problem that faces us, then, is what to select from all that we should teach for inclusion in our various programs. Let me suggest that we can maintain standards and avoid the serious matter of omission by dividing our priorities between two levels—the core curriculum and upper-level studies—as is done at many schools.

It is my opinion that the core curriculum in music theory should contain the following topics in addition to the related skills: (1) fundamentals of music, (2) elementary counterpoint, (3) harmony, and (4) traditional analysis. Studies in advanced counterpoint and harmony, as well as the introduction to linear analysis, can wait for more advanced courses. The one matter requiring immediate clarification here concerns the division between "elementary" and "advanced" studies in counterpoint. It is my feeling that the core curriculum should include counterpoint studies in *at least two parts*. This is an absolute minimum, and I do not mean to imply that counterpoint instruction should end

8. Salzer and Schachter, *Counterpoint in Composition*, p. ix.

there. However, species counterpoint in two parts does introduce the important concept of dissonance as an elaboration of consonance, and in that sense is sufficient as a foundation for the study of more complex relationships. This would mean that studies in counterpoint in three and more parts, including mixed species, could be delayed until later, possibly as part of an advanced course that includes stylistic writing as well. My only concern here is that these more advanced studies might be omitted rather than simply delayed. It may have been such a concern that prompted Felix Salzer and Carl Schachter to present two- and three-part writing together for each of the five species rather than follow the normal procedure of separating the two. Three-part counterpoint *is* important and should be available to those who intend to pursue more advanced studies in musical analysis. In light of this comment I would now like to offer an additional example.

The first phrase of Bach's Prelude in B major (BWV 868) from the *Well-Tempered Clavier*, book 1, is given in part (a) of example 3. A metric reduction and interpretation of the voice leading is given below at (b). Certain features of this reduction require explanation. First, one should note that the inner-voice pattern in m.2 is given a dual interpretation, as indicated by the figures $7<^{8}_{6}$. Later, when the same pattern appears in the bass, the interpretation of the 7 as a displacement of 6 is supported by the motion in the top voice. Second, it should be noted that certain notes are indicated as substitutions or extensions of others. For example, the e♯ on the downbeat of m.3 and later the one on the downbeat of m.5 are interpreted as extensions of the g♯'s preceding them. This means that the f♯ in the top voice in m.5, though heard in the immediate context as an upper neighbor-note, functions as a passing note in the larger context. Finally the bass progressions by fifths in mm.3–4, which are characteristic of free composition as opposed to strict counterpoint, are shown as substitutions for those shown in parentheses. A further reduction, with substitutions omitted, is given at (c). The solid and dotted brackets indicate the invertible counterpoint between the upper two parts. Note, however, that this feature is disguised somewhat by the extension of m.3 into m.4, requiring that the latter be shortened accordingly to bring the pattern back into synchronization with the meter. This rhythmic shift, which occurs at the second beat of bar 4, emphasizes the return of the 7–6 suspension mentioned above; it also forces the rhythmic drive to continue until the cadence in m.6. Elimination of this rhythmic feature results in the reduction at (d), the purpose of which is to demonstrate the contrapuntal origin of this remarkable phrase. The

Example 3: Bach, *Well-Tempered Clavier* I, Prelude 23 (BWV 868), 1–6.

bass line from the middle of m.4 on is put in parentheses to indicate that it, as a manifestation of free composition, could also be eliminated; in its place the descending tetrachord has been repeated (here notated as a tenor part), thus emphasizing the invertibility of the upper parts. Hopefully this example has offered adequate proof of the importance counterpoint plays in tonal composition. We must know strict counterpoint to understand its expression in free composition, and in this instance knowledge of counterpoint in three parts, not just two, is quite necessary.

Most of the discussion so far has centered on the teaching of counterpoint, since I think it is the one area that is most often neglected or at least given a secondary role. The study of harmony, on the other hand, is a fundamental ingredient in all theory programs with which I am acquainted. It is not a question of whether or not to teach harmony, nor even of the amount to be presented (though that is always an important issue), but rather *how* to teach it. The number of approaches to the subject that have been developed over the years is truly astounding. However, I think it is safe to say, though I may be oversimplifying, that most of the texts available today fall somewhere between two poles, the origins of which can be traced back to the eighteenth century. One pole is the vertical approach, while the other is the linear approach to harmony. The vertical approach is characterized by the labelling of each and every chord, usually by a Roman numeral to indicate its "root" within a key. Unless some additional level of interpretation is indicated, perhaps some higher form of organization, the task is simply mechanical and would be better performed by a computer. As an end in itself the mechanical labelling of chords is a gross oversimplification, actually a misinterpretation of musical structure. Such an approach really has no place in higher education, and cannot be taken seriously by anyone interested in teaching Schenker's approach to music. The linear approach, on the other hand, is characterized by a recognition of the contrapuntal nature of certain chords. Not all verticalities are labelled according to the same principle, nor are they considered equal; rather, some are seen as connecting those of greater significance, thus fitting into a larger scheme. Such an approach, where contrapuntal motion or voice leading is understood as the means by which harmony is extended in time, is basic to Schenker's thought.

There are certain textbooks on harmony that are particularly well suited for preparing the student for more advanced studies in Schenkerian analysis. Though there are several that might qualify in this respect, I would like to mention two that I think are particularly appropriate: *Tonal Harmony in Concept and Practice* by Allen Forte[9] and *Harmony and Voice Leading* by Edward Aldwell and Carl Schachter.[10] Though neither is a book on Schenkerian analysis nor intended as an introduction to his theories, both reflect a strong orientation in that direction. Except for certain portions of Forte's book, particularly the section "Linear Intervallic Patterns" and the chapter "Large-Scale Arpeggiations, Passing and Auxiliary Notes," the influence is rather subtle. Both avoid unnecessary use of Schenkerian terminology but in their own ways introduce the underlying concepts. Also, though both can be used as self-contained textbooks on harmony, they could easily be used in conjunction with studies in strict counterpoint, thus preparing the student all the better for more advanced studies in analysis.

After having decided what is to be accomplished in a particular course or program, it is then important to choose a text or texts that will help in accomplishing these goals, which is one reason I have mentioned specific books here and elsewhere. However, I am also aware that it is not the text but the teacher who makes the difference in the long run. That is, a person well trained in harmony and counterpoint, for example, could communicate that knowledge with the aid of most any text, though of course it would be preferable if the teaching materials were consistent with the ideas presented. Also, it is not too difficult to envision a situation in which a teacher would like to introduce some basic Schenkerian concepts into an undergraduate harmony course but, through no fault of his own, is saddled with a text that approaches the subject in an entirely different manner. The good teacher will usually find a creative solution to the dilemma. Consider, for instance, the first eight measures of the second movement of Beethoven's Piano Sonata, Op. 10, No. 1, which is given in part (a) of example 4.

---

9. Allen Forte, *Tonal Harmony in Concept and Practice*, third edition, New York: Holt, Rinehart and Winston, 1979.
10. Edward Aldwell and Carl Schachter, *Harmony and Voice Leading*, two vols. with workbooks, New York: Harcourt, Brace and Jovanovich, 1978 and 1979.

Example 4: Beethoven, Piano Sonata, Op. 10, No. 1 (II), 1–8.

Let us assume that the text being used requires that the student label each chord directly below the music, as has been done at level 1. If the "analysis" were to begin and end here, the student would learn little about this phrase, except possibly that Beethoven could do wonders with three harmonies. Realizing the inadequacy of this primitive analysis, the teacher might then show the student how these chords are organized at increasingly larger levels. It is not difficult for the student to understand, for example, that the first four measures are formed by two two-measure units, the second of which is derived from the first. Furthermore, each of these units, though consisting of three chords, can be understood as controlled by a single harmony, as is shown at level 2. This interpretation is based on a recognition of the contrapuntal function of these intervening chords, as shown at (b). That is, the V^6 chord in m.1 supports the upper neighbor of $a^{\flat 1}$, which, with the tonic harmony, is prolonged through the first unit; similarly, the tonic chord in m.3 supports the upper neighbor of $b^{\flat 1}$, which, with the dominant harmony, is prolonged through mm.3–4 until the arrival at c^2 and the tonic harmony in m.5. A further interpretation of these measures is given at (c), which shows that the $b^{\flat 1}$ prolonged through mm.3–4 is actually a passing note leading to the c^2 in m.5.[11] Likewise, the dominant harmony that supports this passing note must eventually be understood as prolonging a larger-scale tonic harmony, as is shown at level 3 of the harmonic analysis. Interpretation of the remainder of the phrase is more problematic, and is thus more appropriate for an advanced analysis class than a basic harmony course. However, having understood the hierarchical nature of the harmony in mm.1–5, it should not be difficult to do the same for the remainder of the phrase. More specifically, I think it is possible to demonstrate the passing nature of the chords in the second half of m.7,[12] clearing the way for the interpretation given at level 3, namely that the phrase is controlled by a larger-scale harmonic motion of I–IV–V.

This example illustrates a number of important points. First, I think it is extremely important that a student learn that not all tonic chords nor all dominant chords are equal, but rather depend on context for their meaning. For example, it is important to understand that the tonic chord in m.3 cannot be equated with the tonic chords in mm.1–2 or m.5; and, at a higher level, the dominant in mm.3–4 cannot be considered as significant as the one in m.8. Second, it is important to understand that our interpretation of harmony depends on a recognition of its linear nature, which is the main reason I have included the graphs at (b) and (c). Certainly these graphs come closer to what we hear than the harmonic analysis at level 1. This does not mean that I am advocating the teaching of such analytic procedures at an early stage; on the contrary, I think they could cause more confusion than good. Rather, I would be happy to see the student do a two- or three-tiered harmonic analysis, as has been done here. But, whatever you do, please don't let the student stop at level 1.

11. See example 516 (p. 428) in Forte, *Tonal Harmony in Concept and Practice,* third edition.
12. Cf. example 443 in Salzer, *Structural Hearing,* vol. 2.

II. THE TEACHING OF SCHENKER ANALYSIS

The following discussion is based on my own experience of teaching Schenker analysis at both the graduate and undergraduate levels, and in general it follows the outline of a two-term course that I have taught for the past five years at the Eastman School of Music. This particular course is designed primarily for graduate students with solid training in traditional harmony and counterpoint but with little or no background in Schenkerian theory. Thus much of what I have to say about the first term, which is really an introduction to the topic, would apply just as well to an equivalent course for undergraduates. The main difference, of course, is that one can generally assume a wider base of knowledge and experience from graduate students and can thus expect to progress at a faster rate. On the other hand, graduate students have such diverse backgrounds in theory (and in many cases come to a graduate program with preconceived notions about Schenker's theories) that any such advantage is often negated. In general, then, I will avoid the arbitrary distinction between undergraduate and graduate instruction, and instead will concentrate on the progression from introductory to more advanced studies in tonal analysis.

A secondary though important feature of this course is that it is open to all qualified students from various musical disciplines—composition, conducting, musicology, and performance, as well as theory. I stress this point because diversity of this sort contributes in an important way to our attitude toward the analytic process, namely by encouraging us all to approach a piece from several points of view. We may, for example, concern ourselves primarily with matters of compositional choice and logic at one time, while at another—be it regarding the same or a different piece—we may concentrate more on matters of tonal structure or performance. All of these facets of analysis, not just those that relate directly to tonal structure, are important features of Schenker's work.

A. Introduction to Schenker Analysis

It is my firm conviction that the only meaningful way to present Schenker's ideas is through the study of carefully selected compositions, beginning with those that are short and relatively simple and progressing from there to those that are longer and/or more complex. Choice of specific compositions for study depends in part on demonstrating specific concepts or compositional techniques. It is also most important in this respect not to present too many new ideas at once, particularly at the early stages. Rather, concepts and terminology should be presented as methodically as possible so that the student does not become confused by an overabundance of information, thus possibly receiving the false impression that some analytic decisions are arbitrary. It is imperative that the reasons for Schenker's analytic decisions be understood if one is to learn to make equivalent judgments. Furthermore, the analysis of music will not appear arbitrary as long as the rules that govern its organization and structure are clearly explained and understood.

I usually begin by discussing in a general way what I consider to be the fundamental ingredients of Schenker's view of tonal structure—his concepts of structural levels and prolongation and of the interaction of harmony and voice leading at various levels—and by explaining how his approach differs from others that are commonly taught. To demonstrate these concepts I discuss two or three harmonically closed excerpts from well-known works, for example the opening themes of the first and third movements of Mozart's Piano Sonata in B♭, K. 333 (which offer an interesting comparison), and that of the slow movement of Beethoven's Piano Sonata in C minor, Op. 10, No. 1. Examination and interpretation of these passages raise other important points, such as Schenker's concept of interruption, the noncorrespondence between duration and tonal function, and various voice-leading techniques (e.g., voice exchange, substitution at the cadence, etc.). It would appear as if the result is exactly what I warned against above—presenting too many new concepts at once—and to a certain extent this is true. The only way to overcome this tendency is to proceed slowly and carefully and to explain the reasons for the choices that are made. No matter how pieces are selected, each one presents unique situations that require their own explanations. This pedagogical problem persists, but is particularly acute at the early stages of teaching Schenker analysis.

Several of the shorter pieces I have used to introduce Schenker's concepts, many of which have been analyzed by Schenker himself,[13] are the following: Bach, Prelude in C major (BWV 846);[14] Haydn, St. Anthony Chorale; Mozart, Theme from the Piano Sonata in A, K. 331;

13. For a listing of Schenker's analyses of specific works and their sources, see Larry Laskowski, *Heinrich Schenker: An Annotated Index to his Analyses of Musical Works*, New York: Pendragon Press, 1978.

14. See Schenker, *Five Graphic Music Analyses*, New York: Dover, 1969. Though many of my students have been exposed to this analysis prior to taking my course, I am continually amazed at how few are even aware of some of its most interesting features (e.g., the metric analysis).

Bach, Menuet from the French Suite in C minor (BWV 813); and selected Schubert songs. A slightly longer work, the opening section of which is given in example 5, is the second movement of Mozart's Piano Sonata in C, K. 545. Discussion of this one excerpt should be sufficient to demonstrate the general analytic procedure I would follow at this point.

Example 5: Mozart, Piano Sonata in C, K. 545 (II), 1–16.

The first step in analysis is to identify a work's major divisions and subdivisions, and the corresponding harmonic and melodic goals. In this instance we are dealing with just two eight-measure phrases (an antecedent and a consequent), each of which can be further divided and subdivided into four- and then two-measure units. The phrase division is articulated by a cadence on the dominant, and the final phrase completes the harmonic motion to the tonic. Corresponding to these harmonic goals are melodic motions, first to scale-degree 2 (2) in m.8 and later closing to the tonic in m.16. This is a clear example of Schenker's concept of interruption at the phrase level. That is, the tendency of the $\frac{\hat{2}}{V}$ in m.8 to close to $\frac{\hat{1}}{I}$ is not realized, and instead the initial melodic tone is reinstated before the harmonic and melodic motion is completed. It is important to establish this principle right from the beginning, since its recognition facilitates decisions at later stages.

The next step is to have the student make a metric reduction of the voice leading. The major decision to be made at this stage is to determine which notes are given harmonic support and which are notes of rhythmic or melodic embellishment. Removal of the latter types results in a representation of the voice leading at the metric level, along the lines provided in example 6.[15] Here only the outer parts are shown, except at the cadences where an inner voice has been added to clarify the harmony and voice leading. A three-level interpretation of the harmony, much like that shown at (a) in example 4, is given below the bass staff. Although the harmony itself is relatively simple, its interpretation requires more thought than might first appear, since, as will be indicated below, melodic considerations also contribute to the decisions. The harmony in m.6 offers a good example of what Schenker means by scale-step (as opposed to chord). The e minor chord of the second beat does not have harmonic status (vi); rather, it is there as consonant support for g^2. Thus the contents of m.6 must be understood as representing a single harmonic step, the tonic.[16]

The solid brackets above the melodic line indicate recurrences of a falling-fifth motive that is articulated by a dotted rhythmic figure. The dotted brackets indicate two statements of the motive that are obscured somewhat by surface embellishments. It is a feature of this piece that the motion of the initial measure of each two-measure unit is directed

15. Where embellishing notes have been included they are indicated by nonmetric values (note-heads without stems).

16. See Schenker, *Free Composition*, Supplement: Musical Examples, Figure 104, 2b.

toward the second. That is, the ascending motion of m.1 leads to d^2 in m.2, the arrival at which is articulated by the initial statement of the motive and the dotted rhythmic figure; repetition of this pattern in subsequent even-numbered measures (mm.4 and 6) signals the prolongation of d^2 until its descent at the cadence. Establishment of the fifth scale-degree and its subsequent prolongation by voice leading and motivic repetition are the main characteristics of this excerpt. Since mm.9–14 are melodic embellishments of the opening measures, their metric reduction has not been given. However, there are certain features of the final cadence (mm.15–16) that require explanation. First, it is important to understand that the sixth stated as an appoggiatura on the last beat of m.15 results from the delay of the sixth that would normally have occurred on the second beat, as shown by the note in parentheses in example 6. Also, in anticipation of the next analytic step, I have indicated that this delayed b^1 ($\hat{3}$) is introduced by the c^2 on the second half of the preceding beat. This interpretation is facilitated by prior decisions regarding the prolongation of d^2($\hat{5}$) in mm.10–14 (as in mm.2–6) and the closure of the melodic line, at least at this level, in m.16.

The third and final step in the analytic process is the interpretation of the contents of the metric reduction and the representation of this interpretation by means of an analytic graph. In this case much of the interpretation has already been done in conjunction with prior stages of analysis. What remains, then, is to determine how best to represent the relationships you want to show. Here I think it is important to keep in mind that many of the more detailed relationships have already been demonstrated, and thus it would be appropriate at this stage to concentrate on the larger-scale voice-leading connections. In example 7 I have intentionally employed different notational procedures to represent corresponding relationships in the two phrases. Normally one should do the opposite, that is, strive for consistency of notation throughout. My reason for following this unusual procedure here is to demonstrate that there is more than one way to represent these ideas. The notational procedures themselves will be discussed in some detail below.

Though the contents of example 7 are self-explanatory, there are certain features that warrant further comment. First, note that the upper neighbor-notes in the bass (mm.1 and 5) are interpreted at different levels, which is consistent with the distinction between levels 1 and 2 of the harmonic analysis provided in example 6. The first one supports the melodic passing tone c^2, whereas the latter supports the same pitch as

Example 6

Example 7

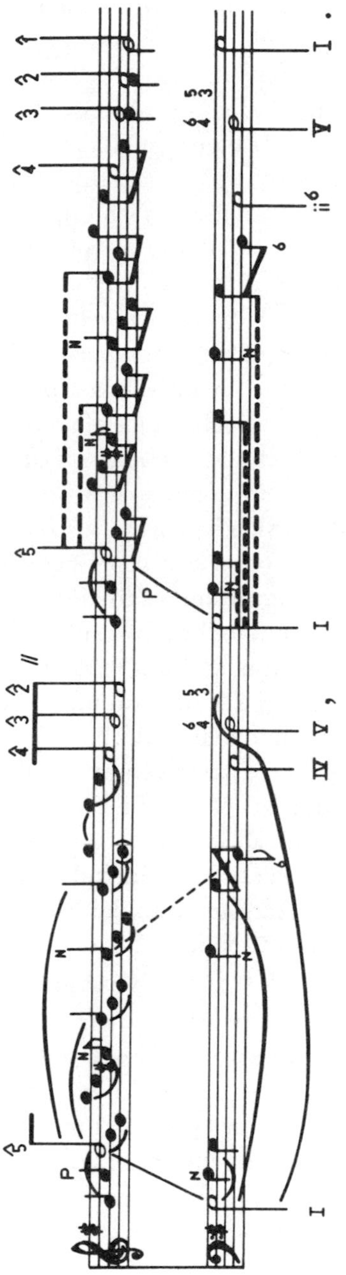

the lower neighbor-note to the prolonged $d^2(\hat{5})$. Because of the harmony in m.5, the expectation is that the c^2 will resolve down to b^1 in the next measure. This resolution is delayed and transferred to the bass (shown by a dotted line), while the melodic line is pushed back up to d^2 by motivic repetition. This interpretation is based on an understanding of the underlying voice leading and, in general, the role it plays in both strict and free composition.

As mentioned above, my selection of pieces for analysis is made in an attempt to introduce specific concepts and voice-leading techniques in a systematic fashion. Each subsequent piece is intended to reinforce ideas previously introduced as well as to present new situations. I also think that it is important to emphasize a newly introduced concept directly by several examples from the literature, preferably in diverse styles. This means developing over the years a list of excerpts, many of which can be taken from *Free Composition* or other sources, of the various techniques of voice leading and prolongation. In general I think that the alternation of analyses (prepared by the students) and such presentations by the instructor lead to the most coherent presentation of Schenker's ideas.

There are also times when the interpretation of a particular passage causes problems for some of the students, in which case I have found it helpful to show in a subsequent meeting how a similar or equivalent progression operates in another piece or two. Let us consider, for example, Schenker's interpretation of the middle section (mm.11–19) of the St. Anthony Chorale.[17] (A score reduction and an interpretation of this passage are given in example 8). Schenker's reason for introducing his analysis of this piece in *Free Composition* was to demonstrate motion from an inner voice (from f^1 up to d^2 in mm.11–14). This motion is followed by the introduction of the upper neighbor-note of $d^2(\hat{3})$, which is prolonged by a descent into an inner voice until its resolution in m.19. This prolongation of the $e^\flat$, which is supported by the progression IV^6 V^7, is an expansion of the neighbor-note relationships stated at the outset of the piece. Though eventually convinced of this interpretation, two or three of the students had difficulty at first with the idea that a note can be prolonged without being restated or present throughout. To overcome this misconception I found it helpful to find other musical passages where the same type of progression occurs. One such passage is

17. Ibid., Figure 42, 2. See also Forte, *Tonal Harmony in Concept and Practice*, third edition, example 522.

Example 8: Haydn, St. Anthony Chorale, 11–19.

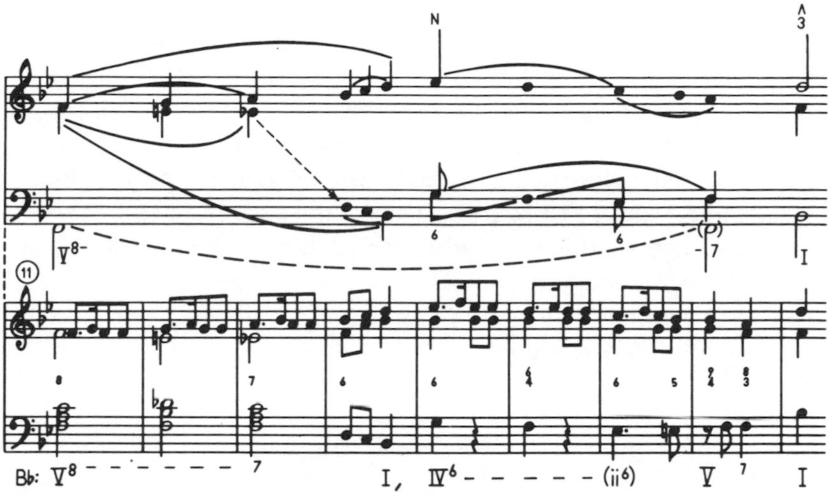

found at the beginning of the Allegro of Beethoven's Piano Sonata in E♭, Op. 81a. As shown in example 9, scale-degree 3 ($\hat{3}$) is introduced by a prolonged upper neighbor-note, which is supported by the harmonic progression IV^6–V^7.[18] (Not shown is the preparation in the preceding measures for the linear connection between the inner and top voices.) Here the prolongation of the upper neighbor is made obvious by its repetition just prior to its resolution. A somewhat different though comparable use of this same progression occurs in the opening movement of

Example 9: Beethoven, Piano Sonata in E♭, Op. 81a (I), 17–21.

18. Schenker, *Free Composition*, Supplement: Musical Examples, Figure 119, 7. See also Salzer, *Structural Hearing*, example 289.

Beethoven's Piano Sonata in C, Op. 53. As shown in example 10, the progression that actually establishes the key of C major is IV^6 V^7 I, the tonic coinciding with the repetition of the opening material. Quite interestingly this same harmonic progression is used to establish the new key area of E major (prepared as e minor) for statement of the second theme. Considered from one point of view this harmonic progression supports the prolonged upper neighbor-note of $\hat{5}$ (actually $\hat{5}$ to $\sharp\hat{5}$). However, it is also important to note the emphasis given to the b and the subsequent descent of a third from there to the g♯ in m.35 (see bracket). The significance of this descending third becomes immediately apparent by its repetition (inner voice) in mm.38–39 (not shown). Thus the surface in this case establishes an important relationship that obscures the underlying voice leading.

Example 10: Beethoven, Piano Sonata in C, Op. 53 (I), 1–35.

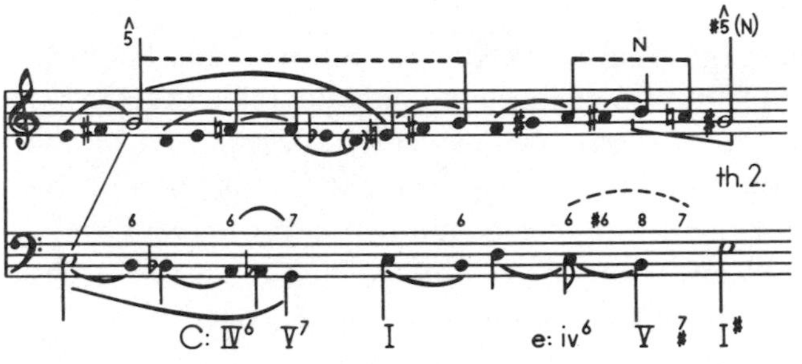

Readings about Schenker's theories should not be assigned, I feel, until after the basic concepts and terms have been presented through analysis. (Once again my reasoning is to control the flow of information, thus avoiding unnecessary confusion.) First I suggest reading my "Schenker Bibliography" and its recently updated version, which contain information about Schenker's own publications as well as the secondary literature.[19] Next I assign what I consider to be the best and most

19. David Beach, "A Schenker Bibliography," *Journal of Music Theory* **13** (1969); reprinted in *Readings in Schenker Analysis*, edited by Maury Yeston, New Haven: Yale University Press, 1977; and "A Schenker Bibliography: 1969–1979," *Journal of Music Theory* **23** (1979).

concise summaries of Schenker's theories in English.[20] They are: (1) Allen Forte, "Schenker's Conception of Musical Structure," *Journal of Music Theory* 3 (1959);[21] (2) Oswald Jonas, Introduction to the English translation of Schenker's *Harmonielehre*;[22] and (3) Adele Katz, "Heinrich Schenker's Method of Analysis," *The Musical Quarterly* 31 (1935). A more lengthy description of Schenker's work is contained in the first volume of Sylvan Kalib's dissertation.[23] Though there are many other important sources, several of which are cited below, these are more than sufficient to provide the student with an overview of Schenker's ideas and their significance.

While the students are occupied with assigned readings I take this opportunity to acquaint them with some of the problems associated with chromatic voice leading. Though there is not enough time to treat this subject thoroughly at this point in the course, we do take the time to examine several shorter works of Chopin and others. Also, since some of the students in my class are limited by other degree requirements to only one term of tonal analysis, I make sure that enough time is left at the end of the first semester to examine at least two larger works or movements of works in some detail. (Last year we analyzed the first movements of Mozart's Piano Sonata in A minor, K. 310, and Beethoven's Piano Sonata in A♭, Op. 110.) It is important for every student to realize that the techniques of voice leading and prolongation described by Schenker apply to the more remote as well as to the more immediate levels of structure. Though it would be unwise to proceed too quickly to a consideration of larger-scale tonal structure, it would also be unfortunate if the student of Schenker's theories were denied an opportunity to apply these concepts to a work of major proportions. After all, Schenker's main concern was with what he considered to be the "masterworks of music," the great pieces of the tonal period that are still performed regularly today.

20. For the most complete discussion of Schenker's theories, see Oswald Jonas, *Einführung in die Lehre Heinrich Schenkers: Das Wesen des musikalischen Kunstwerkes*, revised edition, Vienna: Universal, 1972; English translation by John Rothgeb, New York and London: Longman, 1982.

21. Reprinted in Yeston, *Readings in Schenker Analysis*.

22. Heinrich Schenker, *Harmony*, edited and annotated by Oswald Jonas, translated by Elisabeth Mann Borgese, Chicago: The University of Chicago Press, 1954; paperback edition, Cambridge: M.I.T. Press, 1973.

23. Sylvan Kalib, *Thirteen Essays from the Three Yearbooks "Das Meisterwerk in der Musik" by Heinrich Schenker: An Annotated Translation*, three vols., Ann Arbor: University Microfilms, 1973 (publ. no. 73-30, 626).

By way of concluding my thoughts on the teaching of Schenker analysis at this level I would like to stress two points that I consider extremely important. The first concerns Schenker's conception and our understanding of his conception of the relationship between strict and free composition. It is crucial for us to realize that in dealing with real composition the strict model on which it is based is never far from Schenker's mind. Only in this way can we comprehend and thus communicate the significance of much of what he says and does. The second concerns the role the ear plays in analysis. There can be no doubt that the ear does and should play an important part in the analytic process. However, it must be made clear right from the beginning that what a Schenker graph represents is not necessarily what we hear on the surface but the underlying voice-leading structure, which is subject to the rules of counterpoint. It is a fact that the surface characteristics of a particular work, which is what we often hear as most significant, can obscure the voice leading that supports these characteristics. Thus in constructing a musical graph we must be careful not to rely solely on our ear as the final judge of what is or is not important. Rather, we must strive to expand our perception and understanding beyond the surface to include other levels and types of musical organization.

B. Principles of Graphic Notation

One of the most commonly held misconceptions about Schenker analysis is that the secret of success lies in learning the principles of graphic notation. Nothing could be farther from the truth. The secret of learning Schenker analysis, that is, of learning to represent musical relationships in graphic notation, lies in understanding the music and the principles that govern *its* structure. On most every occasion when a student has complained to me that he or she would have done a better job if I had only been more explicit about notational matters, it has soon become apparent that the problem is not the notation but the student's understanding of the piece. If one understands the structure of a work and thus knows exactly what he wants to show, it is not a difficult matter to represent those relationships in musical notation. The problem arises when one does not understand the music or is unsure about the voice leading. I do not mean to imply that there is nothing one can teach about notation, since surely there are certain basic principles that everyone must know. But these principles are rudimentary and easy to learn. What is not so easy is learning to apply them.

The use of music notation to represent musical relationships is a unique feature of Schenker's work. Since his ideas about music developed so dramatically over the span of his career, it is only natural that his notation of its relationships would also change. This becomes immediately apparent if one compares the graphs published in *Tonwille* (1921-24), for example, to those in *Free Composition* (1935). Even within the latter work Schenker did not attempt to standardize his notation nor explain his procedures, though his use of certain symbols was quite consistent. Rather, Schenker's use of notation seems to have been dependent upon the requirements of the particular situation, and thus quite flexible.

Allen Forte has pointed out that Schenker's graphs fall into two basic categories, which he has labelled "rhythmic" and "structural."[24] In the former, which is often referred to as a metric reduction, the notes retain their relative durational values. (See example 6.) However, in the structural graph, note values do not indicate duration but structural significance. The more remote or deeper levels of structure are indicated by the larger note values, and the more immediate levels by the shorter ones. For example, in *Free Composition* half notes (but sometimes whole notes) are used for the fundamental structure—the fundamental line, which is further designated by scale-degree numbers with carets above them, and its supporting bass. Quarter notes indicate the components of the middleground—the linear progressions and their supporting bass lines—and note values without stems indicate events belonging to the foreground. The eighth note is most often used to indicate an embellishing tone, such as a neighbor-note, or the stepwise approach to the dominant in the bass. (See example 4.) Beams and slurs are used to connect and group together components belonging to the same structural level, and the double curved slur is used to indicate motion to the dominant in the bass. (See examples 1, 4, and 7.) These are the main components of graphic notation. Other special symbols used by Schenker (for interruption, omission, etc.) are mentioned by Forte, and thus need not be discussed here.

The symbols used in graphic notation are quite simple, and thus cause little difficulty in themselves. The main problem, alluded to above, is determining which events belong to a particular structural level. In this respect we must realize that what constitute the various

24. Allen Forte, "Introduction to the English Edition" of *Free Composition*, pp. xix-xx.

levels for a sixteen-measure theme, for example, are significantly different than those for a whole section or movement. If the principles of notation are used consistently, the two structural graphs might look quite similar. This is exactly what one finds in *Free Composition*.[25] It is also true that what is shown as a middleground motion in the graph of a smaller section of a piece may appear as a foreground event in a graph of the entire piece. (Particularly with longer works Schenker preferred to construct several graphs so that he could show a certain amount of detail as well as the long-range connections.) This is not an inconsistency but a reinterpretation in relation to a larger context. Schenker was, in fact, quite consistent in using the notational symbols but flexible in his interpretation of what constitutes the foreground, middleground, and background. That is, the principles of notation remain constant, but what the symbols represent varies with the magnitude of the piece or section being considered. It is important to be aware of this fact when studying Schenker's graphs, particularly when comparing those of the same as well as different pieces.

A somewhat different system of graphic notation was developed by Felix Salzer to accommodate his adaptation and expansion of Schenker's ideas in *Structural Hearing*.[26] Several new terms and their symbols, such as "embellishing chord" (Em) and "contrapuntal-structural chord" (CS), appear for the first time in this work. A most interesting feature of the notation itself is the use of note stems of varying lengths to differentiate between structural levels. The advantage of this method is that one can show several different levels of the middleground in a single graph. In conjunction with this procedure Salzer uses a variety of dotted and solid lines, slurs, arrows, and beams, much more than Schenker used, to indicate relationships among components of the same structural level. A clear explanation of this system of notation is given at the end of the first volume of *The Music Forum*.[27] Though this system of notation is quite accessible to those accustomed to Schenker's graphs, I recommend that you study this glossary carefully since it will facilitate your reading of the analytic graphs of Salzer and others who have adopted its use.

---

25. Compare, for example, Figure 153, 1 (Chopin, Ballade in G minor, Op. 23) and Figure 157 (Mozart, Sonata in A major, K. 331, first movement, Theme).
26. See "Notes and Glossary for the Voice-Leading Graphs," *Structural Hearing*, vol. 2, pp. xiii–xiv. The same type of notation is employed by Salzer and Carl Schachter in *Counterpoint in Composition*.
27. William Mitchell and Felix Salzer (editors), "A Glossary of the Elements of Graphic Analysis," *The Music Forum* 1 (1967), pp. 260–268.

The ultimate purpose of an analytic graph is to communicate our interpretation of a work's structure, and thus it is important that we develop a method of notation that represents our ideas as clearly as possible. Since Schenker did not provide us with a unified notational system—though, as mentioned, he was consistent in following certain principles—it is not surprising that variants of his graphic notation would appear in the sketches of his students and others. The result is that more than one way of representing various kinds of relationships has been developed. Consider again, if you will, the two notational procedures employed in example 7. The notation of the first phrase is based directly on Schenker's method, though modified by the use of stem lengths as well as slurs to distinguish between two different orders of prolongation at the middleground level. The notation of the second phrase reflects more clearly the innovations of Salzer and others. The primary difference between this and the first notation is the change of the slurs to solid and dotted beams, except for the initial ascent to d^2. (Solid beams connect different pitches, while dotted beams indicate the connection and prolongation of a single pitch or harmony.) Though different in appearance, the two communicate the desired information with equal clarity. The point, then, is that there are different methods of graphic notation, and it is our responsibility to learn these variants in the process of developing our own ability to represent and communicate our ideas.[28]

C. Advanced Studies in Schenker Analysis

In some respects the teaching of Schenker analysis at the intermediate and advanced levels is easier than at the introductory stage, where much of the energy is spent on the careful presentation and explanation of new ideas. Later, however, it can be assumed that the students are acquainted with the important concepts and terminology, and thus the time can be devoted almost exclusively to the analysis of music of increasing complexity and length and of different styles and periods. This is the time when the student really begins to comprehend and

28. My own notation (see phrase 1 of example 7) reflects several influences, primarily Schenker but also Allen Forte and Ernst Oster, with whom I studied Schenker analysis. At times, particularly when I want to show several different levels of connection simultaneously, I find it useful to adopt some of the modifications introduced by Salzer. No matter what techniques I might employ at a given time my main concern always is to communicate my ideas as clearly as possible without violating the basic principles of graphic notation inherent in Schenker's work.

appreciate the meaning and breadth of Schenker's thought. When he sees, for example, that a particular voice-leading technique occurs in the music of Chopin and Brahms just as it does in that of Bach and Beethoven and that it also occurs at more remote as well as at immediate levels of structure, the meaning and significance of that technique become increasingly apparent. As we progress with our analytic studies, the student also gains experience at making difficult judgments independently and, in the process, begins to cope at a more sophisticated level than ever before with the difficulties of representing his observations in graphic notation.

For the second term of analysis, I limit the selection of pieces to those that fall within the boundaries of Schenker's own investigations. Extensions of Schenker's theories are best considered, I feel, at a later time. (See section III below.) Normally I begin with a few relatively short works of Bach, works that are more intricate contrapuntally than those studied during the first term. Among others, some of the preludes from the *Well-Tempered Clavier* are well suited for this purpose. Next we study two or three movements from works of the Classical period. Recently I have been looking at the Mozart piano sonatas in some detail and have found several movements that contain a wealth of material for comparative analysis. In conjunction with the analysis of these movements I have involved the class during the past two years in a research project, the thrust of which is described below. Since we are dealing here with works that pose few harmonic problems for the student, we can concentrate our efforts on structural matters. However, for the remainder of the term the emphasis shifts to works of increasing harmonic complexity and scope. For this purpose I normally concentrate on selected works of Chopin and Brahms.

It is important, I think, that the students have an opportunity to examine at least one of Schenker's more extensive analyses in some detail during the course of their studies. Choosing from the numerous possibilities depends, of course, on the circumstances. Two that are readily available and appropriate for use in the latter portion of the program of study outlined above are the analyses of Chopin's Etude in F major, Op. 10, No. 8, and his Etude in C minor, Op. 10, No. 12, which are contained in the *Five Graphic Music Analyses*.[29] An extensive analysis of Beethoven's Third Symphony is published in *Das Meisterwerk* III. In past years we have studied a small portion of this analysis, for

29. Analyses of some of the other Chopin Etudes can be found in *Das Meisterwerk* I, and *Free Composition*.

example that of the exposition of the first movement. However, I have decided against doing so again, since one can hardly do justice to the analysis itself in this way. There is more than enough information there for an entire course.

One feature of Schenker's work that I find particularly fascinating, and thus one that I stress in teaching, is his description of "motivic parallelism."[30] Schenker has demonstrated that the motive, a melodic figure defined by pitch rather than rhythm, often appears at different structural levels of a piece as a result of the expansion or contraction of its "pattern." Examples of this compositional technique surface at various times during the course of the year, and some have been mentioned in passing in the previous sections of this paper. For example, a specific instance of motivic expansion was noted in reference to the Menuet from Bach's French Suite in C minor. (See examples 1 and 2 and the accompanying discussion.) Also it was noted that the prolongation of the e♭ in mm.15–18 of the St. Anthony Chorale (see example 8) is an expansion of the neighbor-note relationship first stated and expanded in the opening two measures of that work. Clear examples of large-scale motivic expansion can be found in several of Beethoven's works in particular. It can be demonstrated, for example, that much of Beethoven's Sonata in A♭, Op. 110, is derived from relationships stated in the opening four measures of the piece. (One might also note that the fourth measure contains a contraction of the middleground melodic structure of the entire phrase.) And Schenker has pointed out that the primary melodic structure of the opening phrase (mm.1–8) of the first movement of Beethoven's Op. 2, No. 1, is subsequently elaborated and extended over the first portion (mm.49–81) of the development secton.[31] Discovery of such relationships provides real insight into the structure of a particular work and, in a more general sense, into the compositional process.

A related matter that has fascinated me for several years, ever since my days studying with Ernst Oster, is the meaning of the large-scale harmonic progression that transverses the development section of Mozart's Piano Sonata in F, K. 280 (I). As shown in example 11, the initial part of this progression is a motion from the dominant down to the major triad a

30. For a detailed discussion of this feature of Schenker's work see Charles Burkhart, "Schenker's 'Motivic Parallelisms,'" *Journal of Music Theory* **22** (1978).

31. *Der Tonwille* 2 (1922), pp. 25–48.

third below, which is approached through the augmented-sixth chord on B♭. The A major chord, rather than leading as expected to the submediant, continues through a passing four-three chord to the tonic, thus completing the large-scale descending arpeggiation of the tonic triad. Acting many years later on Oster's suggestion, I discovered that this same or equivalent progression occurs in several other movements of Mozart's piano sonatas, and subsequently I assigned my students the task of explaining (or at least attempting to explain) the meaning of its individual as well as multiple appearances.[32] The variants of this progression are too numerous to list here, and the results of the study are far from conclusive.[33] However, there is strong evidence to support the idea that many of the occurrences of this large-scale arpeggiation are expansions of the primary motives of their respective movements.

Example 11

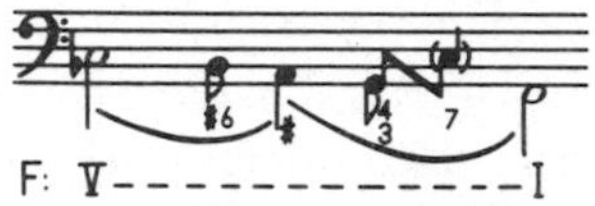

Though analytic studies of the various sorts outlined above occupy most of our time, there are certain readings that are most appropriate at this stage. In addition to Charles Burkhart's enlightening discussion of Schenker's theory of motivic parallelism (see footnote 30), I heartily recommend the following three articles: Ernst Oster, "Register and Large-Scale Connection," *Journal of Music Theory* 5 (1961); John Rothgeb, "Design as a Key to Structure in Tonal Music," *Journal of Music Theory* 15 (1971); and John Rothgeb, "Strict Counterpoint and Tonal Theory," *Journal of Music Theory* 19 (1975).[34] This is also the time to recommend reading Schenker's *Free Composition*, now that the students have enough background to understand and appreciate its contents.

32. Though difficult for many, I think all the students enjoyed the challenge of attempting to answer questions at this level. If nothing else, I hope they learned that meaningful answers can result only from asking interesting questions.
33. The eventual results of this study will be documented in a subsequent article.
34. The first two of these are reprinted in Yeston, *Readings in Schenker Analysis*.

III. READINGS AND RELATED STUDIES

In the preceding sections I have stressed the study of Schenker's theories through analysis, since I think that is the only way one can really come to understand the content and significance of what he has written. Though it is clear that years of study and practice are required to become proficient at Schenker analysis, the studies outlined above should provide sufficient background for the serious student to pursue further work on his own. Ideally, of course, it would be preferable if there were an opportunity for an additional course (e.g., a graduate seminar) devoted to the study of the most important sources. Rather than attempt to be exhaustive in considering the available literature I will indicate in the discussion below certain topics that I think should be given serious consideration in designing such a course (or one's own program of study). These comments are divided into two sections, the first dealing with Schenker's writings and the other with the secondary literature. This division is merely a convenience, since such a course would quite naturally include the most important sources from both categories.

A. Schenker's Writings

Schenker's writings reflect his lifelong interest in the practical as well as theoretical aspects of music. Though it is certainly possible to characterize some of his works as primarily theoretical and others as primarily practical in nature, most of his writings are products of his interest in both areas. So far we have concentrated on Schenker's theoretical views (primarily as expressed in *Free Composition*) as well as their analytic applications. It is important, however, that we do not ignore his work in other areas, for example his important contribution to the science of autograph study. It was Schenker who set the standards for modern editorial practice in music by his consultation of autographs, first editions, and other authoritative sources. This aspect of Schenker's work is reflected in his various editions of music, including the selected keyboard works of C. P. E. Bach[35] and the piano sonatas of Beethoven.[36] Particularly interesting in this and other respects are his explanatory editions of four of the last five piano sonatas of Beethoven, each of which is

35. Ph. Em. Bach, *Klavierwerke*, Neue kritische Ausgabe, Vienna: Universal, 1902-3. See also *Ein Beitrag zur Ornamentik, als Einführung zu Ph. Em. Bachs Klavierwerken*, Vienna: Universal, 1904; neue revidierte und vermehrte Auflage, 1908. English translation by Hedi Siegel, *The Music Forum* 4, pp. 1-139.
36. Beethoven, *Sämtliche Klaviersonaten*, nach den Autographen reconstruiert von Heinrich Schenker, Vienna: Universal, 192-; revised edition, 1947. Reissued as the *Complete Piano Sonatas*, with a new introduction by Carl Schachter, New York: Dover, 1975.

accompanied by an extensive commentary.[37] In addition to information about the various sources and his critical evaluation of the literature, Schenker provides his own analysis of each work and comments on various aspects of performance. These works, though primarily practical in orientation, are excellent examples of the bond between theory and practice in Schenker's writings. This relationship is also evident in many of his other works, most notably in his extensive analyses of Beethoven's Third, Fifth, and Ninth symphonies, and Mozart's Symphony in G minor.[38] Here again we find extensive commentary on sources, literature, and matters of performance along with his analytic observations. Of these major studies I would recommend the first listed (Beethoven's Third Symphony) since it represents Schenker's views and analytic procedures in their most mature form.

There is more than enough material and variety of information in Schenker's writings for several seminars. One possible area of investigation would be to trace the development of Schenker's theoretical views and analytic procedures through study of selected essays and analyses in *Der Tonwille* and the three volumes of *Das Meisterwerk in der Musik*.[39] Also, the matter of autograph study (by Schenker as well as others) and its relationship to analytic and performance decisions could form the nucleus of an interesting course. It seems to me that a topic involving application of acquired analytic skills, perhaps concentrating on one or two of the late Beethoven sonatas, would be particularly appropriate at this stage. As part of this study one would consult Schenker's critical editions of these works as well as the important sources and pertinent literature. Also one might decide to focus in part on the types of motivic relationships described by Schenker in his analyses of some of the earlier Beethoven sonatas.[40] Such a topic, though focused on a particular work or small group of works, leads to several different yet related areas of investigation, all of which play a vital role in Schenker's own work.

---

37. *Erläuterungsausgaben der letzten fünf Sonaten Beethovens*, Vienna: Universal: Op. 109, 1913; Op. 110, 1914; Op. 111, 1915; Op. 101, 1920. Reissued as *Die letzten Sonaten*, edited by Oswald Jonas, 1971–72.
38. "Beethovens dritte Sinfonie," *Das Meisterwerk* III (1930).
Beethovens fünfte Sinfonie, Vienna: Universal, 1925; reprinted 1969. Originally published in three installments in the first, fifth, and sixth issues of *Der Tonwille*.
Beethovens neunte Sinfonie, Vienna: Universal, 1912; reprinted 1969.
"Mozart: Sinfonie G-Moll," *Das Meisterwerk* II (1926). Translated in Kalib (see footnote 23), vol. 2, pp. 321–429.
39. Several of these are now available in translation. See David Beach, "A Schenker Bibliography: 1969-1979," *Journal of Music Theory* 23 (1979), p. 278.
40. See, for example, his analyses of the Sonatas, Op. 2, No. 1, and Op. 57, in the second and seventh issues of *Der Tonwille*, respectively.

B. Secondary Sources

In two previous publications (see footnote 19) I have listed and classified the large amount of literature that has grown out of Schenker's work. My purpose here is not to review this material but rather to specify those sources that I find particularly worthy of our attention. I have already mentioned what I consider to be the best summaries of Schenker's work and explanations of various aspects of his theories. Yet to be considered, though also important, are the various extensions and criticisms of Schenker's theories.[41] In the following paragraphs I will discuss briefly the applications and extensions of Schenker's theories to the analysis of pre-Baroque music, twentieth-century music, and rhythmic structure in tonal music. The most important sources in each of these categories are listed following the end of this essay.

The first to advocate the extension of Schenker's ideas to music beyond the scope of Schenker's own investigation was Felix Salzer. According to Salzer, the basic principle of tonality, which he defines as "directed motion within the framework of a single prolonged sonority,"[42] is characteristic of much of the music written from the middle of the twelfth century on. This view is expressed clearly in the following passage from *Structural Hearing*:

> The inception of the principle of tonality and certain of its techniques expressing themselves in the construction of tonal units of various length and complexity goes as far back as the Organa of St. Martial and Santiago de Compostela. A continuous development of structural polyphony from the twelfth to the twentieth century may with justification be assumed. Whether we encounter the use of modes or the major-minor system, whether the contrapuntal voice leadings are different from those of later periods or whether harmonic thinking expresses itself in a different manner than later on in the eighteenth century, the music of the Middle Ages and Renaissance demonstrates the same basic principles of direction, continuity and coherence as music from the Baroque period to the twentieth century. (I, p. 281)

41. The most recent critique of Schenker's ideas is Eugene Narmour, *Beyond Schenkerism: The Need for Alternatives in Music Analysis*, Chicago: The University of Chicago Press, 1977. To understand Narmour's criticisms as well as his proposed alternatives one should first become well acquainted with what Schenker himself has said. Also I would recommend reading several of the reviews of this book. (See John Rothgeb in *Theory and Practice* 3 and in the *Journal of Research in Music Education* **26**; Ruth Solie in *Notes* **34**; Kay Dreyfus in *The Journal of Aesthetics and Art Criticism* **36**; James McCalla in *19th Century Music* **2**; and Steven Haflich in the *Journal of Music Theory* **23**.)
42. Felix Salzer, "Tonality in Medieval Polyphony," *The Music Forum* **1** (1967), p. 54.

Salzer's discussion of his view of the historical development of tonal coherence is accompanied by several analyses of pre-Baroque works. (See *Structural Hearing*, II, examples 511–539.) Additional analyses can be found in the tenth chapter of *Counterpoint in Composition* and in several articles by Salzer and others in the first two volumes of *The Music Forum*.

Extensions and applications of Schenker's theories to music of the twentieth century are considerably more varied. In some cases the association is tenuous, the only similarity being the use of musical graphs to show linear connections at various levels. In other cases, however, the association is more direct in that the hierarchy of levels is shown to be governed by some predefined principle(s) of tonality. The difference lies in the definition of tonality itself. For Schenker a work is tonal only if it is governed by the unfolding of the tonic triad. A much more inclusive definition is given by Roy Travis, who must be regarded as the central figure in the extension of Schenker's ideas to music of this century. Travis states that "music is tonal when its motion unfolds through time a particular tone, interval, or chord."[43] Examination of his writings reveals that this prolonged interval or chord (often referred to as the "tonic sonority") can be dissonant as well as consonant.

As an introduction to this topic I would suggest reading the first two articles by Travis listed following this essay. In the first article he discusses several short works, including numbers 124 and 133 from Bartok's *Mikrokosmos* and the opening of Stravinsky's *Le Sacre du Printemps*. The second article discusses directed motion in two additional short works for piano: Schoenberg's Op. 19, No. 2, and the second movement of Webern's *Variations for Piano*, Op. 27. Travis's analysis of the former piece is not only interesting in itself but also particularly useful as a point of departure for further study and analysis.[44]

---

43. Roy Travis, "Towards a New Concept of Tonality," *Journal of Music Theory* 3 (1959), p. 261.

44. It is interesting to compare Travis's analysis of this piece with those contained in the following sources: Allen Forte, "Context and Continuity in an Atonal Work: A Set-Theoretic Approach," *Perspectives of New Music* 1 (1963), pp. 79–81; Hugo Leichtentritt, *Musical Form*, Cambridge: Harvard University Press, 1961, pp. 445–446; and Robert Suderburg, *Tonal Cohesion in Schoenberg's Twelve-Tone Music*, Ann Arbor: University Microfilms, 1966 (publ. no. 66-10, 672), pp. 82–85.

One of the most common misconceptions regarding Schenkerian analysis is that it minimizes the importance rhythm plays in musical structure. Though it is true that Schenker did not formulate a theory of rhythm and that he did indeed describe background structure as being arhythmic, he most certainly did not ignore the significance of rhythm at more immediate levels of structure. As has already been noted, many of his analytic graphs are metric reductions of voice leading, and others, like that of the C major Prelude of Bach, show larger-scale metric organization. In addition, several of his analytic essays contain extensive commentary about rhythmic detail, quite often related in some way with matters of performance. From these sources it becomes clear that Schenker was most interested in rhythmic detail and organization. Unfortunately, his only separate discussion of the topic is the rather brief fourth chapter in part III of *Free Composition*, a fact that most likely is the source of the abovementioned misconception.

In recent years various individuals have become interested in extending Schenker's ideas about rhythm with the idea of formulating a theory that is analagous in some way to the hierarchical nature of pitch organization in tonal music. Two such extensions are Arthur Komar's *Theory of Suspensions* and Maury Yeston's *The Stratification of Musical Rhythm*. Before studying these works I would suggest first reading Carl Schachter's extended essay on "Rhythm and Linear Analysis" in the fourth and fifth volumes of *The Music Forum*.[45] If time permits one should read these as well as some other recent sources,[46] since they too contain many interesting ideas about a topic that is of vital interest to us all.

45. A third and final part is scheduled for publication in vol. 6 of *The Music Forum*.
46. See, for example, David Epstein's *Beyond Orpheus: Studies in Musical Structure*, Cambridge: M.I.T. Press, 1979.

EXTENSIONS OF SCHENKER'S THEORIES

A. Pre-Baroque Music

Salzer, Felix. *Structural Hearing: Tonal Coherence in Music,* two vols. New York: Charles Boni, 1952; New York: Dover Publications, 1962.

Salzer, Felix and Carl Schachter. "Voice-leading Techniques in Historical Perspective (ca. 1450–ca. 1900)," chapter 10 of *Counterpoint in Composition.* New York: McGraw-Hill, 1969.

The Music Forum, edited by William Mitchell and Felix Salzer.

1: Articles by Peter Bergquist and Felix Salzer.

2: Articles by William Mitchell, Saul Novack, and Carl Schachter.

B. Twentieth-Century Music

Baker, James. "Scriabin's Implicit Tonality," *Music Theory Spectrum* **2** (1980).

Forte, Allen. *Contemporary Tone Structures.* New York: Bureau of Publications, Teacher's College, Columbia University, 1955.

______. "Schoenberg's Creative Evolution: The Path to Atonality," *The Musical Quarterly* **64** (1978).

Katz, Adele. *Challenge to Musical Tradition: A New Concept of Tonality.* New York: Alfred A. Knopf, 1945.

Lester, Joel. *A Theory of Atonal Prolongations as Used in an Analysis of the Serenade, Op. 24, by Arnold Schoenberg.* Ann Arbor: University Microfilms, pub. no. 71-1615, 1971.

Morgan, Robert P. "Dissonant Prolongations: Theoretical and Compositional Precedents," *Journal of Music Theory* **20** (1976).

Salzer, Felix. (See entry above.)

Travis, Roy. "Towards a New Concept of Tonality," *Journal of Music Theory* **3** (1959).

______. "Directed Motion in Schoenberg and Webern," *Perspectives of New Music* **4** (1966).

______. "Tonal Coherence in the First Movement of Bartok's Fourth String Quartet," *The Music Forum* **2** (1970).

______. [Analysis of Movement I ("Bewegt") of Webern's Orchestral Pieces (1913)], *Journal of Music Theory* **18** (1974).

C. Rhythm

Komar, Arthur. *Theory of Suspension: A Study of Metrical Pitch Relations in Tonal Music.* Princeton: Princeton University Press, 1971; Austin, Texas: Peer Publications, 1980.

Schachter, Carl. "Rhythm and Linear Analysis: A Preliminary Study," *The Music Forum* **4** (1976); and "Rhythm and Linear Analysis: Durational Reduction," *The Music Forum* **5** (1980).

Yeston, Maury. *The Stratification of Musical Rhythm.* New Haven: Yale University Press, 1976.

concealed repetition (structural patterns at middleground
— expansions of same
— contractions in melodic structures

Thematic Content: A Schenkerian View

JOHN ROTHGEB

". . . music was destined to reach its culmination in the likeness of itself . . ."
Schenker, *Free Composition*

If a "Schenkerian view" of thematic content is taken to mean a view set forth by Schenker himself, or one that can be directly inferred from his theory of tonal organization, then the title of this article imposes narrow limits on the kinds of generalizations it can make. For Schenker's theory neither proposes nor implies a theory of thematic construction or relations for music. This does not, however, mean that it can contribute nothing to their elucidation. In the paragraphs that follow I should like first to sketch briefly Schenker's basic conception of the thematic dimension with the aid of some quotations from his writings, and then to illustrate with several examples from the literature the sorts of thematic features whose recognition and understanding seem to me to be fostered by a Schenkerian view of tonal organization in general.

Schenkerian thought recognizes only one imperative for thematic content: the necessity of repetition. Music, lacking access to the kinds of direct association with the phenomenal world central to most other art forms, was able to satisfy the universal requirement of association only through the "likeness of itself"—through self-repetition.[1] The rise of polyphony, as is well known, brought with it an emphasis on repetition through imitation. During this epoch, "repetition lay always on the surface; it was immediately and constantly perceptible to eye and ear as inversions, augmentations, and contractions."[2] Early polyphony provided in ample measure the "pleasure the ear derived from repetition—a joy in recognition itself."[3]

Later, musical art was enriched when simple and literal repetitions—including both temporally distant repetitions of form-defining significance and the more immediate and local repetitions from bar to bar and phrase to phrase—began to be supplemented by other less obvious forms:

1. Heinrich Schenker, *Free Composition,* translated and edited by E. Oster, New York and London: Longman, 1979, p. 93. See also Oswald Jonas, *Einführung in die Lehre H. Schenkers,* revised edition, Vienna: Universal, 1972, pp. 1–8 and passim. A valuable recent contribution to the Schenker-oriented study of thematic organization is Charles Burkhart, "Schenker's 'Motivic Parallelisms,' " *Journal of Music Theory* 22 (1978).
2. Schenker, p. 99.
3. Ibid.

> New types of repetition . . . revealed themselves to composers of genius. Although these new types seem to lie just as clearly before eye and ear as the repetitions that occurred within the imitative forms, they remained less accessible because they did not offer creator and listener the same ease of perception. They were fully as effective as the simpler repetitions; they, too, sprang only from the blood relationship of statement and variant, almost beyond the composer's volition—but they remained concealed.[4]

If there is a single aspect of Schenker's work that could be described as the hallmark of his view of thematic content, it would be his recognition of the concealed repetition (*verborgene Wiederholung*), both as an abstraction and in the innumerable concrete manifestations revealed in his analytical and critical essays.

Schenker's notion of the phenomenon of concealed repetition is unique in two respects. First, it is inextricably bound to his theory of structural levels and the compositional unfolding of triads. Second, Schenkerian theory nowhere specifies in an abstract way exactly how or where such repetitions shall or must occur in a work, or how we are to look for them. Schenkerian theory therefore has less in common than is widely believed with the Schoenbergian *Grundgestalt* (basic shape) or derivative ideas, which are based on various formulations of the premise that "the whole collection of themes in a work, though apparently independent of one another, can be traced back to a single basic idea. . . ."[5] Such conceptions impose unwelcome and often explicit prior constraints on our analytical thought processes.[6] Indeed, by suggesting all too specifically where relationships should be sought (i.e., in the underlying unity of the apparently contrasting "themes"), they can and often do divert attention from the true loci of association, the concealed repetitions that cut across formal boundaries, thematic entities, and voice-leading strata.

Although a Schenkerian approach to the study of association in music sets no requirements as to where or how relationships are to be discovered, it does impose a different kind of obligation on those who adopt

4. Ibid.

5. Joseph Rufer, *Composition with Twelve Notes Related Only to One Another,* trans. by H. Searle; third impression, revised, London: Barrie and Rockliff, 1965, p. 29. See also David Epstein, *Beyond Orpheus: Studies in Musical Structure,* Cambridge, Mass., and London: M.I.T. Press, 1979.

6. For example, according to Alan Walker, "in a masterpiece, ideas give birth to ideas and these in turn to still newer ones; a network of relationships is established, everything belongs to everything else and ultimately to a single progenitor. The fundamental task of analysis *must be* to show how a piece of music hangs together *by demonstrating this progenitor.*" (Alan Walker, *A Study in Musical Analysis,* New York: The Free Press of Glencoe, 1963, p. 47; emphasis added.)

it. The uncovering of a nonobvious repetition usually entails simplification of at least one of the tone-successions involved; a Schenkerian approach requires that such simplification—the selection (*Auslese*, Schenker would say) of relatively few tones as a basis of association from relatively many—be founded on fixed and indisputable principles of relation (ultimately those of basic counterpoint) between simple and complex tone-successions. In other words, a Schenkerian approach encourages the discovery of relationships (possibly unexpected) by "reading through" diminution to underlying shape, but with the restriction that the "reading" process must be informed by principles that are independent of any specific configuration one may believe "ought" to be present.

What this implies may best be shown with reference to a specific case. In a monograph on Mozart's "Jupiter" symphony, Johann Nepomuk David presents the following example in support of his contention that "the second theme of the [first] movement immediately uses all ten notes of the cantus firmus."[7] One need not refer to the lower voice that appears in the score to sense that tones 5, 6, and 7 of the cantus firmus are represented in the music by incomplete neighboring tones (echappées in their purest form), and that note 8 is represented by a passing tone. The theme by itself, and especially in combination with its bass, makes clear that the upbeat to bar 5 stands for g, not a, and that the tonal succession in bars 5–6 must be heard as f–e–d, not g–f–e. A

Example 1

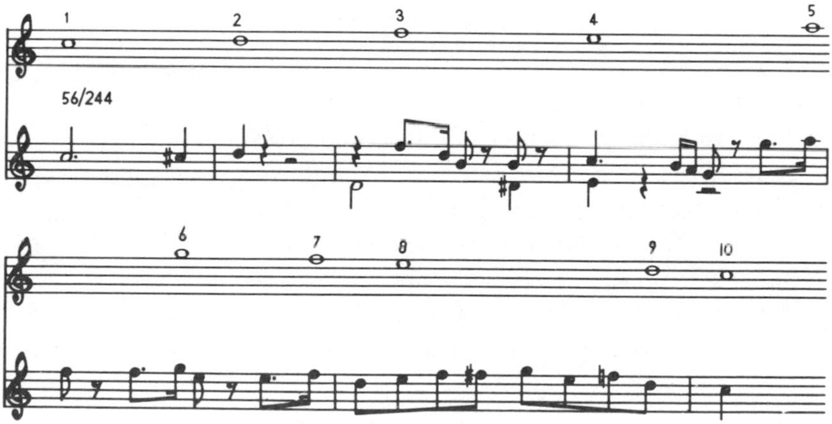

7. Johann Nepomuk David, *Die Jupiter-Symphonie: Eine Studie über die thematisch-melodischen Zusammenhänge,* fourth printing, Göttingen: Vandenhoeck & Ruprecht, 1960, p. 12.

Schenkerian approach to the study of this music, without denying the possible relationship of this theme to other themes in the symphony, would disallow David's particular interpretation of it. A Schenkerian analyst who expected to find the whole cantus firmus in this theme would meet with disappointment and would be forced to abandon that expectation.

This example is an unusually simple one; but although generalizations are hazardous, I think one can say that it illustrates, in a small way, a principle of some generality: Proposed thematic relationships must bear scrutiny in the light of the Schenkerian theory of structural strata, along with the evidence provided by immediate features of the musical surface. The levels by themselves will not necessarily constitute criterial evidence in favor of a hypothesized relationship, but one that is incompatible with the levels in the sense that example 1 is should be dismissed as spurious. Because Schenkerian theory specifies the "*strictly logical precision of relationship* between simple tone-successions and more complex ones,"[8] it supplies an indispensable testing ground for thematic hypotheses; more importantly, it promotes the hearing and identification of relationships wherever and however they may be manifested. This, it seems to me, is what differentiates a Schenkerian approach essentially from investigations that set out with the interrelatedness of all "themes" as an initial premise, and adjust their methods of interpreting diminution as the occasion demands.

ILLUSTRATIONS

The analytical discussions that follow are intended to illustrate above all the principle of concealed repetition in a variety of manifestations. The phenomena to be exhibited should stimulate further study; the reader is invited to investigate any generalizations that suggest themselves by testing them against further examples from the tonal literature.

Consider first the Courante of Handel's Suite No. 8 in F minor. This movement is in a type of ternary form that in many ways comes close to sonata form. At the beginning of the B ("development") section, in bar 21, Handel introduces a free inversion of the movement's opening

---

8. Schenker, p. 18.

motive. (See example 2, parts (a) and (b).) Association through repetition is thus realized in an obvious way. But the inverted motive of bars 21-23 is at the same time still more intimately connected with what immediately preceded it. The diminution[9] associated with the cadence in bars 19-20 describes two descending thirds, the second of them slightly augmented rhythmically. The latter of these, e♭-d-c, is redrawn in still larger rhythmic values by the inverted motive, with a beautiful inflection of the d to d♭ (in agreement with the local expansion of A♭ major). (See example 2, level (c).) The use of motivic inversion by itself is commonplace, accessible to any composition student; it is the integration into such an inversion of a concealed repetition that elevates Handel's idea and its execution to a higher artistic plane.

Example 2: Handel, Suite No. 8, Courante.

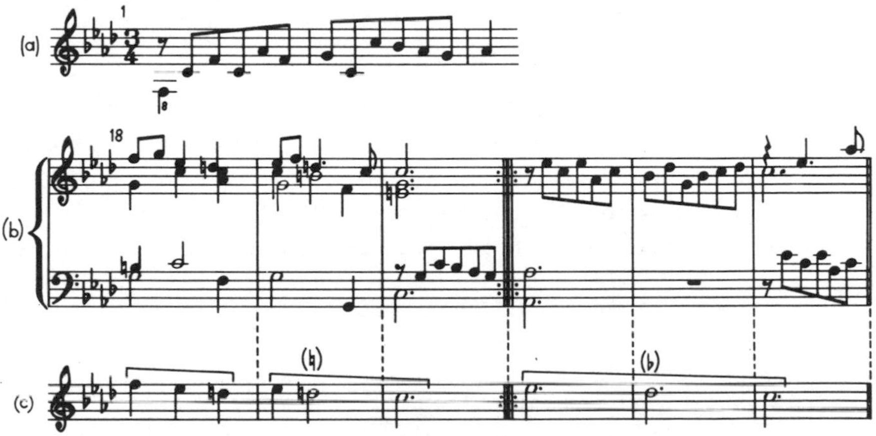

9. I will use the term "diminution" throughout this paper in the Schenkerian sense, in which it designates "embellishment in a general, broad sense." See Schenker, p. 93, footnote 6 (by Ernst Oster).

A closely related procedure is found at the principal division (bar 36) of Bach's G minor Sinfonia. (See example 3.) Bars 37–40 augment the descending third of the cadence, f–e–d, internally articulating it into two tone-pairs and inflecting the passing tone downward to e♭. (The surface diminutions of the right hand in bars 38 and 40 derive ultimately from the middle voice of bars 2–3.)

Example 3: Bach, Sinfonia No. 11.

In Mozart's Sonata in B♭, K. 333, first movement, the last cadence of the exposition not only grows out of what has preceded it in the second theme group (in particular the many occurrences in different guises of $\hat{6}$ as an upper neighbor to $\hat{5}$) but prefigures the first theme itself as it appears, transposed, at the head of the development! (See example 4.)

Example 4: Mozart, Sonata in B♭, K. 333.

The examples presented so far illustrate a particular use of concealed repetition, a procedure that Schenker termed "linkage technique,"[10] which establishes continuity across formal divisions. Repeti-

10. *Knüpftechnik.* See Jonas, pp. 6–8, for additional examples.

tions introduced for this purpose need not involve restatement of the same pitch succession: They may instead be expressed by sequential continuation, as in the following example from Chopin's Mazurka in G minor, Op. 24, No. 1. (The music of bars 25–34 is given at (a) in example 5.) A cadence in bar 32 marks the end of a B♭ major section; B♭ now becomes an applied dominant to the E♭ of the ensuing section. As revealed at level (b), the basic outlines of bars 25–32 (descending thirds embellished by upper auxiliaries) press onward into the E♭ section, in spite of the change in diminution occasioned by the return to the dotted rhythm of the opening. The parallel sixths above the bass F in bars 30–31 originate in those of bars 25–26 (repeating 17–18); they engender parallel thirds above B♭ in bars 33–34. The chromatic passing tone b♮ of bar 32 is recalled by the inner voice (left hand) in bars 36–37.

Example 5: Chopin, Mazurka, Op. 24, No. 1.

The linkage techniques shown in the Handel and the Bach examples, especially the latter, involve a repetition with some lengthening of durational values. Often a repetition involves expansion of larger proportions, so that the expansion must be understood as belonging to a deeper structural level than the original configuration; in such cases it appears that *enlargement* is an effect sought for its own sake rather than merely resulting from the adjustment of durations to fit a new metric or phrasing situation.[11] The Larghetto of the second sonata from C. P. E. Bach's first collection of *Sonatas for Connoisseurs and Amateurs* contains a remarkable example of this in its first eight-bar group. (The first twelve bars of the music are given at (a) in example 6.) The voice leading in bars 3-5 moves essentially in parallel tenths:

a♭-g /g♭-f
f - e♭ -d♭ ;

the top voice is melodically elaborated by a diminution comprising a rising broken sixth followed by a stepwise descent through a third, as is shown at (b). Bar 4 already shows a variation in comparison with bar 3: the middle tone of the broken sixth is omitted, with the result that the descending third's passing tone (d♭ in bar 4) is now unaccented rather than accented as in bar 3; this provides an opportunity to touch on g♭³ in the last beat of bar 4, strengthening the preparation already begun in bar 3 of the higher register that is to figure more prominently in bars 9-12 and in the second theme (not shown). Bars 5-7 now continue the sequential transposition of the motive of bar 3, but with an expansion of its duration (originally two beats) across the greater part of three bars! The motive's descending-third component (now d♭-c-b♭) is carried out first in dotted quarters (bars 6-7) and then immediately in eighth notes; it returns in the left hand at the end of bar 8.

The Larghetto merits further discussion because of the special way the motivic enlargement relates to underlying structural levels. A graphic reconstruction illuminates this relationship. Example 7 shows three middleground strata in order of increasing detail. At (a) it is shown that the motion of the bass from the tonic F to its fifth C—in essence an ascending fifth—is expressed as a descending fourth; the V is introduced by ♮IV⁷, whose bass tone B♮ is reached by a descending arpeggiation through D♭ set as the bass of VI (bar 5). At level (b), the space between I and VI is filled with a passing tone; the resulting third progression is accompanied in parallel motion by the upper voice, giving rise to the parallel tenths of bars 3-5 mentioned above. The upper voice's f¹ will become a diminished fifth within ♮IV⁷ at bar 7 and will consequently be drawn down to e♮ over V. At this point Bach employs a technique of reaching-over,[12] which enables the upper voice to arrive at $\hat{2}$ (g¹) over V and which also gives rise to a second descending third, b♭-a♭-g, paralleling the first one (see the brackets); this higher-order association is more

11. For other examples of enlargement, see Burkhart, pp. 147 ff.
12. See Schenker, *Free Composition,* pp. 47-49 and p. 83, and especially Ernst Oster's helpful clarification on pp. 48-49. Level (b) exemplifies Schenker's "boundary-play" (*Ränderspiel*); see *Free Composition,* pp. 103-105.

Example 6: C. P. E. Bach, *Sonatas for Connoisseurs and Amateurs.* First Collection: Sonata No. 2, Second Movement.

Example 7

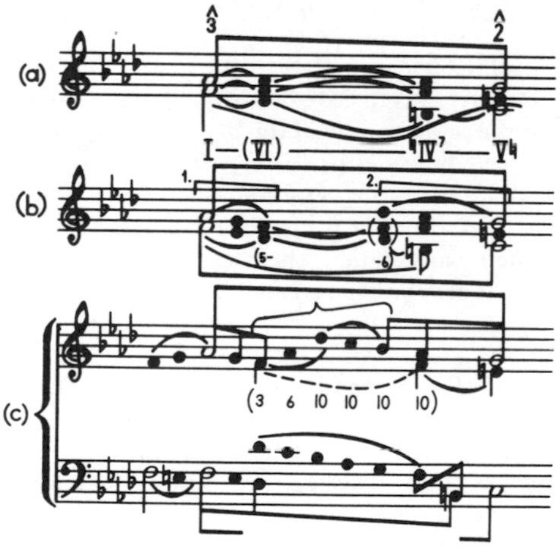

difficult to perceive, but it coexists with those of the foreground described above.[13] At (c) the left hand fills the space between $d^{\flat 1}$ and f with a linear progression. As a counterpoint to this, the upper voice arpeggiates upward to $d^{\flat 2}$ and thereafter follows the bass in parallel tenths, so that the $b^{\flat 1}$ of bar 7 is itself introduced by a motion from above. Thus in a level-oriented derivation of these measures, the enlargement in bars 5–8 (see the curly bracket in level (c)) arises at a level deeper than that of the motive's surface appearances in bars 3 and 4. It seems probable that from the viewpoint of compositional "chronology" the diminution of bars 3 and 4 influenced the higher-level configuration of bars 5–8, but this cannot be proved; compositional features such as these may have been in Schenker's mind when he wrote, "I would not presume to say how inspiration comes upon the genius, to declare with certainty which part of the middleground or foreground first presents itself to his imagination: the ultimate secrets will always remain inaccessible to us."[14] A final observation on the Larghetto, whose wealth of associations cannot be fully discussed here: a beautiful linkage is carried out across the formal division between bars 8 and 9, as the right hand of bar 9 initiates its melodic line with the tones c^{1}–$d^{\flat 1}$–$e^{\natural 1}$ (especially striking because of the piquancy of the augmented second)—a restatement of the same tones, an octave lower, in the left hand of bar 8.

An enlargement in J. S. Bach's F major Sinfonia bears witness to his titanic contrapuntal powers. (The music of the first twelve bars is provided at (a) in example 8.) This work features an especially dense imitative thematic saturation; observe in particular the canonic stretto with its dovetailing thematic entrances that begins in bar 7, and, even more remarkably, the complete thematic entrances embedded in the first episodic passage (bars 5–7).[15] The most striking element in this elaborate

13. A word in explanation of this analysis may be helpful. Among the reasons for assigning $b^{\flat}$–$a^{\flat}$–g to a deeper level than the $d^{\flat}$–c which precedes it is the metric location and "agogic accent" of the $b^{\flat}$, which falls at the beginning of a relatively strong bar in a four-bar group and has an effective duration of a dotted half note. Another consideration is the specific prolongation of the $b^{\flat}$, involving (as noted above) a restatement of the immediately preceding $d^{\flat}$–c–$b^{\flat}$. The $b^{\flat}$ emerges as the "target," so to speak, of both descending thirds. The abrupt reduction of dynamic level to *p* underscores the significance of $b^{\flat}$–$a^{\flat}$–g in a poignant and ironic way. (In bars 31–32, just before the recapitulation, these same tones appear prominently at the conclusion of a four-bar group that is strongly associated in many respects with bars 5–8.)

14. Schenker, p. 9.

15. These entrances, in part for reasons discussed below, are almost comparable to the subject entrance in the bass in bar 7 of Bach's C minor Fugue from the *Well-Tempered Clavier,* vol. 2, described by Ernst Oster in "Register and the Large-Scale Connection," *Journal of Music Theory* 5 (1961), reprinted in Yeston, ed., *Readings in Schenker Analysis and Other Approaches,* New Haven: Yale University Press, 1977, pp. 54–71.

Example 8: Bach, Sinfonia No. 8.

counterpoint, however, is the enlargement in the top voice of bars 5–6 (simultaneously with the "smuggled" thematic entrance in the bass!) of the head of the theme (*comes* form, as in bar 2), as is shown at (b).[16] The vitality of this relationship is secured by the overall registral disposition (especially the abandonment of the high register in bar 6); it binds the soprano entrance of bar 7 to the enlargement in bars 5–6 and thus causes the entrance in bar 7 to sound like the retrieval and completion of something left unfinished by the enlargement. Levels (c) and (d) of example 8 show how the enlargement (bracketed) fits into the more comprehensive middleground configuration of bars 1–7.

Contraction—repetition within a foreshortened span of time, and hence the opposite of enlargement—serves a variety of purposes even outside the realm of fugal composition, where it might be considered most indigenous. Perhaps the most spectacular example in the literature is the one in the fourth bar of Beethoven's Piano Sonata in A♭, Op. 110: The tones beginning with the thirty-second note c^2 and ending with the last note of the small "cadenza" repeat in condensed form the contents of the upper voice from the very beginning to the middle of bar 4.[17] The example is unusual in that contraction is applied to a relatively extended series of tones. A perhaps loosely related phenomenon occurs on a more modest scale in Beethoven's other piano sonata in A♭, Op. 26, bars 4–5, where the head of the second four-bar group presents a contraction, a step higher, of the voice leading of bars 1–4 (see example 9).[18]

Example 9: Beethoven, Piano Sonata in A♭, Op. 26.

16. This sinfonia appears in Bach's handwriting, under the title *Fantasia,* in Friedemann Bach's *Clavierbüchlein.* The version given there differs in a few small details from the final one. Interestingly, it is clear from the manuscript that Bach first wrote the f^2 in bar 5 as a half note. I would speculate that Bach's addition of sixteenth notes in bar 5 was intended to suppress the overly strong association with bar 3 (which would obscure the more important one with bar 2) that would have resulted from repeating the half-note–quarter-note rhythm.
17. As far as I am aware Oswald Jonas was the first to describe this in print. (See *Einführung,* p. 5). More recently this relationship has been cited by Roger Kamien in "Aspects of the Recapitulation in Beethoven's Piano Sonatas," *The Music Forum* 4 (1976).
18. The parallelism of the ascending third b♭–c–d that begins the second phrase to the a♭–b♭–c which underlies bars 1–4—and the continuation of that parallelism in the form of another ascending third, c–d♮–e♭, in the B section of the theme—is noted by Schenker (see *Free Composition,* p. 75 and Figure 85); but he does not mention the exact correspondence of the embellishment of bars 4–5 to the tones of bars 1–4.

Examples of this kind come close to ornamentation in the old, narrow sense of *Manieren*; they manifest a kinship with the music of C. P. E. Bach, where the ornaments often play a role that is far more than merely decorative. For example, in the opening measures of the third movement of C. P. E. Bach's fourth "Essay" sonata (see example 10), the upper voice's initial $c\sharp^2$ is embellished by an upper neighbor d^2 (in large notation, expressing the *siciliano* rhythm); in the middleground voice leading of the first eight bars this first $c\sharp^2$ moves to d^2 above IV (bar 7) and returns to $c\sharp^2$ above V (bar 8), producing an enlargement of the opening figure. In a sense, then, the d^2 of bar 7 is a direct successor of the opening $c\sharp^2$, and this is clarified by Bach's application to it of a neighboring-tone figure (not a complete trill!) written *as an ornament*. It is not difficult to believe that such an organic use of ornamentation would have been among the features of C. P. E. Bach's music that were

Example 10: C. P. E. Bach, "Essay" Sonata (*Probestück*) No. 4, Third Movement.

admired by Haydn, Mozart, and Beethoven. The same C. P. E. Bach movement, incidentally, provides an interesting example of contraction applied to a four-tone succession, as shown in example 11. (The curly brackets point out a miniscule application of rhythm-preserving enlargement!)

Example 11: C. P. E. Bach, "Essay" Sonata (*Probestück*) No. 4, Third Movement.

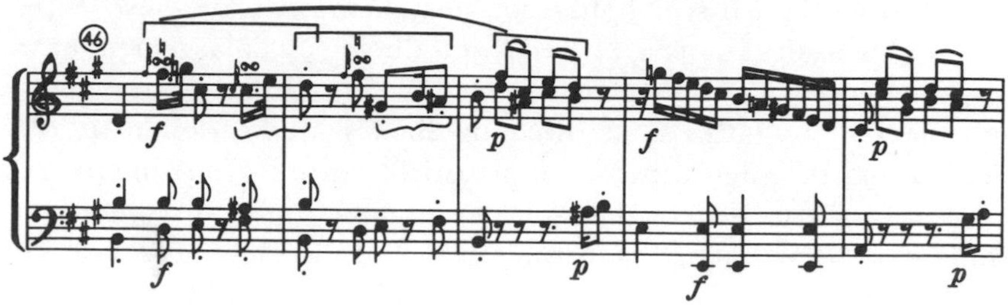

Each of the examples of contraction presented above involves contraction of a tone-succession that is already more or less explicitly thematic at its first appearance. There is another type that is perhaps of more general importance. It occasionally happens that a succession of tones that either belongs to the general voice leading or is otherwise relatively "incidental" in a work is elevated to the status of a motive by virtue of a compressed repetition. This is the case in the closing bars of the exposition of Mozart's Piano Sonata in D major, K. 576, first movement. The definitive cadence of the A major (second theme) section occurs at bar 53. A closing section based on sixteenth-note passages rises to the high register, introducing c♯³ at bar 55; the immediately ensuing repetition of this two-bar group is modified to conclude on a². (See example 12.) The two tones, c♯³ and a², are at once drawn together (bar 57) into an entity that is continued with a chromatic inflection of the c♯ to c♮ (and later of e♮ to e♭) to form the transition into the development. Mozart thus "hooks onto" the c♯³–a² succession of bars 55 and 57—a potentially insignificant juxtaposition—and uses it as the basis of a new figure that will play an important role later on in the development.

Example 12: Mozart, Sonata in D, K. 576.

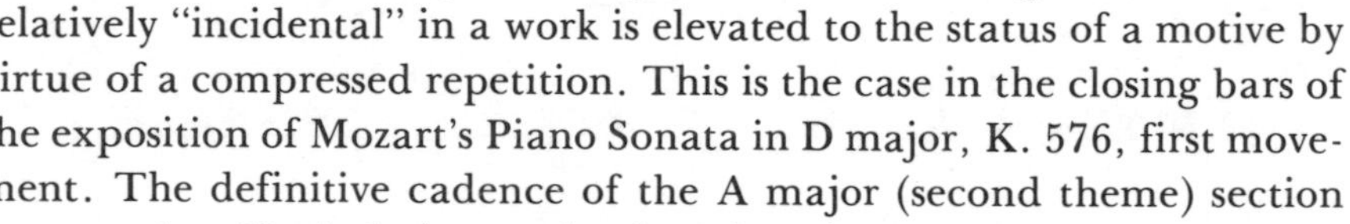

In Scarlatti's G major Sonata K. 471 the descending fourth d^2-c^2-b^1-a^1 that unfolds slowly at the middleground level in bars 43-54 emerges in the foreground in bars 56-58 (see (a) in example 13 and the interpretation at level (b)); the return of the "second theme" diminution in bars 59-60 traverses the same fourth descent an octave higher. The association of the first two descents—bars 43-54 and 56-58—is strengthened by the surface-level application of lower neighbor-tone embellishments, as indicated by the brackets in (a).

Example 13: Scarlatti, Sonata in G, K. 471.

Example 14: Beethoven, Symphony No. 3.

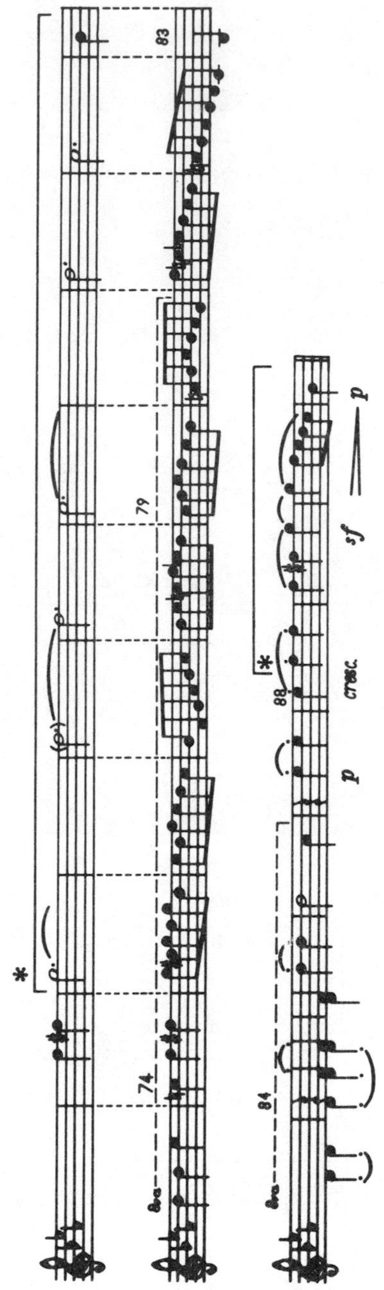

In the first movement of Beethoven's Eroica Symphony, the conclusion of the first "period" of the second group (bars 88–91) shows a contraction of the large-scale upper neighbor g (approached by the chromatic passing tone f♯) and the subsequent fifth descent of bars 74–83. Example 14 displays this relationship. (This association is revealed by Schenker in his Eroica Symphony monograph,[19] and is mentioned even more explicitly by Jonas in his review of the latter.[20] Jonas cites it as an example that "clearly illustrates the influence of background on foreground.")

Finally it should be remarked that the seeds of the motivic events discussed earlier in the first section of C. P. E. Bach's F minor Larghetto movement (see example 6) lie in the contraction of the ascending third f–g–a♭ (bars 2–3) into eighth-note values in bar 3 (see example 15). The first ascent is carried out by two successive applications of reaching-over; these produce third arpeggiations, which in turn evoke the sixth arpeggiation of bar 3, and the descending third that follows it provides a counterpoint to the rising third and its contraction. The interaction of contraction and enlargement in these opening measures is subtle and complex; obviously the ramifications with respect to rhythmic organization are profound.

Example 15

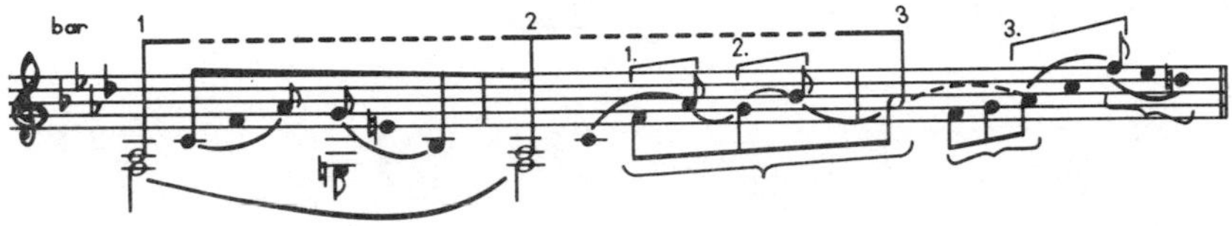

Contraction is applied in an obvious way in the opening measures of Beethoven's Piano Trio in B♭, Op. 97 (the "Archduke"). Bars 3–4 are immediately compressed, by the deletion of passing tones, in bar 5. What is less obvious is the series of enlargements (at various tonal levels) of the ascending sixth (articulated as a third plus a fourth: d^2–f^2 and f^2–$b^{\flat 2}$ at its first occurrence in bars 2–3) that figures prominently in the

19. Heinrich Schenker, *Das Meisterwerk in der Musik* III, Munich: Drei Masken Verlag, 1930, p. 36 and the foreground graph.
20. In "Bücherschau," *Zeitschrift für Musikwissenschaft* 15 (1932–33), p. 94.

continuation. The first expansion appears in bars 6–8 (a^2–f^3), where the dotted rhythm of the first segment is augmented. The modulation replicates this ascending sixth on a much larger scale, beginning with $f\sharp^1$ in bar 39 and ending with a climactic D, expressed in six different registers, at bar 49. This passage preserves, by obvious foreground features, the articulation of the sixth as a rising third followed by a stepwise ascent through a fourth. (In the absence of such preservation the relationship could not be said to hold.) The second theme, which begins with the upbeat to bar 52, describes a sixth space from B upward to G with the same articulation, and the ascending-fourth segment, D–G, emerges on the surface, singing beautifully (*dolce*) in the cello in bars 60–61. The progress of this rising-sixth idea can be shown best with a series of illustrations, which are provided in example 16.

Example 16: Beethoven, Piano Trio in B♭, Op. 97.

In conclusion I should like to discuss in some detail certain thematic features of Mozart's Piano Sonata in F, K. 332, third movement, with particular attention to the way they influence changes in the recapitulation. In any sonata movement having a significant cadential articulation before the entrance of the second theme group, it is in principle possible to satisfy the requirements of the recapitulation's tonal adjustment (which, of course, in almost all classical sonatas assigns the recapitulation of the second theme group to the tonic area) by simply transposing all of the music following the so-articulated formal juncture. Yet this "easy" solution is almost never encountered in major works, because its application will necessarily vitiate, in the recapitulation, essential thematic associations composed into the exposition. It is the task of the composer to establish new and equally convincing relationships in the recapitulation. As Ernst Oster has expressed it, "Mozart would always modify the reprise by a variety of means, adding emphasis to the section, letting the previous material appear in a new light, establishing new relationships, or doing whatever else might appear necessary."[21]

One thing that evidently appeared necessary to Mozart in this recapitulation was some reordering of the material from the exposition. The most conspicuous change in the recapitulation is the omission of bars 22-35 of the exposition; these measures are transplanted to the very end, where they serve as a coda for the movement as a whole. The reason for this change has to do with the specific tonal level of the modulation as it appears in the exposition, beginning in bar 36. The tones a^2-g^2-f^2 with which the modulation begins link directly to the succession a^1-g^1-f^1 in bars 34-35; these tones are important because they complete the fifth progression twice initiated, but not completed, by the c^2-$b\flat^1$ successions of bars 32 and 33. The sharp disjunction at bar 36 created by the radical change in surface texture and the abrupt *forte* dynamic is bridged over by this linkage technique. The modulation is so constructed that another stepwise descent from a^2 — in augmented rhythm — is initiated at bar 46; the return at this point of a^2 is accomplished through a chromatic passing tone $g\sharp^2$ — the progression of g^2-$g\sharp^2$-a^2 in bars 45-46 being obviously a consequence of the f^2-$f\sharp^2$-g^2 of bars 40-41. (Example 17 displays these features with the aid of a rhythmic simplification.) This seemingly insignificant detail takes on additional meaning in the recapitulation, as we shall presently see.

Example 17: Mozart, Sonata in F, K. 332, Third Movement.

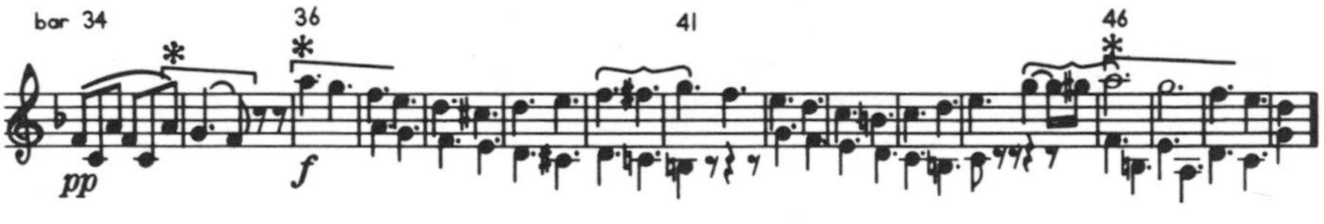

21. Ernst Oster, "Analysis Symposium I: Mozart, Menuetto K.V. 355," *Journal of Music Theory* **10** (1966), p. 49; reprinted in Yeston, op. cit.

A transposition of the modulation to fit the needs of the recapitulation would dictate a melodic beginning on the tone d^3 (corresponding to the a^2 of bar 36 in the exposition). This is in fact the choice that Mozart makes, although he alters slightly the total course of voice leading in the modulation, extending it by one bar (see below). The beginning on d^3 clearly could not relate to the preceding material in the same way that the a^2 of the exposition did. In particular, the linkage of first-theme conclusion and modulation could not exist as it had existed in the exposition: the succession d^3-c^3-$b^{\flat 2}$ could not be motivated in the way that a^2-g^2-f^2 had been. For this reason Mozart omitted the concluding part of the first theme group and ended with the abrupt cadence at bar 169—an incomplete closure, because of the gap from $b^{\flat 1}$ to g^1 in bar 168. It is just the abruptness, the incompleteness, of this cadence that gives prominence to the chromatic succession c–c♯–d (counterpointed by f–e♭–d in the bass) in bars 167–170. Through this chromatic succession Mozart succeeds in tying together the formal parts, and, moreover, in establishing a new association proper to the recapitulation: At the return to d^3 in bar 180 (with its subsequent augmentation of the descending line from the first d^3) the chromatic detail from bars 45–46 becomes, under transposition, c^3-$c^{\sharp 3}$- d^3, which is now heard as a contraction of bars 167–170! (See example 18.) The association of the two descending motions from d^3 is thus strengthened in that both are approached in the same way.

Example 18: Mozart, Sonata in F, K. 332, Third Movement.

This new association in the recapitulation may, however, have arisen partly as a by-product of Mozart's solution of a deeper problem. In the exposition, the a^2 at bar 36 was not only motivated thematically by virtue of the linkage with the preceding bars: It stood in a clear harmonic relation to the F major conclusion of the first theme; it was the upper third of that F major, a relation not obscured by the fact that in the subsequent unfolding it is interpreted as the octave of a major triad. If we imagine an exact transposition at bar 170 of the original modulation — a beginning on an open octave d^3/d^2 without the intervening augmented-sixth chord on E♭, we find that the significance of this pitch-class D is thoroughly ambiguous. It does not enter into a self-explanatory harmonic relationship with the preceding F major as the analogous A of the exposition did. The ear will attempt to interpret it as a local upper neighbor returning to C already in bar 170, but will of course be frustrated in this attempt by the retained d^2 in the right hand (see the score) on the second beat of that bar; the net result will be a momentary confusion, an unwanted insecurity. The d^3 in bar 170 is, indeed, an upper neighbor to c^3, but not to the one that immediately follows it: It is prolonged as the analogous a^2 was prolonged in the exposition, until the parallel descent from c^3 begins at bar 175. By setting d^3 in bar 170 over an explicit D major chord (strengthened by the approach through the augmented-sixth chord) Mozart has secured for it a "foothold" which clarifies its significance as a relatively long-range upper neighbor. The pitch d^3, in both of its occurrences in the modulation (bars 170 and 180), serves as an upper neighbor — a function completely different from that of the corresponding a^2's in the exposition, and this places the whole modulating

Example 19

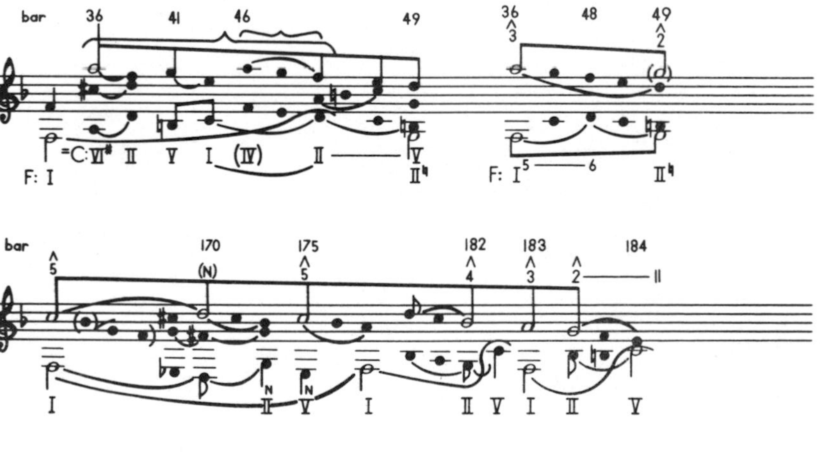

section in a different light as it appears in the altered environment of the recapitulation. One result of these new relationships is that the F major chords in bars 179 and 183 are both genuine tonics, in contrast to the analogous C triads in the exposition (bars 44–45 and 48), both of which are passing-tone chords without structural connection to the tonicized C area (it turns out to be initially C minor) of the second theme group. The complete difference in significance between the C harmonies of the exposition's modulation and the corresponding F harmonies of the recapitulation is made clear by middleground voice-leading graphs presented in example 19. This difference accounts for the expansion of bar 182 (which places the F major chord on the first beat of bar 183) as compared with bar 48, and, consequently, for the addition of the extra bar to the recapitulation's transition passage.

Motive and Text in Four Schubert Songs

CARL SCHACHTER

Music set to words can reflect them in many different ways. Perhaps the most fascinating and greatest settings are those where the tonal and rhythmic structure, the form, and the motivic design embody equivalents for salient features of the text: grammar and syntax, rhyme schemes and other patterns of sound, imagery, and so forth. Structural connections between words and music occur frequently in the art-song repertory—above all, in the songs of Schubert. Yet they seem to have attracted less attention, at least in the published literature, than prosody, tone painting, and affect.[1] In this paper I shall concentrate on one type of connection—that between the imagery of the poem and the motivic design of the music. The examples come from four Schubert songs: (1) *Der Jüngling an der Quelle* (D. 300), (2) *Dass sie hier gewesen*, Op. 59, No. 2 (D. 775), (3) *Der Tod und das Mädchen*, Op. 7, No. 3 (D. 531), and (4) *Nacht und Träume*, Op. 43, No. 2 (D. 827).

Der Jüngling an der Quelle

Our simplest example comes from the coda of this early song.[2] The poem is by the Swiss writer Johann von Salis-Seewis; since I am going to discuss only one detail, I shall not quote the whole text, but only the last two lines. The words are those of a boy, unhappy in love, who tries to

1. A notable exception occurs in Anhang A of Oswald Jonas, *Einführung in die Lehre Heinrich Schenkers*, revised edition, Vienna: Universal, 1972. Jonas was the first to discuss in a systematic way the implications of Schenker's ideas for the analysis of music composed to a text; his treatment of the subject contains many remarkable insights. A splendid study of a Brahms song is to be found in Edward Laufer, "Brahms: 'Wie Melodien zieht es mir,' Op. 105/1," *Journal of Music Theory* 15 (1971), pp. 34-57; reprinted in Maury Yeston, editor, *Readings in Schenker Analysis and Other Approaches*, New Haven: Yale University Press, 1977, pp. 254-272. In my opinion, the most profound insights into the relation of music and words—especially in Schubert songs—were achieved by the late Ernst Oster. It is a great misfortune that he published none of his work in this area.
2. The date of composition is unknown; according to the revised Deutsch catalog, it was probably written in 1816 or 1817. See Otto Erich Deutsch, *Franz Schubert: Thematisches Verzeichnis seiner Werke in chronologischer Folge*, revised by Werner Aderhold, Walther Dürr, Arnold Feil, and Christa Landon, Kassel: Bärenreiter, 1978, pp. 183-184.

forget his coy friend in the beauties of nature. But they bring renewed desire rather than consolation; the poplar leaves and the brook seem to sigh her name, Luise. The final lines, as Schubert set them,[3] go as follows:

ach, und Blätter und Bach	ah, and leaves and brook
seufzen: Luise! dir nach.	sigh, Luise, for you.

The song is pervaded by a typically murmuring accompaniment pattern, which imitates the sound of the leaves and brook. Example 1, which quotes the beginning of the introduction, illustrates. Note that the right-hand part centers on the broken third c♯^{2} -e^2.

Example 1: ***Der Jüngling an der Quelle,*** **1–3.**

The introductory material returns in bars 23–26 to become the main part of the coda. Rather unusually, this coda is not a simple postlude for the piano; the singer joins in, repeating the name Luise (example 2). His exclamations are set to the very pitches—c♯^{2} and e^2—that have pervaded the accompaniment. There is even a return to the c♯^{2}, which recalls the oscillating piano figuration (see the brackets in example 2). Like the boy in the poem, the listener hears an indistinct pattern transformed into a clear one; the sounds of nature become the girl's name, and the murmuring accompaniment becomes a melodic figure of definite shape. Schubert creates his musical image out of a structural connection between accompaniment and melody: Both center on the

3. Schubert made a slight change in the words either inadvertently or to produce a rhyming couplet at the end (the original is unrhymed). Salis had written "mir zu" (to me) and not "dir nach" (for you). But either way, the leaves and brook speak her name.

prominent pitches c♯^{2} and e^2. This connection is underlined during the last three bars, in which the piano continues alone with only c♯^{2}–e^2 in the right-hand part; the murmuring dies away into a final block chord, which, rather unusually, has the fifth, e^2, on top.

Example 2: *Der Jüngling an der Quelle,* 23–29.

Artless as it is, the musical image that Schubert creates in *Der Jüngling an der Quelle* has points of similarity with some of his subtler and more complex settings of words. As a consequence, the passage is a good introductory example of his practice. The following features deserve mention:

1. The transformation of the accompaniment into a melodic idea has nothing to do with "tone painting," although the accompaniment itself, of course, is intended to summon up the sound of leaves and water. Nor does it convey a "mood," although few listeners, I suspect, would complain that Schubert had failed to match the emotional tone of the words.

2. By associating accompaniment and vocal line Schubert creates a musical analogy to the sequence of ideas in the poem; the accompaniment is to the melodic figure derived from it as the indistinct sounds of nature are to the specific name that they evoke. Without the words, any extramusical association would disappear, but the connection between accompaniment and melody would remain perfectly comprehensible as a musical relationship. This is typical of Schubert's method, which sustains a remarkable equilibrium between sensitivity to the text and compositional integrity.

Yet it would probably be going too far to maintain that *Der Jüngling an der Quelle*, played as an instrumental piece, would sound completely natural. This is because the pervasive $c\sharp^2$–e^2 is too neutral a figure and is treated with too little emphasis to justify its very conspicuous transformation into a melodic idea at the end of the piece. It is the words, which begin by invoking the murmuring spring and whispering poplars, that draw the listener's attention to the accompaniment and thus supply the necessary emphasis.

3. In creating his musical image Schubert reaches a far higher level of artistry than Salis-Seewis, for the poem, charming as it is, merely asserts that the leaves and brook sigh the girl's name. Of course the name itself—"Luise"—sounds more like whispering leaves and water than, say, "Katinka" would. But this is the easiest kind of onomatopoetic effect, with little inner connection to the poem as a whole. In Schubert's song, on the other hand, the musical image *is*, in symbolic form, what the words talk about; it grows out of the earlier part of the song with wonderful naturalness.

Dass sie hier gewesen

This song is set to a beautiful poem by Rückert. Schubert probably wrote it in 1823; it was published in 1826.[4] I am going to discuss the first stanza, composed to the following text:

Dass der Ostwind Düfte	That the east wind
Hauchet in die Lüfte	Breathes fragrance into the air
Dadurch tut er kund	In that way he makes it known
Dass du hier gewesen.	That you have been here.

4. Revised Deutsch catalog, p. 466.

The musical style of *Dass sie hier gewesen* could hardly be more different from that of *Der Jüngling an der Quelle*. The tonal ambiguity of the opening bars is such that a listener hearing them without knowing where they come from could easily date them from the 1890s rather than the 1820s.[5] No tonic triad appears until bar 14; indeed, the listener receives not even a clue that the piece is in C major for six bars at a very slow tempo (example 3). The very first sound is doubtful. It turns out to be a diminished-seventh chord with an appoggiatura, f^3, in the top voice, but for a bar or so the listener might hear the chord as G–B♭–D♭–F rather than the G–B♭–C♯–E sonority that in fact it is. After we have our bearings about the diminished seventh, we remain in the dark as to the function of the D minor chord to which it resolves; a listener might easily take it for a tonic. The attraction of C as center begins to be felt only in bars 7–8 and is not evident beyond a doubt until the authentic cadence of bars 13–14. Comparing Schubert's music with the words, we can see how

Example 3: *Das sie hier gewesen*, 1–16.

5. Richard Capell finds the opening similar to Wolf's "Herr, was trägt der Boden"—a similarity that seems rather external to me. See Richard Capell, *Schubert's Songs*, London: Ernest Benn, 1928, p. 200.

marvelously it embodies the semantic and syntactic structure of this involuted sentence, whose import becomes clear only with the key predicate clause—"that you have been here"—the clause to which Schubert sets the clinching authentic cadence of bars 13–14.[6]

Although the motivic design of this passage is not as strikingly original as the tonal organization, it too connects with the words in a most wonderful way. The piano's opening statement contains a four-note figure in an extremely high register: f³–e³–d³–c♯³. The four notes belong together, for they project into the melodic line the prevailing diminished-seventh chord, of which the e³ and c♯³ are members. But the very slow pace and the strong subdivision into twos make it easier to hear two groups of two notes each than a coherent four-note figure. As example 4 shows, the vocal line uses the four-note figure as a motive, quoting it directly (bars 3–4) and elaborating on it (bars 5–8 and 9–12). When the tonally definitive cadence of bars 13–14 arrives, the character of the melodic line begins to change: the pace quickens; there are no chromatics and no dissonant leaps. Yet for all the contrast, there is a connecting thread: the melodic line over the V⁷ of bar 12 is our four-note figure—at a new pitch level, in a different harmonic context, in quicker time values, but nonetheless the same figure. Even the distribution of nonchord and chord tones remains the same. In its new form the motive no longer divides into two times two notes; the coherence of the four-note group has become manifest.

Example 4

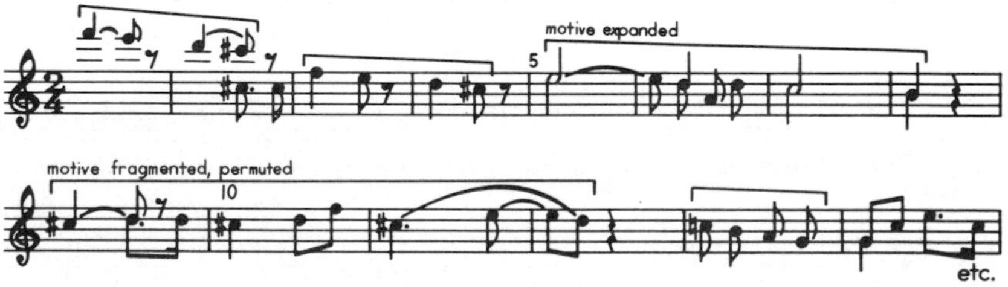

6. Both Capell (*Schubert's Songs*, p. 200) and Tovey have commented perceptively on the relation of the music's tonal structure to the syntax of the poem. See Donald Francis Tovey, *Essays and Lectures on Music*, London: Oxford University Press, 1949, p. 132.

Let us now compare the central image of the poem and the motivic aspects of its setting. A perfume in the air signifies that the beloved has been here. The perfume—a melodic idea barely perceptible as such, floating in an improbably high register within a tonal context of the utmost ambiguity. The person—the same melodic idea but now with distinct outlines, a definite rhythmic shape, the greatest possible clarity of tonal direction. Certainly many compositional elements contribute to this astonishing example of text setting: rhythm, texture, register, and tonal organization, as well as motivic design. But only the motivic aspect conveys the *connection* between perfume and person, conveys the notion that, in a sense, the two—sign and signified—are one.

Der Tod und das Mädchen

The song was written in February 1817 and was published in 1821. The text, a poem by Matthias Claudius, is as follows:

Das Mädchen

Vorüber, ach vorüber
Geh, wilder Knochenmann!
Ich bin noch jung! Geh, Lieber,
Und rühre mich nicht an!

Der Tod

Gib deine Hand, du schön und zart Gebild!
Bin Freund und komme nicht zu strafen.
Sei gutes Muts! Ich bin nicht wild!
Sollst sanft in meinen Armen schlafen!

The Maiden

Go past, ah, go past
Wild skeleton!
I am still young! Go, dear,
And do not touch me!

Death

Give me your hand, you beautiful and tender creature!
I am a friend and do not come to punish.
Be of good courage! I am not wild!
You shall sleep softly in my arms!

The poem is a dialogue, and Schubert, altogether appropriately, composes the song as a dramatic scene.[7] The piano introduction clearly represents a vision of Death; the Maiden's outcry is an agitated recitative; Death's reply is set to a recomposition of the introductory material. In a piece as short as *Der Tod und das Mädchen* marked contrasts between sections can prove disruptive. That Schubert creates a continuous musical discourse despite the changes in tempo, rhythm, and texture is partly due to the presence throughout most of the song of a basic motive, which serves as a link between the contrasting sections. The first statement of the motive occurs at the very beginning of the introduction in the next-to-highest part. The motive is a double-neighbor figure decorating a: a–b♭–g–a (example 5). Note that this figure is the main melodic event at the beginning of the song, for the uppermost part, prefiguring the monotone character of Death's speech, simply repeats a single pitch.

Example 5: *Der Tod und das Mädchen*, 1–2.

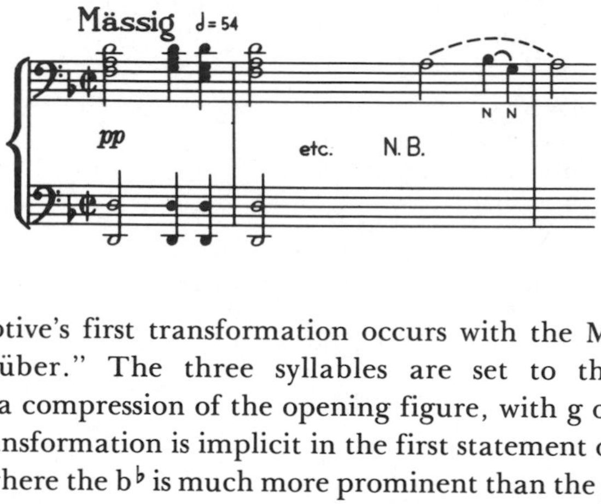

The motive's first transformation occurs with the Maiden's first word, "Vorüber." The three syllables are set to three notes—a^1–$b^{\flat 1}$–a^1—a compression of the opening figure, with g omitted. In a sense this transformation is implicit in the first statement of the motive (bars 1–2), where the b♭ is much more prominent than the g on account of its higher pitch and stronger metrical position. As example 6 shows, the first half of the Maiden's speech is permeated by the neighbor-note figure. After the first "Vorüber" an expansion of it stretches over four bars (9–12) of the middle voice. And with the despairing cry "Ich bin noch jung!" of bars 12–14 the figure breaks out into the open, transposed up a fourth.

7. Professor Christoph Wolff, in a highly interesting lecture at the International Schubert Congress (Detroit, November 1978), pointed out the operatic character of this song and suggested possible antecedents in the oracle scenes of Gluck's *Alceste* and Mozart's *Idomeneo* and in the two statue scenes of *Don Giovanni*.

Example 6

In the second half of the Maiden's speech (bars 15–21) the motive does not appear. But it pervades the accompaniment to Death's reply, as can be seen in example 7. The figure resumes its original four-note form, but is altered by rhythmic enlargement (bars 22–25, 25–29, etc.), voice exchange (bars 26–27 and 34–36), and the chromatic transformations B♭/B♮ and G♮/G♯ (bars 34–36, 37, and 40). In addition the phrase in B♭ (bars 30–33) most probably contains a statement of the motive, transposed up a fourth and with the two neighbors in reverse order. The similarity of the accompaniment at "Ich bin nicht wild" to the Maiden's "Ich bin noch jung" certainly seems to reflect the parallelism in the text.

Example 7

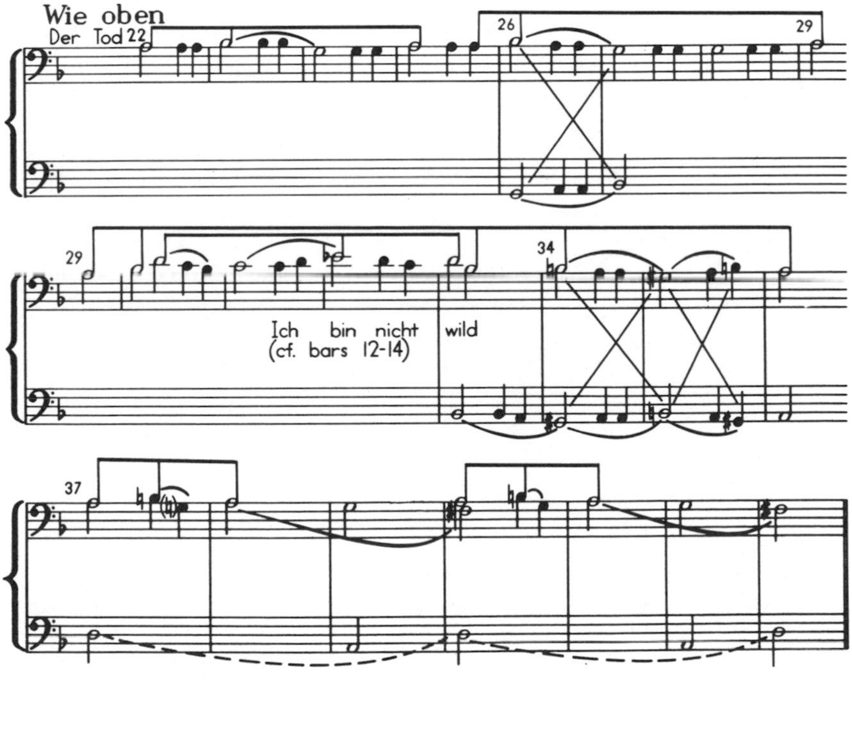

The motivic design of *Der Tod und das Mädchen* parallels the emotional progress of the poem in a remarkable way. The basic motive itself—the double-neighbor figure—is a most appropriate one for a song about death. Its most prominent tones—A-B♭-A—form a musical idiom that has had an age-old association with ideas of death, grief, and lamentation. The musical basis of this association is surely the descending half-step (6-5 in minor) with its goal-directed and downward motion, its semitonal intensity, and the "sighing" quality it can so easily assume. Note that the three-note figure with its descending half-step occurs literally only when the Maiden speaks; Death's reply softens the B♭-A with the interpolated G and the very slow melodic pace. As Death continues to speak the motive undergoes subtle tonal changes. With his promise of sleep (bars 33-34), the B♭ changes to B♮; the despairing half-step descent is heard no more. At the same time the G changes to G♯. Owing to this upward inflection a half-step still remains in the double-neighbor figure, and with it melodic tension and goal-oriented progression. But now it is a rising half-step (G♯-A), signifying hope rather than despair.[8] With the d of bar 37, the Maiden surely dies. (This low tonic is far more expressive than the alternative higher one; any singer who can reach it should certainly choose it.) At the Maiden's death, the double-neighbor figure appears in its original rhythmic shape for the first time since the introduction. It decorates a major tonic chord, and both neighboring notes lie a whole step from the main note. In this final statement there is no half-step, no strongly goal-oriented progression; the music, like the Maiden, is at peace.

8. I would certainly not maintain that every rising half-step in music denotes hope and every falling one, despair. But in connection with a text that deals with death, upward and downward motion can easily take on extramusical significance, especially if the composer draws attention to it by varying previously heard material.

Nacht und Träume

Universally regarded as one of Schubert's greatest songs, *Nacht und Träume* appeared in print in 1825, but was written much earlier, probably in 1822 or 1823.[9] The author of the poem was Matthäus von Collin, a friend of Schubert's, some of whose songs were first performed at Collin's home. According to the *Neue Schubert Ausgabe* Schubert possibly had the poem in manuscript, for the text of the song differs considerably from the published version of the poem.[10] The text, as Schubert set it, appears below.

Heil'ge Nacht, du sinkest nieder;
Nieder wallen auch die Träume,
Wie dein Mondlicht durch die Räume,
Durch der Menschen stille Brust.

Die belauschen sie mit Lust,
Rufen, wenn der Tag erwacht:
Kehre wieder, holde Nacht!
Holde Träume, kehret wieder!

Holy night, you descend
Dreams, too, float down,
Like your moonlight through space,
Through people's quiet breasts.

They listen in with pleasure,
And call out when day awakens:
Come back, lovely night!
Lovely dreams, come back!

Like *Der Tod und das Mädchen, Nacht und Träume* contains a tonal pattern that permeates the song and that helps to connect music and text. Here, however, the design is much less obvious than in the earlier song. The basic tonal pattern does not take on the form of a concrete melodic figure with a definite rhythmic shape, as does the double-neighbor figure at the beginning and end of *Der Tod und das Mädchen*. It is therefore not a pattern that would become evident through a conventional motivic analysis.[11] And it does not occur only at the fore-

9. Revised Deutsch catalog, pp. 522–523.
10. Franz Schubert, *Neue Ausgabe sämtlicher Werke*, Serie IV: Band 2, Teil b, edited by Walther Dürr, Kassel: Bärenreiter, 1975, p. 323.
11. A detailed analysis of *Nacht und Träume* appears in Diether de la Motte, *Musikalische Analyse (mit kritischen Anmerkungen von Carl Dahlhaus)*, 2 vols., Kassel: Bärenreiter, 1968, vol. 1, pp. 61–71. There is no mention of the basic motive.

ground, but penetrates deep into the underlying tonal structure. Therefore the motivic design becomes accessible only if we take into account the song's large-scale linear and harmonic organization.

A good place to begin is with the G major passage of bars 15–19. The passage is extraordinarily beautiful and is obviously of central significance to the song—"central" in an almost literal way, for the passage begins at the midpoint of the poem and, more or less, of the music. Its importance is underscored by the striking chromatic chord progression B major–G major of bars 14–15, by the long silence in the vocal part, and by the very slow pace of the chord progressions—six bars (14–19) of just one chord per bar.

What is the function of the prolonged G major chord? At first one would probably think of it as $\flat$VI ($\natural$VI)—the submediant triad borrowed from B minor. As a descriptive label, $\flat$VI would not be wrong, but it would not give us much insight into the behavior of this G major chord. That the behavior is most unusual can be seen from example 8. The progressions shown at (a) and (b) are typical for $\flat$VI. At (a) the bass moves down in thirds (bass arpeggio) to the II$^6_5$ borrowed from the minor. At (b) the bass is sustained, and an augmented sixth is added above it. In both progressions, $\flat\hat{6}$ eventually *descends* to $\hat{5}$, either in the bass or in an upper part. This is what one would expect a chromatically *lowered* sound to do. How different is the progression shown at (c), a reduction of bars 14–21 of *Nacht und Träume*. "$\flat$VI" does not occur within a connected bass line, either arpeggiated or scalar, for its lowest tone moves up an augmented second (bar 20). Nor does $\flat\hat{6}$ resolve to $\hat{5}$, either in the bass or in an upper part. In the bass, the augmented second leaves the G$\natural$ hanging. In the "tenor" the g$\natural$ is sustained into a diminished-seventh chord (bar 20), then transformed enharmonically to f$^{\times}$, which *ascends* (bar 21) to g♯.

Example 8

A glance at the score will show that a melodic progression F♯–F×–G♯ occurs in bars 2–3 of the introduction; the F× functions as a chromatic passing tone. In bar 4 the reverse progression, G♯–G♮–F♯, answers the chromatic ascent; here the G♮ is a chromatic passing tone. In its rising form (F♯–F×–G♯) the chromatic progression recurs twice before the G major passage (in bars 7–8 and 9–10). It appears again immediately after the G major passage as a consequence of the fact that bars 21–27 form an almost unaltered repetition of 8–14. And the postlude contains two G♮'s, which obviously refer back to the F×'s and G♮'s heard earlier on. F×/G♮ appears far more often than any other chromatically altered sound—so often, in fact, and so characteristically that it must be regarded as a motivic element. In example 9, a voice-leading graph of the entire song, asterisks point out the various statements of F×/G♮.

The interpretation of the piece shown in example 9 hinges on the idea that the section in G major derives from the earlier passages containing F× or G♮. This idea is corroborated by the fact that the section is followed immediately by the restatement of one of these passages. And a careful study of the voice-leading context provides further substantiation. As example 9 shows, the prolonged G chord of bars 15–19 contains a middle-voice G♮ that comes from F♯ (bar 14) and that changes to F× before moving up to G♯ in bar 21. This melodic progression is the fantastic enlargement of the motivic F♯–F×–G♯ that occurs three times earlier in the song, as well as once in inversion (see the brackets on the lower stave of example 9). In this enlargement, the F×, a chromatic passing tone, becomes transformed enharmonically; as part of a locally consonant triad it is stabilized and extended in time so that its passing function is disguised. Now we can begin to understand why ♭VI behaves so differently here from the typical usages shown at (a) and (b) in example 8: it is because the guiding idea of the passage is the rising middle-voice progression F♯–F×–G♯. The G♮ of the middle voice represents the foreground transformation of an underlying F×; that is why it moves up. And the G♮ of the bass does not function linearly—hence its lack of connection with the material that follows. Its purpose is to produce a root-position major triad—the most stable of all chords—and thus to provide support and emphasis for the G♮ (F×) of the middle voice.

By combining in a single sonority two different and contrasting orders of musical reality, Schubert gives this song a great central image; the song embodies a musical symbol of dreams. The G major section crystallizes around a most transitory musical event—a chromatic passing tone. Yet, while we are immersed in it, it assumes the guise of that most

Example 9

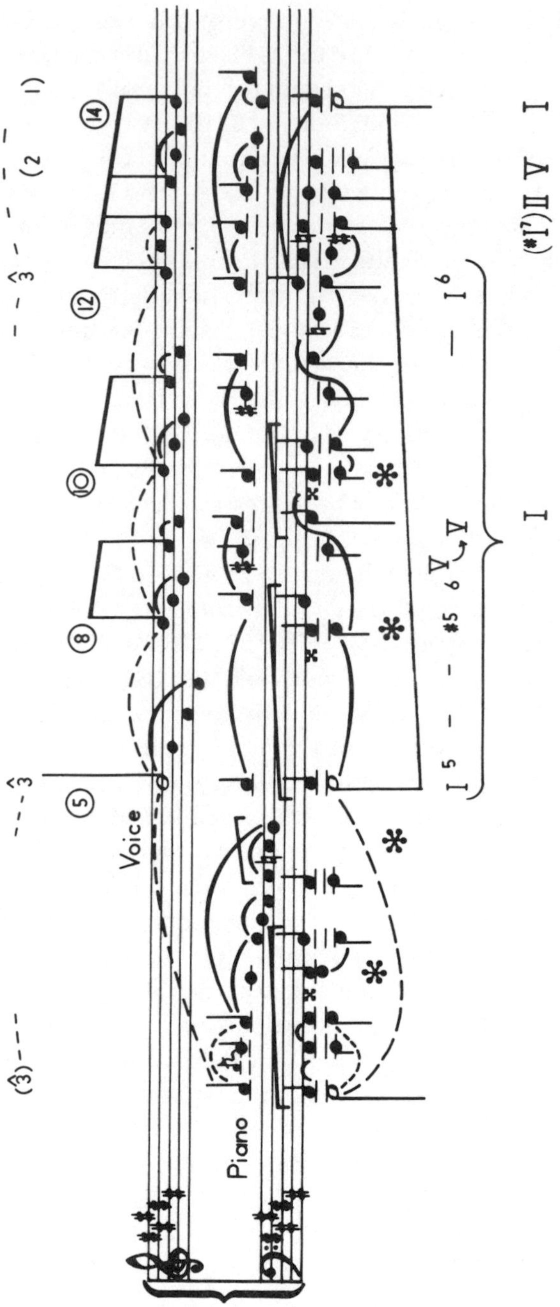

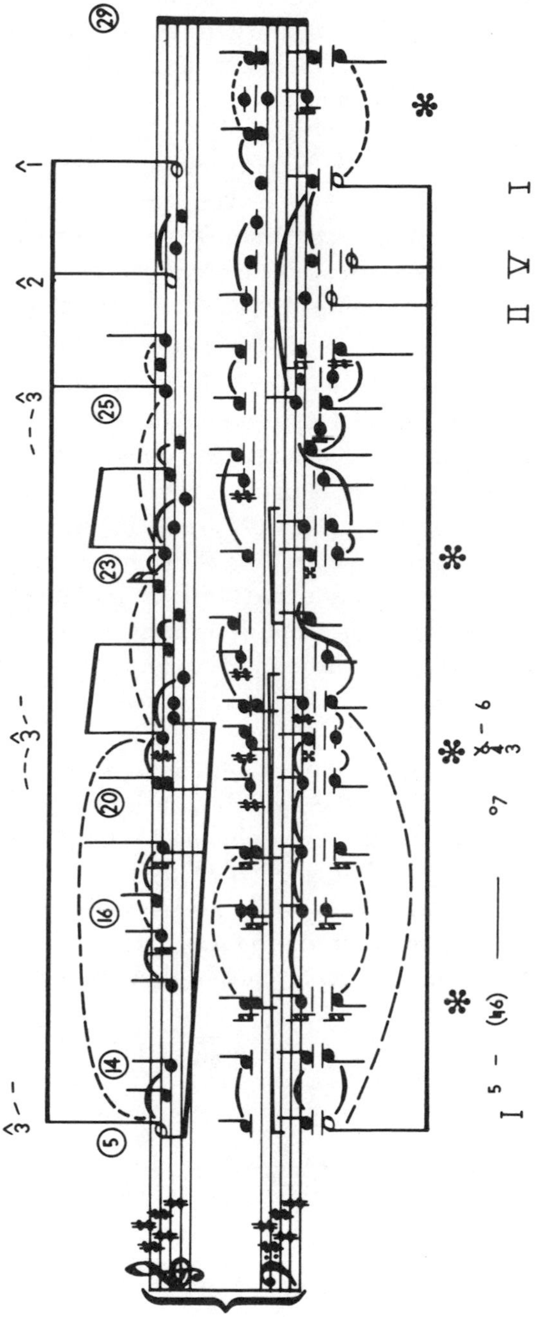

solid tonal structure, the major triad. Only at "wenn der Tag erwacht" does its insubstantiality become manifest; it vanishes, never to return except as an indistinct memory in the G♮'s of the coda. In *Nacht und Träume*, it seems to me, Schubert approaches the limits of what music composed to a text can achieve.

Quite apart from its fantastic relation to the text, the G major passage is most remarkable, for the principles of tonal combination and succession that govern it are applied in a very special, perhaps unique, manner. Since its complex voice leading cannot be demonstrated adequately in a single graph of the whole piece, I should like to close this article by presenting a contrapuntal explanation of the passage (example 10). The graph proceeds from background to foreground and contains five levels:

a. The basis of the passage is the connection of the prolonged B major tonic of bars 1–14 to the G♯ minor six-three of bar 21. The inner-voice progression f♯–g♯ forms the intervals of a fifth and sixth (5–6) above the sustained tonic in the bass.

b. The motivic f♯–f×–g♯ arises in the tenor, caused by the chromatic passing tone f×. The f× is incorporated into a diminished-seventh chord that leads to the G♯ minor six-three. Note that the upper voice splits into two parts, one decorating d♯^{2} with its upper neighbor e^2, the other descending through c♯^{2} to an inner-voice b^1.

c. Another chromatic passing tone, d♮^{2}, appears in the uppermost voice.

d. The f× of the tenor is anticipated so that it coincides with the soprano's d♮^{2}. Thus the two chromatic passing tones occur simultaneously, their coincidence producing a "chord" enharmonically equivalent to a G major six-three (B–f×–d♮^{2}).

e. The apparent G major chord is stabilized. The f× changes enharmonically to g♮ in order to produce a triadic structure. And G♮ is added in the bass, thus making a root-position sonority.

Example 10

Aspects of Motivic Elaboration in the Opening Movement of Haydn's Piano Sonata in C♯ Minor

ROGER KAMIEN

It is now widely accepted that Schenkerian analytic procedures can lead to a more profound understanding of motivic relationships in tonal music. Analyses by Schenker and his disciples often reveal hidden motivic connections between themes or sections that are quite different in character.[1] Such motivic parallelisms appear both on the same and on different structural levels. As Carl Schachter has observed, a foreground motive will sometimes be "expanded to cover a considerable stretch of the middleground."[2]

The present study will deal with aspects of motivic elaboration in the opening movement of Haydn's Piano Sonata in C♯ minor (Hob. XVI:36). It will discuss the ways in which motives are rhythmically transformed and used on various structural levels. We will show how a motive may be presented several times in succession, each time unfolding over a longer time span. This important procedure, which we shall refer to as "progressive motivic enlargement," has received insufficient attention in the analytical literature.[3] Our study will also consider another procedure that has been slighted in most discussions of eighteenth-century music—the reharmonization of specific melodic pitches during the course of a movement.[4]

---

1. For a valuable discussion of Schenker's approach to motivic relationships, see Charles Burkhart, "Schenker's Motivic Parallelisms," *Journal of Music Theory* 22 (1978), pp. 145-75.
2. "Rhythm and Linear Analysis: A Preliminary Study," *The Music Forum* 4 (1976), p. 286.
3. For a discussion of progressive motivic enlargement in Beethoven's Piano Sonata in A♭ major, Op. 110, see Roger Kamien, "Aspects of the Recapitulation in Beethoven Piano Sonatas," *The Music Forum* 4 (1976), pp. 215-18.
4. For brief descriptions of reharmonization in works by Haydn, see Charles Rosen, *The Classical Style: Haydn, Mozart, Beethoven*, New York: The Viking Press, 1971, pp. 115-16 (String Quartet in B minor, Op. 33, No. 1, opening movement) and p. 136 (String Quartet in F♯ minor, Op. 50, No. 4, opening movement); and *idem*, *Sonata Forms*, New York: W. W. Norton, 1980, pp. 264-68 (Symphony No. 55 in E♭ major, opening movement).

The Sonata in C♯ minor is part of a set of six piano sonatas (Hob. XVI:35-39 and 20) first published as Op. 30 by Artaria in Vienna in 1780. Though the precise composition date of this sonata is unknown, most Haydn scholars believe that it was written during the 1770s.[5] The first of its three movements is a Moderato characterized by irregular phrase structure and by rhythmic, harmonic, and dynamic surprises. This sonata-form movement is composed of an exposition, development, and recapitulation that are almost equal in length—33, 31, and 33 bars, respectively.

THE EXPOSITION

The exposition begins with two sharply delineated thematic units—a six-bar opening theme and a five-bar bridge (bars 7-11) ending on V^6_5 of the relative major, the key of the second theme group. The second theme group extends from bar 12 to the downbeat of bar 31, and it contains a series of contrasting but interrelated musical ideas. The end of the second theme group overlaps with the beginning of the brief closing unit of the exposition (bars 31-33).

Much of the exposition's thematic material is derived from motivic elements presented in the motto-like opening bar (see example 1). Of primary importance is the interval of a third, c♯-e, particularly the ascending third c♯-d♯-e of beats 1-2. This third is filled in by a decorative figure that includes the upper neighbor d♯, the lower neighbor b♯, and the passing tone d♯. The decorative figure and ascending third are immediately elaborated in the continuation of the first theme, which contrasts with the opening unison statement in dynamics, texture, and register. The repeated-note pattern in the top voice of bars 2-4 contains ornaments that echo the decorative figure of bar 1 (see the brackets in example 2). (Whether these ornaments are executed as turns starting on the upper notes or as mordents, they are still derived from the decorative figure of bar 1.)

5. See, for example, H. C. Robbins Landon, *Haydn: Chronicle and Works*, Vol. II: *Haydn at Eszterháza 1766-1791*, Bloomington: Indiana University Press, 1978, p. 584.

Example 1

Example 2

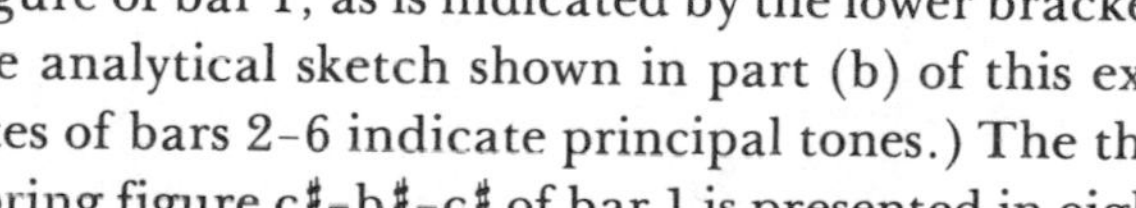

In this movement, the process of progressive motivic enlargement begins within the opening theme. The bass of bars 2-4 expands the decorative figure of bar 1, as is indicated by the lower brackets in example 1. (In the analytical sketch shown in part (b) of this example, the stemmed notes of bars 2-6 indicate principal tones.) The thirty-second note neighboring figure c♯-b♯-c♯ of bar 1 is presented in eighth notes in bar 2, and the fleeting passing tone d♯ is extended to a whole measure in bar 3, where it is decorated by the neighboring tone c♯. Thus the rising third $c\sharp^1$-$d\sharp^1$-e^1 of bars 2-4 is an expansion of the rising third in the first two beats of bar 1. Another example of motivic expansion occurs at the end of the first theme: The upper brackets in example 1 indicate that the top line of bars 4-6 is a varied enlargement of the pattern c♯-e-d♯-c♯ in bar 1.[6]

6. Also, the larger arpeggio pattern in the top voice of bars 2-6—$g\sharp^1$ of bars 2-3, $c\sharp^2$-e^2 of bar 4, and $c\sharp^2$ of bar 6—is prefigured by the arpeggio pattern g♯-$c\sharp^1$-e^1-$c\sharp^1$ in the last three eighth notes of bar 1 and first eighth note of bar 2.

Example 3

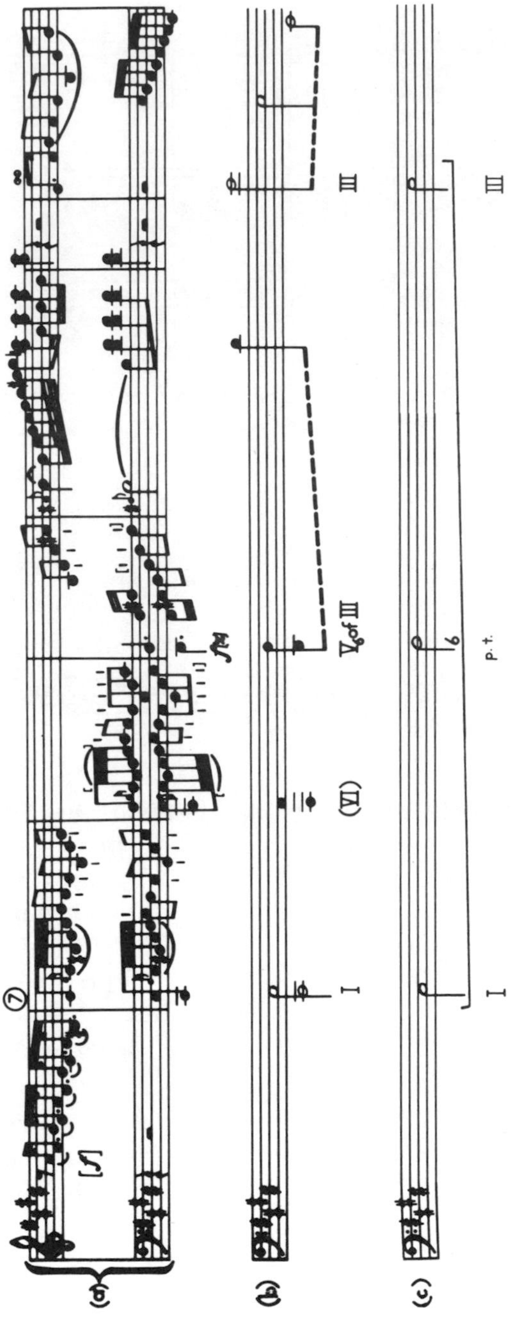

The bridge and the beginning of the second theme group bring a further rhythmic expansion of the ascending third c♯-d♯-e heard in bar 1 and in the bass of bars 2-4. At the beginning of the bridge (bars 7-8) the opening bar is presented twice, first on the tonic and then a third lower (see example 3). The VI of bar 8 is a contrapuntal chord that connects the tonic of bar 7 with the V $^6_3$ of III in bar 9. Therefore, the underlying bass motion of bars 7-12 is the ascending third c♯-d♯-e, as shown at level (c). Haydn has unified the opening of the exposition with a succession of ascending thirds which take longer and longer to unfold. In bar 1 the third c♯-d♯-e takes two beats to unfold; in bars 2-4, three measures; and finally in the bridge, bars 7-12, six measures. In this example of progressive motivic enlargement, a foreground motive is repeated on a higher structural level within the bridge.

Ascending thirds are used in a variety of ways within the remainder of the exposition. For example, a legato version of bar 1 is presented three times in ascending sequence at the beginning of the second theme group (bars 12-14). This sequence produces the ascending third e^1-$f♯^1$-$g♯^1$, as shown at level (b) in example 4. This ascent grows out of the rising third in the left hand of bars 2-4, which becomes even more explicit when this idea returns in E major within the second theme group, shown at level (c).

Example 4

At the beginning of the development section (see example 5, part (b)), the opening three bars of the second theme group reappear an octave higher. This reappearance is prepared most artfully within the closing unit of the exposition through progressive motivic enlargement (see example 5, part (a)). In the top voice of bars 31 and 32, the ascending thirds e^2-f♯^{2}-g♯^{2} take only three eighth notes to unfold, as shown by the brackets. In bar 33, the ascending third takes three quarter notes to unfold, and at the beginning of the development it unfolds within three whole bars.

Example 5

We have seen that the ascending third e-f♯-g♯ has undergone various rhythmic transformations within the E major section of the exposition. Haydn also succeeds in integrating the original third, c♯-d♯-e, within the E major section, a far more difficult task. Near the end of the second theme group, the original third c♯-e makes a brilliant appearance at the highest register of the movement (see example 6).[7]

Example 6

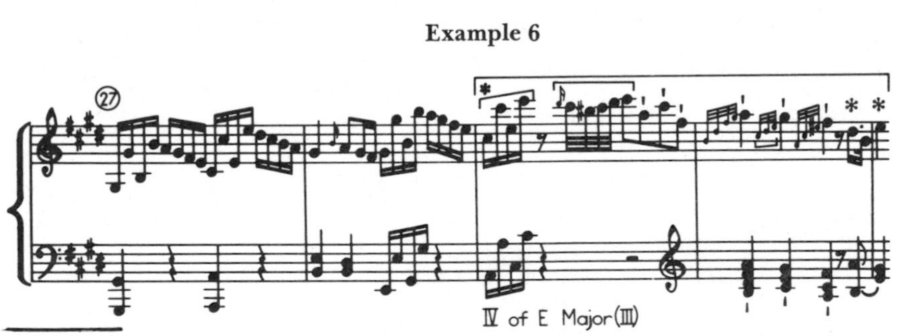

7. Observe that the e^3 in bar 29, first beat, is prepared by the e^3 of bar 25, second beat.

After the broken octaves c$\sharp$-e at the beginning of bar 29, Haydn unexpectedly interrupts the rhythmic motion with a brief pause. This pause highlights both the rising third and the following varied repetition of the third. This varied repetition takes the form of a witty quotation of the opening decorative figure, two octaves higher. Here the third c$\sharp$-e appears within a major chord (IV of E major), in contrast to bar 1, where it is in C$\sharp$ minor. The thirds c$\sharp$-e of bar 29 are embedded within a longer-range ascending third (see the asterisks in example 6). This third ascends from the $c\sharp^2$ on the first beat of bar 29 through the $d\sharp^2$ on the last eighth note of bar 30 to the e^2 of bar 31, first beat.[8] This amazing passage even contains a reminder of the third c$\sharp$-d$\sharp$-e in the thirty-second note prefix to the second beat of bar 30.

There is an extraordinary relationship between bars 22–24 (*dolce*) and the brilliant ending of the second theme group, bars 28–31. Parts (a) and (b) of example 7 juxtapose these two units and part (c) shows some of their common elements. Both units begin with the same chord progression (I^6–IV) and top voice (b–c$\sharp$). The melodic descent a^2–$g\sharp^2$–$f\sharp^2$–$d\sharp^2$–e^2 occurs in bars 23–24 and bars 30–31, and in each case the melodic descent $f\sharp^2$–$d\sharp^2$ is supported by the chord progression II^6–V^7 at the identical register. Both passages employ $b\sharp^2$ as a decorative tone within a IV chord. Finally, the right hand of the *dolce* unit employs octave doubling, while both hands of bars 28–29 contain broken octaves. This relationship between the *dolce* phrase and the end of the second theme group is a marvelous example of Haydn's variation technique.

The phrase structure at the end of the second theme group (bars 27–30/31) is highly irregular (see example 6). Here a four-bar phrase, closing into a fifth bar, is asymmetrically subdivided into a subphrase lasting a bar and a half (bars 27–28) and an expanded repetition of this subphrase lasting two and a half bars (bar 28, third beat, to bar 31). By beginning the repetition in the middle of bar 28 Haydn gains the time to recall the opening decorative figure in bar 29 as well as the concluding tones of the *dolce* unit (bar 23) in bar 30. Since the repetition of the subphrase begins in the middle of bar 28, the second half of this bar is not heard as metrically weak, as would normally be the case, but as metrically strong. The beginning of bar 29 is also heard as metrically strong owing to the pause after the first quarter of the bar.[9]

8. As shown in example 8, this third, which is an inner voice, occurs within the context of a larger structural descent of a fifth from b^2 (m.28) to e^2 (m.31). The connection between the tones of this third is reinforced by identity of register and by rhythmic prominence of the $d\sharp^2$ (m.30), owing to the preceding eighth-note rest.

9. I am indebted to Professor Carl Schachter and Mr. Channan Willner for helpful comments on this passage.

Example 7

Both the first subphrase and its expanded repetition contain the harmonic progression I^6-IV-V (in III). In the first subphrase the IV lasts half a bar (bar 27, beats 3-4), but in the second subphrase the IV is greatly extended. On the surface the extension seems to last for one bar (bar 29). However, on a higher structural level the IV is retained through the third quarter of bar 30, where it becomes II^6 (see example 8). Observe that the A in the bass of bar 29 is transferred up to the a on the third beat of bar 30. The bass ascent b-c$\sharp^1$ (bar 30), which supports the foreground progression V^7-VI, is actually a motion into an inner voice.

Example 8

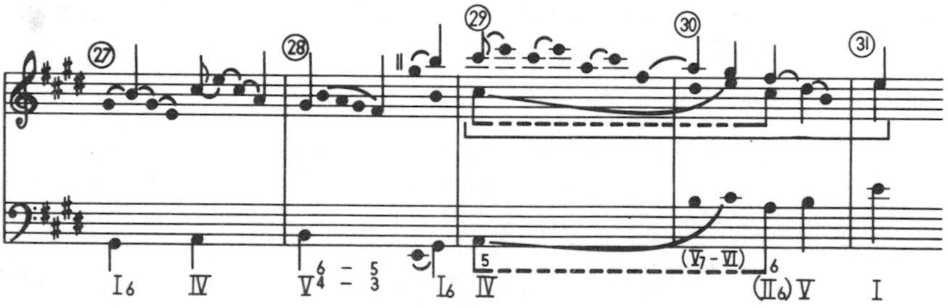

THE DEVELOPMENT SECTION

The development section is clearly divided into two parts of unequal length, bars 34–43 and bars 44–64. The first part begins in III and moves through a passing IV (bar 37) to a V♯ chord (bar 43) that is followed by a long pause (see example 9).[10] The second part begins with the first theme, not in the expected tonic key, but in V minor (G♯ minor). This creates a sharp harmonic jolt. Later in the development the minor dominant is transformed into the major dominant to prepare for the recapitulation of the opening theme in the tonic.

We have already observed that the top voice of the development begins with an ascending third, e^2–$f\sharp^2$–$g\sharp^2$, that takes three bars to unfold (see examples 5, part (b), and 9). This ascending third reappears in the bass within both parts of the development section. In the first part,

Example 9

10. Through a voice exchange, the bass tone f♯ of bar 37 is taken over by the upper voice as $f^{\times 2}$ in bar 42 while the a^2 of the top voice in bar 40 is transferred to the a of the bass in bar 42. (This is shown by the diagonal lines in the graph of example 9.)

the underlying bass motion over a span of ten measures (bars 34–43) is e-(e♯)-f♯^{1}-g♯ (see the large bracket in example 9). In the second part (bars 51–55) the ascending third is traversed more rapidly and now contains two chromatic passing tones: E-(E♯)-F♯-(F×)-G♯. Though different in figuration and duration, bars 51–55 and bars 34–43 are similar in register and harmonic content. (Cf. bar 34 with bar 51; bar 36, beats 3–4 with bar 52; bar 37 with bar 53; and bars 42–43 with bars 54–55.)

A fascinating example of motivic enlargement occurs near the end of the first part of the development. In bar 40 there is a strange progression from an F♯ minor $^6_3$ chord (*piano*) to an A major chord (*forte*). This harmonic and dynamic jolt highlights the top voice a^2, which is an upper neighbor to the g♯^{2} of bar 43 (see the bracket in example 9). The melodic line a^2-g^2-f×^{2}-g♯^{2} of bars 40–43 is a bold enlargement of the ornament in bar 2 (see example 10)! This enlargement exploits the repeated eighth-note figure that is associated with the ornament. The prominent a^2 of bars 40–41 has been prepared by striking appearances of a^2—with the same rhythmic pattern—in bars 10–11, at the end of the bridge, and in bars 15–16, within the second theme group (see example 11).

Example 10

The neighboring tone a^2 is also prominent with the second part of the development. In bars 56–59 it is sustained in the top voice for four bars over a chromatically descending bass (see example 9). This sustained a^2 is followed by a progressive rhythmic acceleration in the top voice that intensifies the drive toward the recapitulation, as shown in example 12.

Example 11

Example 12: Rhythmic Reduction of Top Voice (bars 55–64)

THE RECAPITULATION

Exposition motives are treated in new ways in every section of the recapitulation. In the opening theme of the recapitulation (bars 65–72), the neighboring-tone figures in the left hand (bars 66–68) are now imitated in the right hand (bars 68–71). The original bridge and first five bars of the second theme group are omitted. Haydn uses the long upbeat figure to the original bridge (bar 6) as the basis for a new bridge (bars 73–77) that leads directly into the second subsection of the second theme group (bar 78). Thereafter the recapitulation is roughly parallel to the exposition, but with many significant departures in motivic detail.

In the recapitulation, Haydn provides new harmonic support for pitches retained from melodic lines in the exposition. Through reharmonization, subtle sonoric associations between the two sections are created. Parts (a) and (b) of example 13 show the beginning of the bridge in the exposition and recapitulation, respectively. The top voice of each bridge executes the identical melodic descent: a^1-g♯^{1}-f♯^{1}-e^1. In the recapitulation the descending second a^1-g♯^{1} is given greater emphasis because of its new metrical placement and accompanying bass. The a^1 of bar 6 appears without harmonic support, but the a^1 of bar 72 is part of a diminished-seventh chord. Parts (a) and (b) of example 14 show the *dolce* phrase of the second theme group in the exposition and recapitulation. Both passages contain the melodic descent c♯^{3}-b^2-a^2-g♯^{2}-f♯^{2}, and in both passages the top voice f♯^{2} is supported by an F♯ minor $^6_3$ chord. The harmonic context and musical effect of each descent is quite different, however. Bars 22–23 are within the context of E major, while bars 82–83 are within C♯ minor. This minor key makes the "sigh" figures seem much more pathetic in the recapitulation.

The return of the *dolce* phrase (bars 82–86) in the recapitulation is prepared in a most imaginative way. Parts (a) and (b) of example 15 show how the new bridge in the recapitulation subtly prefigures the *dolce* phrase of the second theme group. The melodic pattern of bars 74–75 is expanded within bars 82–85 (see the tones marked with asterisks). Both passages contain a progression from I to IV and the bass ascent e-f♯-g♯-a. In addition, the connection between the two passages is reinforced by the use of the same register in the top voice. Through these varied repetitions of melodic and harmonic patterns, Haydn has unified sections that are quite different in character.

Example 13

Example 14

Example 15

Perhaps the most significant exploitation of reharmonization may be found at the end of the second theme group (see parts (a) and (b) of example 16). In bar 91, third beat, Haydn preserves the striking third $c\sharp^2$ -e^2 from bar 29; this third is now supported by a tonic $^6_3$ chord rather than by the IV of E major. Unlike bar 29, bar 91 does not contain a rhythmic interruption after the ascending third, or a quotation of the opening decorative figure. Instead, the top line descends stepwise after the third, creating the pattern c♯-e-d♯-c♯ within the last two beats of bar 91. This pattern recalls the first three beats of bar 1 (cf. example 1, level (a), and example 16, part (b)). The broken octaves in the second half of bar 91 should be played as a climax because they bring the motive c♯-e-d♯-c♯ into the highest register for the first time in the movement.

Example 16

Haydn masterfully weaves recollections of other basic motives into the continuation of this phrase. Bar 92 contains an augmentation of the turn figure a^1-$g\sharp^1$-$f{\times}^1$-$g\sharp^1$ from bar 2, and this turn figure is embedded within an enlargement of the repeated-note motive from the same bar. Haydn even preserves the accompanying neighboring tone figure in thirds. The thirty-second note decorative figure of bar 29 that does *not* appear in the analogous bar 91 is used *three* times in bar 93.

In the recapitulation, as in the development section, the neighboring tone a is of special importance. The neighboring-tone pattern g♯-a-g♯ appears on various structural levels and unifies different sections. Three related passages from the recapitulation will illustrate contrasting uses of this pattern. Example 17 shows the neighboring tone a as a fleeting detail at the beginning of the bridge. Observe that the neighboring tone appears at two different registers—a^1 at the last eighth of bar 72 and a^2 at the last eighth of bar 73. The neighboring tone a is extended over a longer time span within the second theme group (see example 18). The graph at level (b) shows a as a neighboring tone that is retained through six bars as the top voice of an underlying F♯ minor chord and diminished-seventh chord (bars 83-88). Though this a is not literally sustained through all six bars, it maintains its significance as a top voice until it resolves to the $g\sharp^1$ in the first beat of bar 89. In bars 83-84, the melodic line twice descends a third, a^1-$g\sharp^1$-$f\sharp^1$, into an inner voice. This third is forcefully restated in the double octaves of bar 88. The last appearance of the neighboring-tone figure occurs in bars 93-94, where, for the first time, the figure is followed by a stepwise melodic descent to the tonic that is supported by a cadential bass.

Example 17

Haydn has ingeniously led up to this conclusion through a variety of melodic descents from the neighboring tone a. Toward the end of the development the neighboring tone a^2, extended for four bars, is followed by the descent $g\sharp^2$-$f\sharp^2$-e^2-$d\sharp^2$ (see example 9, bars 55-62). In the recapitulation, the beginning of the bridge brings the fleeting descent a-g♯-f♯-e in two different registers (see example 17). The second theme group in the recapitulation (example 18) contains the descent a^2-$g\sharp^2$-$f\sharp^2$ in the "sigh" figures of bars 83-84 and the descent a^1-$g\sharp^1$-$f\sharp^1$-e^1 in the stark octaves of bars 88-89. Finally, at the end of the recapitulation (bars 94-95), the descent a^2-$g\sharp^2$-$f\sharp^2$-e^2 receives a new harmonic setting and continues definitively to the tonic.

Example 18

82
(a)
dolce
p
[p]
(b)
N
10
5
N (IV)
I6
6
86
[6]
f
[ff]
I.N.
10
6
4#
I6
IV
91
N
V 6 – 5
4 – 3
I6
(IV)5
3
(V4
2)
I6

This study has shown some of the ways in which a motive can be rhythmically transformed and repeated on a higher structural level. We have also observed how Haydn uses progressive motivic enlargement to unify different sections. We have seen that specific pitches from melodic lines are harmonically reinterpreted and that specific registers are used to clarify motivic relationships.

Musical performance is enhanced by sensitivity to hidden motivic connections such as those discussed in this essay. As Heinrich Schenker wrote almost fifty years ago, "The *performance* of a musical work of art can be based only upon a perception of that work's organic coherence."[11]

11. *Free Composition (Der freie Satz),* translated and edited by Ernst Oster, New York: Longman, 1979, p. 8.

Schenker's Theory of Levels and Musical Performance

CHARLES BURKHART

A Schenkerian analysis of a musical work primarily reveals how that work is "composed"—that is, how its components may be viewed in terms of hierarchically ordered structural levels (*Schichten*).[1] I will consider here the elusive question of what bearing the multi-leveled view, once established, has on the way one performs the work and, in so doing, will attempt to put into perspective Schenker's many references to the subject.

While Schenker's life and work as a whole involved performance in many ways, from about 1920 on he came to see it more and more (though far from exclusively!) in terms of the theory of levels, the dominant idea in his theoretical work of that period. In his writings he now approached the subject of performance in two somewhat different ways, depending on whether he was writing an analytic or a theoretic work.[2] In the analytic works, which are essays on individual pieces, he frequently followed

1. Allen Forte long ago pointed out that "Schenker's major concept is not that of the *Ursatz*, as is sometimes maintained, but that of structural levels, a far more inclusive idea." (See his article, "Schenker's Conception of Musical Structure," *Journal of Music Theory* 3 (1959).) To my knowledge Schenker did not use the term *Schichtenlehre* ("theory of levels"), but he made much use of *Schichten*. Very briefly, the theory sees the pitch organization of a work (or passage) as a series of progressively more complex elaborations of a simple foundation. Each successive elaboration is a "level." I will use the terms *background* and *foreground* in a relative sense. Schenker's usage was stricter. For him the background (*Hintergrund*) was only the *Ursatz* and he spoke of *Schichten* only beyond that point. (This distinction is important to the understanding of Schenker's writings, but I do not adhere to it in this paper, which scarcely refers to the *Ursatz* at all.) In Schenker, the term foreground (*Vordergrund*) does not equal "the music," nor does it here. My term "surface" refers to the note-to-note aspect of music—an important aspect!
2. The "analytic" works of the period in question are most of the essays comprising the ten issues of *Der Tonwille* (1921-1924) and the three "yearbooks" *Das Meisterwerk in der Musik* (1925, 1926, and 1930). I will not attempt to report in detail on the large body of performance commentary in these essays, but study of it is to be recommended highly. A sizable sampling of essays from the three *Meisterwerk* volumes is available in English translation. See (1) Sylvan Kalib, *Thirteen Essays from the Three Yearbooks "Das Meisterwerk in der Musik" by Heinrich Schenker: An Annotated Translation*, Ann Arbor: University Microfilms, 1973; (2) the translation by Hedi Siegel of the essay on the Sarabande from J. S. Bach's Third Suite for Unaccompanied Violoncello, *The Music Forum* 2 (1970); and (3) the translation by John Rothgeb of the essay on the Largo from Bach's Third Sonata for Unaccompanied Violin, *The Music Forum* 4 (1976). *(Continued on page 96.)*

the analysis proper with remarks—often quite extensive ones—on how the piece in question should be performed; in the theoretic works he was primarily presenting a theory, not explicating the structure of a particular piece. Therefore he quite naturally did not discuss details of performance here, but often did comment on performance in general. All these writings testify to his strong feeling that his theory has great relevance to performance.

Schenker saw his theory as revealing the music's "content" (*Inhalt*)—its voice-leading, motivic correspondences, harmonic structure—and he believed that the benefit of his exposition of the content was that it provided the performer with valuable objective information applicable to performance, thereby decreasing the performer's need to rely on guesswork and personal fancy. While he often vividly expressed his convictions on the benefits of applying his theory, he did not think that such application would automatically produce a good performance, and he recognized that many decisions would always be left to the individual performer. By no means did he ignore the intuitive side of performing, but in his writings he focused on the objective side. For example, at the beginning of his comments on the performance of Beethoven's F minor Piano Sonata, Op. 57, he writes:

> In my discussion here of the performance (*Vortrag*) of the work, I will attempt not to touch on those matters that are left to the freedom of all performers, including myself; rather, I will discuss it only in terms of the reading established above [*Tonwille* 7, p. 22].

This passage typifies Schenker's use of the word *Vortrag* for performance, a word that might be more precisely rendered as "execution." In the light of the content, how should the composition be executed in terms of articulation, rhythmic emphases, dynamics? After these matters are settled, the performer must next determine how he can best realize them. If one is a pianist (as was Schenker), an important question is what fingering to use. And *then* one practices, now that there is something *to* practice.

(Continued from page 95.)

By "theoretic writings" I refer chiefly to the three volumes of *Neue musikalische Theorien und Phantasien*. This category would also include certain essays on the *Urlinie* in *Der Tonwille* and *Das Meisterwerk*.

It is well known that during this period Schenker also worked on a treatise on musical performance to be entitled *Die Kunst des Vortrages*. Announced as early as 1912 and intended as a major work, it was unfortunately left in a fragmentary state. For an informative report on this interesting item in Schenker's *Nachlass*, see Oswald Jonas's article, "Die Kunst des Vortrages nach Heinrich Schenker," *Musikerziehung* **15**, No. 4 (1962), p. 127.

In his edition of the Beethoven piano sonatas Schenker tried to make the results of his analytic work (not to mention his very significant work in the area of manuscript study) directly available to the performing musician.[3] He accomplished this in various ways, but the most pertinent here is his choice of fingering. The player reading from this edition should be aware that there is a special significance to these fingerings: they are designed to bring out (as much as fingering can) Schenker's view of the work's structure. I offer one typical example. It shows how Schenker's view of the structure in terms of levels has influenced his choice of articulation and how he subsequently achieves this articulation (and induces the player to achieve it) by his choice of fingering.

AN EXAMPLE FROM SCHENKER

In the first movement of Beethoven's Op. 57, Schenker writes the unexpected fingering $^{3}_{1}$ for the right hand in bar 24 (see example 1, which is reproduced from Schenker's edition). (Other editions typically add a slur into bar 24 and give a fingering of, say, $^{5}_{4}$, as shown in example 2.) By means of his fingering, Schenker forces the player to detach the ending of the trill from the following g^{2}–$b^{\flat 2}$. He says the $b^{\flat 2}$ "looks ahead" and "has nothing to do with" the previous $d^{\flat 2}$ (see *Tonwille* 7, p. 23). His reason is that he considers bars 24–32 to be a kind of large "insertion" (*Einschaltung*) that requires a special articulation at its beginning. (See example 3, Schenker's own reduction of this passage, in which the insertion is enclosed in large parentheses.) This articulation serves to set off the $d^{\flat 2}$ of bar 23, a note temporarily abandoned while the insertion features a higher register. When bar 33 brings a return to $d^{\flat 2}$, Schenker wants the ear to relate it to the one left hanging, as it were, in bar 23. This interpretation is based on his conception of those two $D^{\flat}$'s as emanations from a single "higher-level" tone beginning in bar 23 and enduring beyond the insertion to resolve to the c^{2} in bar 36.

3. A full account of the many attributes of this unique edition is given by Carl Schachter in his introduction to the recent reprint of it by Dover Publications (1975).

Example 1: Beethoven, Piano Sonata Op. 57 (I), 17–37.

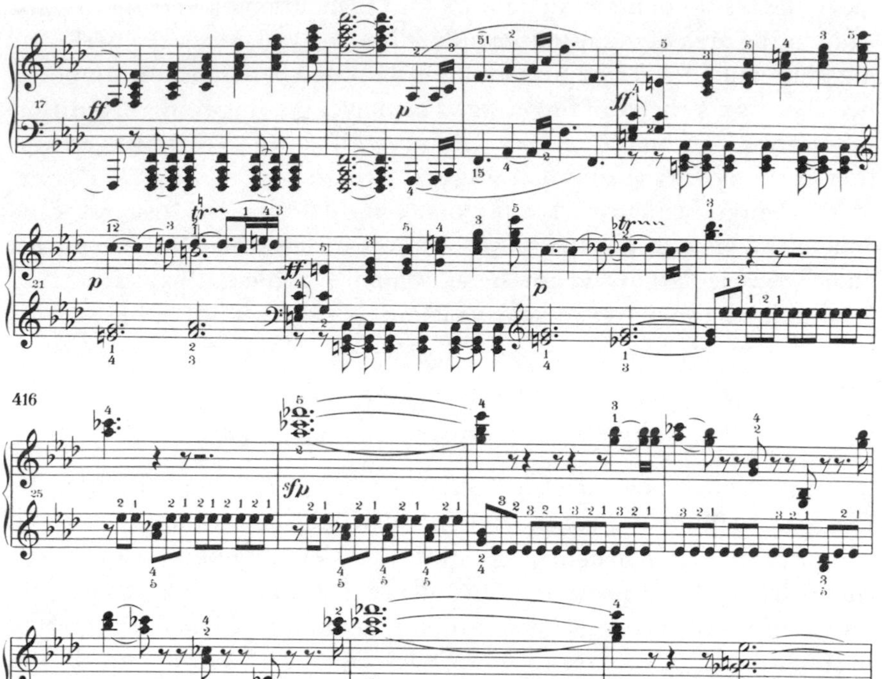

Example 2

Example 3: From Schenker's Analytic Reduction of Beethoven's Op. 57 (*Tonwille* 7).

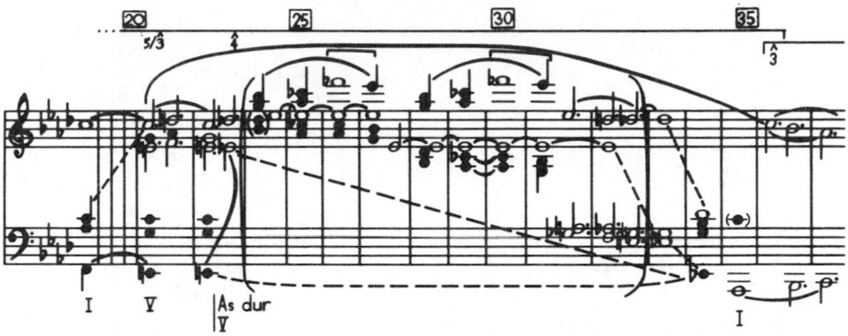

This example is not intended to suggest that there is anything sacred about a particular fingering. The important thing is to produce the desired musical effect, whatever the fingering chosen. But pianists playing from Schenker's editions should be aware that his fingerings are more than simply what worked for his hand. Before replacing his fingering with their own, they should try to discover what the *musical* reason for his fingering is.

ARTICULATING MOTIVIC PARALLELISMS

My analysis of the third movement of Beethoven's Sonata in E♭, Op. 7, provides another example of how the use of Schenker's theory of levels can directly affect the performer's decision on the execution of a specific passage. Notice that throughout most of the first large section (bars 1–95) of the movement the composer has written quite explicit legato slurs (see example 4).[4] But no slurs are given at bars 61 and 62. Here the player must decide what to do, particularly whether or not to

4. Example 4 is reproduced from Schenker's edition. Slurs were a feature that Schenker took great care to reproduce accurately in all his editions, and a matter that he deemed not only of textual but also of great analytic importance. See his essay "Weg mit dem Phrasierungsbogen" ("Away with the Phrasing Slur!") in *Das Meisterwerk* I (p. 41), in which he inveighs against editors that add phrasing slurs and, in so doing, obliterate the original legato slurs.

Example 4: Beethoven, Piano Sonata Op. 7 (III), 1–95.

Example 5

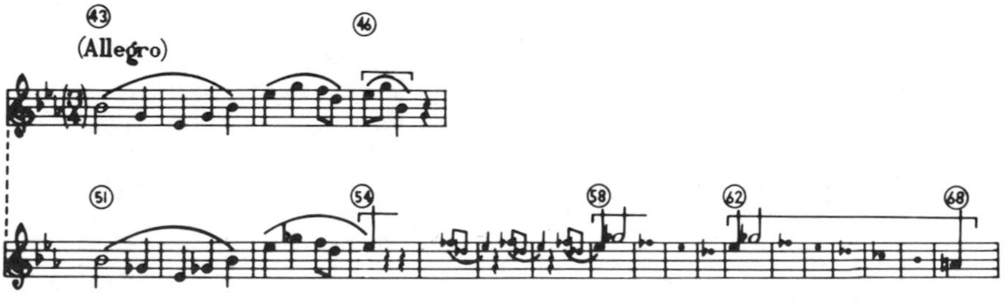

slur the $d^{\flat 2}$ into the $e^{\flat 2}$, as at the turn of bar 58. (Many editors have in fact added a long phrasing slur here that covers these two notes.) I suggest that the player will be better prepared to decide this matter when he realizes that a motivic parallelism[5] exists between bar 46 (originally bar 4) and bars 62-69, as shown in example 5.

If reading a parallelism here at first strikes the reader as unwarranted, it may seem much less so after further examination of the piece. Observe that in the first subsection (bars 1-24) the second phrase (bars 9-24) exhibits considerable "extension." Then notice that the analogous phrase starting in bar 51 is even more drastically extended, not reaching a cadence (comparable to the one in bar 24) until bar 86. The motivic parallelism (bars 62-69)—Schenker called this type of parallelism an "enlargement" (*Vergrösserung*)—is a contribution to this general extending of the material.

Now the "hard" advice that this analysis gives to the player must surely be to "bring out" this enlarged motive somehow. There are various ways to do this, but a very direct one would be to lift the right hand before striking the $e^{\flat 2}$ in bar 62. Slurring into the $e^{\flat 2}$ can easily obscure the motivic relationship.

Motivic parallelisms can lie very near the surface or buried in the remoter levels of structure. The farther toward the background they lie, the less they can be explicitly performed, of course. Yet even the deeply buried ones, I suggest, can influence performance if the performer is aware of them.

Chopin's F♯ major Impromptu, Op. 36, contains motivic parallelisms on many levels (as do most great pieces). My first of three examples from this work lies very near the surface but concealed within a passage that has often puzzled pianists. I refer to bars 59-60, a strange little transition leading from a march-like section in D major that unexpectedly breaks off to a fantasy-like return of the opening theme in the "wrong"

5. The phenomenon of "motivic parallelism," an outgrowth of the concept of structural levels, was one of Schenker's most important discoveries and one which, in my opinion, has been somewhat neglected. (See my article, "Schenker's 'Motivic Parallelisms,' " *Journal of Music Theory* 22 (1978), pp. 145-175.) Motivic parallelism is a compositional feature in which a given motive that occurs more than once is stated at least once beneath the surface. The variety of forms this phenomenon can take is virtually boundless, but example 5 shows a frequently found type: A motive first occurring on the surface is later repeated on a higher level. Schenker gives innumerable examples in his post-1920 works. He refers to them by a variety of names, the most felicitous of which is perhaps *verborgene Wiederholungen* ("hidden repetitions").

key of F major. It is difficult to bring off this part of the piece with a sense of logical progression. While many different considerations will go into its successful execution, only the motivic aspect and its articulation are relevant here. As shown by the brackets in example 6, an inner voice features a motive of a descending second—an element introduced in bar 1 and repeated many times throughout the opening (F♯ major) section. I maintain that this knowledge will help the pianist play this passage more effectively. But before he decides how to do so, he should also be aware of one other bit of objective information, namely, the meaning of Chopin's own slurs in these bars. (They are reproduced in example 6.) Schenker's only published comment on this impromptu[6] concerns these slurs. He makes the insightful observation that the slurring of the *three* notes g♯-e^1-d^1 is to prevent the ear from hearing the e-d as coming from f^1, that is from hearing it as part of a third-progression f-e-d, for to hear

Example 6: Chopin, *Impromptu* Op. 36.

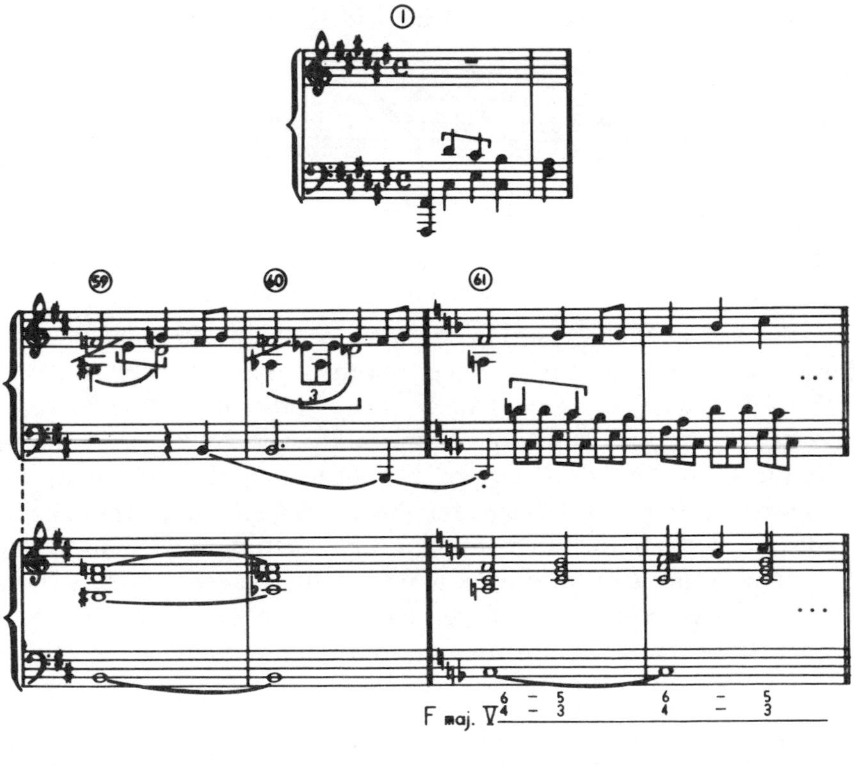

6. *Free Composition*, par. 273, Fig. 128, 5c. The first system of my example 6 is adapted from Schenker's figure.

thus would obliterate the motive. What the player now does with all this information is "left to the freedom of all performers." My own means of keeping the f^1 aurally separate from the e^1-d^1 is to play the two top lines with very different tone quality, giving the top line (the alternating f-g's) the more penetrating color. Further exposure of the two-note motives can be achieved by giving a very slight emphasis (and perhaps a hair's breadth more length) to the first note of each one (the e^1 in bar 59, etc.). Each first note is a weak-beat appoggiatura and its dissonance followed by resolution should be as clear as possible.

My second example is a somewhat higher-level expression of the two-note motive. This one occurs where the key of F♯ major returns in bars 72-73. It is formed by the D♮-C♯ of the bass, differing from my first example in being chromatic. The motive actually starts on the d♮ of the second beat of bar 72, where Chopin placed an accent mark (see example 7). The player should not let the crescendo in these two bars overpower the motive.

Example 7

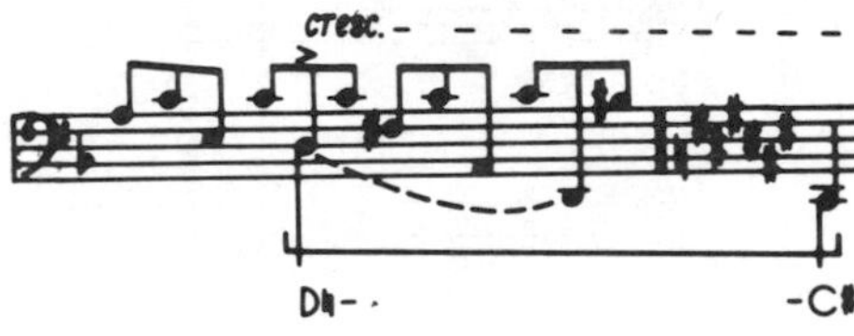

Finally, the highest-level expression of the two-note motive results from relating the D of bar 72 to the D of the D major "march" starting in bar 39. Thus a huge enlargement of the motive may be said to embrace the entire middle section of the work—bars 39-73—as shown in example 8.[7] While such a "motive" cannot be literally performed, will not awareness of it usefully contribute to the conception of the work as a whole—help guide the mind through the unsettling digression beginning at bar 59 toward the return of tonal stability at bars 72-75? If so, will not this awareness inevitably if ever so subtly influence the way the performer shapes the large dimensions of the composition?

---

7. I am indebted to Aldwell and Schachter's *Harmony and Voice Leading,* New York: Harcourt, Brace, Jovanovich, 1979, vol. 2, p. 247, for the idea that there is a *motivic* aspect to the Impromptu's tonal structure.

Example 8

Motivic parallelisms are, of course, only one of many elements that a musical performance in the fullest sense will seek to "bring out." Too great an effort to bring them out can distort the music rather than promote its effective projection, and there are doubtless some cases of parallelism that should receive no overt effort to be expressed. It is all a question of relating the many parts of a work in such a way that they produce a whole greater than the sum of the parts. Motivic parallelism is one of the parts, and understanding this phenomenon can greatly enrich a performance.

THE ROLE OF THE BACKGROUND

Most of the examples offered so far have focused on short, specific applications of level theory to performance. However, the theory also contributes to the solution of more general problems—the kind suggested by such time-honored expressions as "the long line," "hanging together," and "a sense of direction." Indeed, it is from this point of view that level analysis has its most significant effect on performance—and an effect that is at the same time no less relevant to small details.

Consider, for example, the problems involved in arriving at a performance of the first section of the sarabande from J. S. Bach's Partita I in B♭ major (see example 9). It is not difficult to recall performances of this passage that failed because they left the impression of a mass of undifferentiated detail. I propose that a performer who has not perceived "what to do" with all these details can benefit from understanding them as "embellishments," or "diminutions," to use Schenker's term, of the higher-level construct (which I will call the "framework") shown at

(a) in example 10.[8] What does this framework tell us that is applicable to performance, that will affect the way one plays the *surface*—the way one gets from one note of the piece to the next, and in so doing, tries to make them all "hang together"?

Example 9: Bach, Partita I, Sarabande, 1–13.

8. Example 10 is adapted from my own analysis of the Sarabande. The reader will note that both (a) and (b) combine two or more levels.

First of all, one negative conclusion seems clear: It would clearly be tasteless to overemphasize the tones of the framework itself. Schenker repeatedly counsels against such an approach. "It is improper," he writes, "to expressly pursue the *Urlinie* in performance and to single out its tones . . . for the purpose of communicating the *Urlinie* to the listener." Rather, says Schenker, "for the performer, the *Urlinie* provides, first of all, a sense of direction. It serves a somewhat equivalent function to that which a road map serves for a mountain climber . . ."[9] For Schenker, then, it is not so much the "main" tones that the player should expressly bring out, but the diminutions thereof. A simple example of this, and one well known to all musicians, is the way one "leans" on an appoggiatura. The appoggiatura itself may be metrically stronger, louder, and sometimes even longer, than the tone of resolution, but it acquires its meaning and its expressiveness by virtue of the note of resolution. Thus, even though the appoggiatura is the more striking of the two tones, the note of resolution is the *higher-level* one—the one which, in analytic notation, would be written as the *larger* of the two.

While Schenker's advice not to "single out" the tones of the *Urlinie* in performance is certainly sound and generally to be observed, there are undoubtedly many cases of long-range connections that call for some kind of special performance. For example, the opening d^2 of our sarabande is obviously related to the c^2 of bar 13 (see example 9). The performer should take care to play these two points (particularly the chords on the second beat of each bar) with the same quality of tone. (In an orchestral work, two such related bars would be similarly orchestrated.) This is not the kind of excessive emphasis that Schenker warned against. He meant that the *Urlinie* tones should not be exaggerated, nor brought out at the expense of the diminutions.

In the present case there is an avenue quite distinct from level analysis that will begin to guide the searching performer toward an understanding of what to "bring out." I refer simply to the traditional sarabande rhythm with its characteristic stress on the second beat—a stress

9. The quotation is from an essay on the *Urlinie* in *Das Meisterwerk* I, p. 196 (translation from Kalib, op. cit., vol. 2, p. 147). Schenker is here making his point with respect to the kind of "*Urlinie*" represented in (a) of example 10 by the descending stepwise line d^2-f^1. In his later work he will make the same point with respect to the concept of the *Urlinie* as finally formulated. See, for example, *Free Composition (Der freie Satz)*, translated by Ernst Oster, New York: Longman, 1979, p. 8.

Example 10

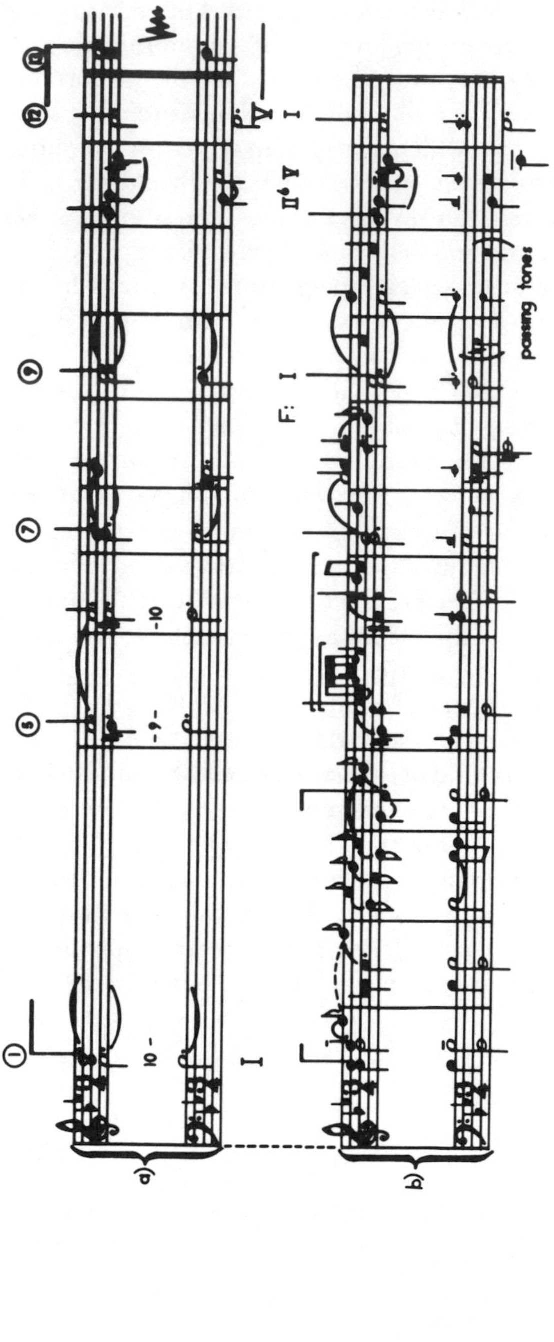

automatically produced in many bars of this sarabande by the thicker texture of the chord on that beat. But notice that not all the high-register tones so stressed are tones of the framework, and that those that are not (for example, the g^2 in bar 8, second beat) are all the more expressive.

I will now go through example 10 from the background toward the surface and consider the effect of each level on the ones that follow it. The highest level shown in line (a) is the $\frac{3}{\mathrm{I}}$-$\frac{2}{\mathrm{V}}$ that embraces bars 1-13 (and, of course, points beyond).[10] The next level shows that the opening d^2, before moving to the c^2 of bar 13, first makes a subordinate motion down to f^1 in bar 12. The player should be aware that this unbroken stepwise descent is the primary factor that articulates the first twelve bars as a unit. The bass line counterpointing this descent causes three events also worthy of the performer's note: 1) the 9-10 suspension in bars 5-6, which propels the motion forward; 2) the tritone $b\flat^1$-$e\natural$ in bar 8 that points toward the key of F major, thus making this bar a "turning point"; and 3) the complete F major cadence (I-II^6-V-I) in bars 9-12, which sets off these bars as a unit and gives them greater stability than the previous four bars.

Line (b) shows the next stage of diminution. The largest event here is the division of the twelve bars into groups of 4 + 8, which occurs because the opening d^2 now receives a diminution of its own. The main element of this complex diminution is the transfer of the d^2 of bar 1 down to the d^1 of bar 4. The player should listen for this transferred tone and let it influence his "phrasing," but then immediately find a way to relate bar 1 with bar 5, where the opening register is restored. In other words, he should take care to preserve the connection between bars 1 and 5 shown in line (a).

10. My view of the structure of the entire piece is as follows:

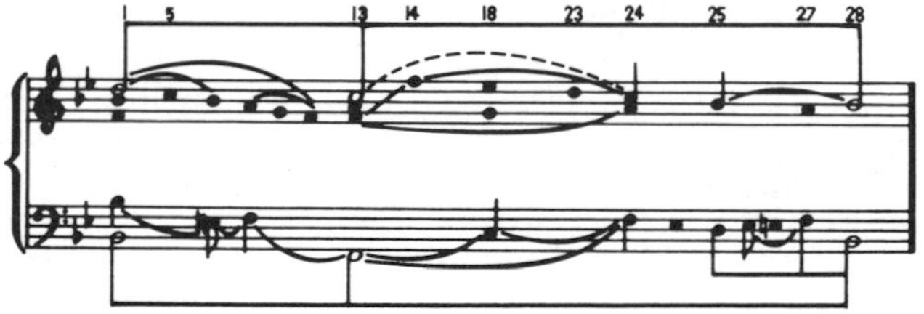

Nearer the foreground, line (b) is replete with motives formed of arpeggiated rising intervals, mostly sixths (indicated with slurs in the example). Occurring on different levels and in different contexts, these rising-sixth motives vary greatly in the extent to which they need to be brought out. Particularly interesting are the low-level sixths $e^{\flat 1}$-c^{2} and d^{1}-$b^{\flat 1}$ that occur in bars 3-4. Notice that the c^{2} at the end of bar 3 is left unresolved as the higher-rank d^{1} enters in bar 4. The need of the c^{2} to resolve to $b^{\flat 1}$ (see arrow) prevents the d^{1} from having too strong an effect of an ending. The player should seek to communicate the suspense of this complex situation, possibly lingering very slightly on the d^{1}, then compensating for this by accelerating on the thirty-second note run up to the $b^{\flat 1}$, and then lingering ever so slightly on that note. The momentum so generated should carry over into, but of course be subordinated to, the performance of the higher-rank rising sixth $e^{\natural 1}$-c^{2} of bar 5.

Bach himself has notated the rising motives in bars 5 and 6 (the filled-in $e^{\natural 1}$-c^{2} and $f^{\sharp 1}$-$e^{\flat 2}$) in a special manner—holding down every key, thus producing a crescendo—that automatically brings them out. (This way of producing a crescendo, very effective on the harpsichord, is lost in a piano performance that uses too much pedal.) Schenker had the imaginative idea that this kind of super-legato notation is also intended to simulate on a keyboard instrument the effect of a vocal portamento—a most suggestive idea for the performer.[11] Strictly speaking, the "portamento" in bar 5 connects the $e^{\natural 1}$ to the c^{2} occurring at the end of the first beat, an anticipation of the c^{2} beginning the second beat.

The enlarged motive ($b^{\flat 1}$-g^{2}) covering bars 7-8 is another factor contributing to the special character of bar 8 (recall the "turning point" noted earlier). Obviously it should be brought out with some kind of increase of intensity up to the g^{2}. Notice how this $b^{\flat 1}$-g^{2} is then "answered" by the a^{1}-f^{2} of the next two bars (9-10), an event which, by linking together bars 7-10, lessens the effect of the break at bar 9 caused by 1) the change of surface figuration to the rhythm  , and 2) the integrity of bars 9-12 as a complete harmonic unit.

The understanding of example 10 will now provide a solid basis for the interpretation of the intricate figuration of the surface. I will mention only two such details, noteworthy because Schenker himself has left

11. See *Kontrapunkt*, vol. 1, pp. 124-126, and examples 105, 109, and 110. See also Schenker's comments in *Ein Beitrag zur Ornamentik* (1904) on C. P. E. Bach's use of this kind of notation. Inveighing against those who miss the artistic basis for it, Schenker writes: "It would be all too easy to be misled into linking such a technique to the meager tone of the instrument!" (translation by Hedi Siegel, *Music Forum* 4, 1976, p. 25.)

some indication of how he played them. Though Schenker never mentioned this sarabande in his published writings, he made various annotations on his own copy of the music, a document I have been fortunate to be able to study.[12]

In bar 5, second beat, the high-level c^2 is embellished by a figure that rises to $e^{\flat 2}$ and falls back again to c^2. The $e^{\flat 2}$ is particularly expressive because of its disagreement with the inner-voice $e^{\natural 1}$. How might one execute this embellishment in the light of the high-level c^2? Schenker gives here the fingering shown in example 11, a fingering which seems at first glance to require needless effort. At the risk of reading too much into it, I propose first of all that the use of the "weak" 4th finger on the expressive $e^{\flat 2}$ suggests that the embellishment is intended to be somewhat less emphasized than the c^2 struck at the start of the second beat. But within this softer dynamic Schenker may have wanted this same weak finger to bring out the $e^{\flat 2}$ slightly. The crossing of 4 over 5 could indicate a slight delay just before striking the $e^{\flat 2}$, followed perhaps by a slight lingering on it. (It is typical of Schenker's approach to keyboard playing that his fingerings give preference to bringing out what he saw as the *musical* gesture rather than to being as physically easy as possible. A player who gives priority to maximum relaxation and ease will find another fingering for this embellishment, but he should not miss the suggestiveness of Schenker's.)

The figure c^2-(d^2)-$e^{\flat 2}$-d^2-c^2 of bar 5 is repeated as an enlargement covering bars 5–6 (see the brackets in example 10 (b)). Schenker's fingering in bar 6 (see example 11) seems designed to express this enlargement. The line he writes connecting finger 5 with 4 suggests that the $e^{\flat 2}$ should somehow be related to the d^2 that begins the third beat.

Example 11

12. It was Schenker's custom to make analytic and performance annotations on his own music (frequently during lessons with students, who would later copy them). The present copy is an undated Peters publication edited by Czerny, Griepenkerl, and Roitzsch. Schenker's markings date from around 1922. I am deeply indebted to the late Ernst Oster not only for his kindness in loaning it to me, but also for many invaluable discussions with me on the relation of Schenker's theories to performance.

The particular means of execution—be it articulation, rhythm, tone color, dynamics,[13] or a combination of these—that the player employs to interpret the diminutions on the surface will depend ultimately on his personal style. But he cannot even recognize the diminutions, much less interpret them, until he knows what is being "diminuted"—has a clear conception of the underlying levels. In other words, only when he is aware of the "main" tones can he perceive the diminutions and perform them in the light of the main tones. When he does so, the surface will benefit, but not only the surface, because proportioning the small with respect to the large has a way of projecting an impression of the large as well. In this sense the background also is "performed"—the "long line" conveyed.

Do good performers already "know" these things? It is surely true that many will intuitively realize something of what Schenker has to tell them about the performance of a given composition. If a theory of art has any value, that theory must arise from a common intuitive understanding. A responsible theory does not seek to substitute principle for intuition, but to confirm intuition with the help of principle—to "improve opinion into knowledge," in Samuel Johnson's phrase. But some principles can take us further: they can make the mind aware of dimensions that have not hitherto been perceived—not even intuitively. Such is Schenker's theory. It can provide the performer with insights not available by other means. It offers no magic formulas, but it can help a good performer become even better.

---

13. Schenker worked at one period on a theory that explicit dynamic levels could be deduced with certainty from the levels of the pitch structure. I consign mention of this astonishing idea to a footnote because it appears little in Schenker's published work and not at all after 1926. In *Das Meisterwerk* I (1925) he applies this idea in analyses of two solo violin pieces of Bach, the F major Largo from Sonata III and the E major Preludio from Partita III. In both analyses he writes dynamics into the voice-leading graphs and gives his reasons for each one. For example, he remarks concerning the F major piece that in approaching the cadences in C major and F major the player should build to *forte,* but only to *mezzo forte* in the case of the cadence in G minor. This is because the G minor section is ultimately only a "dividing fifth" of a higher-level V. That is, since the G minor cadence has a structural function subordinate to those in C and F, it should have a subordinate dynamic. While Schenker's dynamics here are musically persuasive, one can readily imagine situations in which precisely the opposite interpretation—that is, playing the structurally subordinate area louder—would be more appropriate.

According to Jonas, this theory of dynamics is among the subjects discussed in Schenker's unfinished treatise on performance (see note 2). Nonetheless, one wonders if perhaps it was not an idea that Schenker eventually dropped.

The Analysis of Pre-Baroque Music

SAUL NOVACK

In limiting himself to the music from Bach to Brahms, Heinrich Schenker defined his view of the nature and scope of the art of music. He regarded the music of this period as the highest level of diatonic art. All other music was of lesser quality. Schenker therefore chose to ignore so-called "early" music. It is by-passed in his writings, though he makes reference to its shortcomings and outlines its historical role as preparatory to the masterworks of his domain. Since Schenker's death, consideration has been given to the analysis of Medieval and Renaissance music, and within recent years a number of studies utilizing Schenkerian analytical procedure have been made.[1]

Critical evaluation of the application of this approach is twofold. On the one hand, it is argued that Schenker's criteria do not apply for the reasons stated by Schenker himself.[2] On the other hand, it is argued by traditional theorists and musicologists that the polyphony prior to 1600 is modal, not tonal. The prevailing view is that the major-minor system came into being at the beginning of the seventeenth century. The idea of applying an analysis based on triadic tonality to music which is not considered to have that basic quality is totally unacceptable.[3] The latter criticism is considered first. The discussion will center on analyses. Since there now are a number of complete analyses of representative Medieval and Renaissance compositions which clearly apply Schenker's methods, it will not be necessary to offer a host of new analyses as evidence, except in a few cases to illustrate specific points of importance. For the convenience of the reader, most references to compositions will be those contained in the first volume of the *Historical Anthology of Music*, hereafter referred to as *HAM*.

---

1. These analyses have appeared primarily in: Felix Salzer, *Structural Hearing*, 2 vols., New York: Charles Boni, 1952 (reprinted, New York: Dover Publications, 1962); Felix Salzer and Carl Schachter, *Counterpoint in Composition*, New York: McGraw-Hill, 1969; and *The Music Forum* **1** (1967), **2** (1970).
2. Schenker's views on "early" music are scattered throughout his writings from *Harmonielehre* to *Der freie Satz*. A summary, with quotations, is given in Sylvan Kalib, *Thirteen Essays from the Yearbooks "Das Meisterwerk in der Musik,"* Ann Arbor: University Microfilms, 1973, vol. 1, pp. 372–379 and 443–445.
3. Ibid., p. 443. Kalib joins others in distorting music history by referring to "early" music as "pre-diatonic," a basic semantic error.

I. THE HISTORICAL BACKGROUND OF TRIADIC TONALITY

By the time true polyphony began, the concept of the triad as a determining force in composition had already been established. While we do not have adequate documents of secular and folk music prior to the beginnings of polyphony, Gregorian chant, much of which came from secular origins, furnishes evidence. While scholars may shudder at this violation of the sacred corpus to which only formal modal theory has been applied, the evidence speaks for itself.[4] The study of the organizing properties based on pitch relationships has been neglected. Apel, in his admirable survey, devotes a chapter to the "tonality" of chant.[5] He acknowledges the term *tonalis*, primarily relegating its meaning to the identity of the *finalis*. He states at the outset that each of the eight tonalities, known as church modes, "is an octave-segment of the diatonic (C major) scale, with one of its tones playing the role of a central tone, or 'tonic.' " The substantial discussion is devoted to many facets of description, identification, and classifications of the various tones, but never to the nature whereby the concept of a "central tone" is achieved through the relationship among the tones of the chant, one to another. Is it only the *finalis* that creates tonality? It is obvious that the problem of pitch organization has not been engaged systematically. The *ambitus* of each tone or mode provides only a general background of range but not necessarily of structure. Indeed, the study of chant is complex, and only suggestions can be given within this essay. (There are problems related to type, function, and chronology of the chants, comparison of sources, the reliability of the *Liber Usualis*, etc.) Some chant types have specifically designed intervallic frameworks, such as the psalm tones. Among the thousands of chants, however, no general structural properties are discernible. Many, however, have strong characteristics that reveal a background of tonal structure. A few examples are given below.

In the *Alleluia* of Easter Sunday (see example 1) the opening phrases indicate the role of the fifth to which the third as a filler is incidental. In the succeeding phrase (*Pascha nostrum*) the third, b-d^1, asserts itself more strongly. In the latter part of the phrase the ascent to g^1 is

---

4. A convincing case is made by Curt Sachs in his study, "Europe and the road to Major and Minor," *The Rise of Music in the Ancient World*, New York: Norton, 1943, pp. 293-311.
5. Willi Apel, *Gregorian Chant*, Bloomington: Indiana University Press, 1958, pp. 133-178.

made, followed by a stepwise descent from g^1 to d^1. In the last phrases d^1 is prolonged by moving to g, again emphasizing the third, and at the end falling to g, possibly (?) stepwise. The organizing force of the octave, fifth, and third is evident. A summary of the motion is shown at (b).

Example 1: *Alleluia,* Easter Sunday (*Liber Usualis,* p. 779).

Applying the same principles to some of the chants reprinted in *HAM*, similar characteristics of organizing properties emerge. In the Gradual *Haec dies* (*HAM*, no. 12), the unfolding A minor triad dominates, while two other triads are outlined: F (the opening phrase, *Haec dies*, with the stipulated b♭!, and *et laetemur*) and G (in the middle and end of *quoniam*). The Responsorium *Libera me* (no. 14) is based on repeated filling of the descending fifth a–d. There is a delay in attaining the tone a, but once gained (*quando caeli movendi*) it is emphasized and repeated. The descents through the fifth are also filled in stepwise. The *finalis* is d. The Sequence *Victimae paschali laudes* (*HAM*, no. 16b) exhibits the role of stepwise descent through the fifth a–d as a form-creating factor. The rise to d^1 as a point of climax in the concluding stanza is noteworthy.

These examples of Gregorian chant, not chosen very selectively, offer us direct evidence of the importance of the octave and the fifth, the latter far more assertive than the fourth, as the determinant intervals forming a framework within which the melodic motion takes place. The numerous leaps of the third emphasize its importance as an interval of articulation, sometimes in prolonging a tone, other times in filling in the fifth. Neighbor-tone motions are both immediate and prolonged. The principle of descent is evident repeatedly, the descent within an octave sometimes being divided into two segments, 8 to 5 and 5 to 1. The last descent into the *finalis* is frequently definitive, outlining the fifth or octave above the *finalis*. No attempt has been made to provide a systematic analysis of Gregorian chant. The few selections offered are designed to illustrate the presence of tonal structure, probably existing in a significant number of chants, heretofore not considered by scholars.

Monophonic secular composition contemporaneous with Gregorian chant provides additional evidence not only to the emergence of the triad as a background to the melodic motion but also to the realization of the triad as a horizontal or spatial concept. These features are emphasized by rhythmic articulation, thus giving the motion a clearer profile. Two examples of Trouvère chansons are given here. (See *HAM*, no. 19d and e, and examples 2A and 2B.)

In example 2A, the typical divisions of the *Rondeau* into two parts, A and B, and their alternation are given support by the structure, for it is not until the end of B that a definitive close is effected, the tone b (bar 4) acting not unlike the usual motion to the leading-tone as an inner voice immediately prior to the final tone. The final c is more important than the c in bar 4, the *fractio* of the strict rhythmic mode (trochaic) supporting the continuity to the final c. The triad adjusts to the poetic form, divided in its outline into two parts: 5 4 3 / 2 1. The triad is also stated immediately at the outset. The second *Rondeau* (*HAM*, no. 19e) reveals the structural adaptation to a more extended B section, which poetically is in itself divided into parts (example 2B). In part A, the highest tone, c, is prolonged as the fifth degree of the F triad by neighbor and triadic motion. It descends stepwise in part B, but its goal, f, the root of the triad, is only attained in the second of the two phrases. In the first phrase the penultimate g is prolonged by a motion to e, the latter tone having the property of a leading tone. This, in effect, is the principle of interruption applied through the musical device of *overt* and *clos*, similar to the later first and second ending.

Example 2

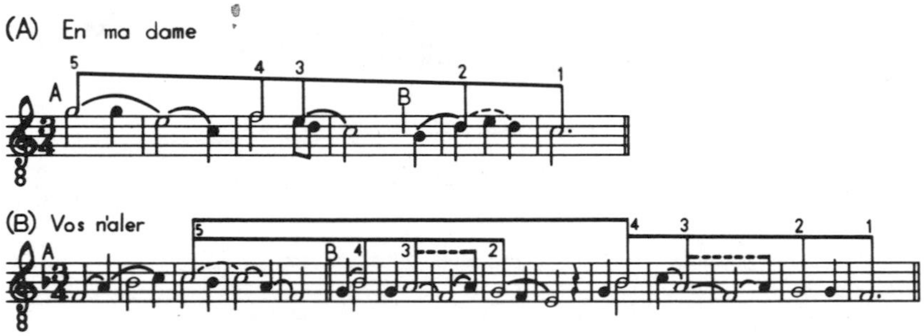

The monophonic dances of the Middle Ages serve as another valuable source for the evaluation of the structure of secular melody. The dance element provides rhythmic impetus to the organization. In the most popular type of dance, the estampie, each section or *punctus* is characterized by a repetition, with different endings not unlike the *overt* and *clos* of the contemporaneous chanson. The dance element results usually in groupings of two accents (with occasional variants), reflecting the outline of physical motion related to the feet in regular alternation. A singular contribution of the dance lies therefore in the repetition of rhythmic fragments reflecting the ordered spatial motion of the dance.

Several *puncti* of an estampie (*HAM*, no. 40c) are given in example 3. Each of the *puncti* cited illustrates a different type of organization. In *punctus 1* the triadic prolongations suggest the succession of an F triad by a C triad, the latter extending over a space comparable to five bars. It is not far-fetched to accept this as an equivalent of I–V–I. In *punctus 5* the initial rise through the triad to the fifth degree establishes c as the top tone from which the descent begins. *Punctus 6* is based on the principle of interruption. In each of these examples the use of an *overt* and *clos* is an expression of musical repetition using interruption, thus creating form through repetition of the design and tonal motion. The rhythmic patterns, emanating from the dance, emphasize stepwise motion through the F triad. Other *puncti* in the same dance are organized in other ways, e.g., *punctus 7*, in which the descent of an octave, f^1–f, is exposed clearly through the use of sequence.

Example 3

The first excursions into polyphony beyond the early experiments in parallel and free organum offer the clues to the concept of interval horizontalization and tonal prolongation. Melismatic organum as practiced in the School of Compostela (c. 1125) is structured on the concept of melodic motion of a number of tones above a given tone. It is significant that the chant melody is the lower of the two voices, thus establishing the principle of the fundamental role of the lowest voice upon which intervals are constructed or measured. Excerpts from the polyphonic realization of the Kyrie trope *Cunctipotens genitor* (*HAM*, no. 27b) illustrate the expansion of an interval and the manner in which it is filled (example 4). Three fragments are shown. Each chant tone in the tenor controls the upper voice, which outlines the triad of the chant tone either in whole or in part. Thus *cunctipotens* is projected by four tones in the *tenor*, a-a-g-a, which form a unit wherein A is the central tone controlling the upper voice. Within this unit the upper voice outlines the A triad, e-d-c-b-a. The concluding *eleison* unit likewise is a chant fragment moving away from and returning to the tone a. The falling stepwise line moving through the triad at the end of the setting is again very significant. Also noteworthy in this concluding phrase is the spatial displacement of the consonances, which become dissonances through anticipation.

Example 4

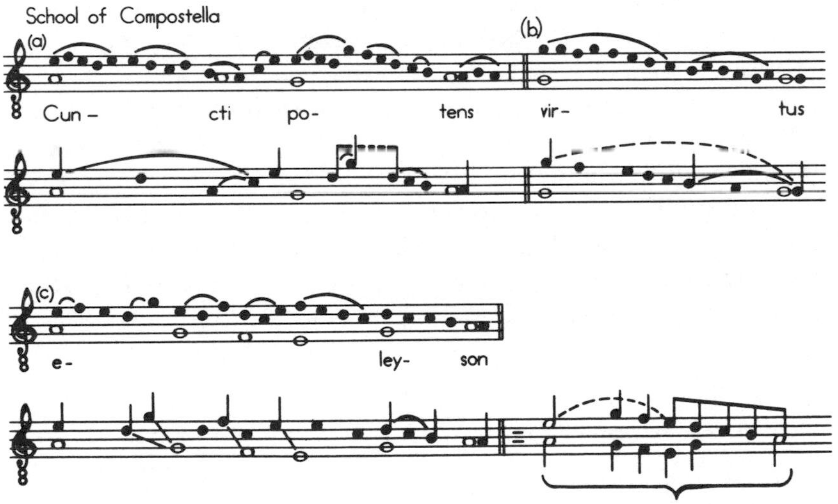

The concluding phrase of the two-voice setting of *Benedicamus Domino* (*HAM,* no. 28c) and its interpretation are given in example 5. Now that durational values are regularized, there can be no doubt about the emphasis given to the tones moving above the sustained tone d. This early example of rhythmically articulated sequence is also significant, reflecting the fusion of thematic design and directed motion. This cannot be regarded as casual counterpoint with a somewhat amorphous upper line without a goal. The sequential motion within a fixed interval strongly implies the presence of an inner voice. The outlined octave and the emphasized fifth and third combine to effect a genuine manifestation of triadic tonality, a fitting climax to the polyphonic setting of this melody, which itself is strongly tonal.[6]

Example 5

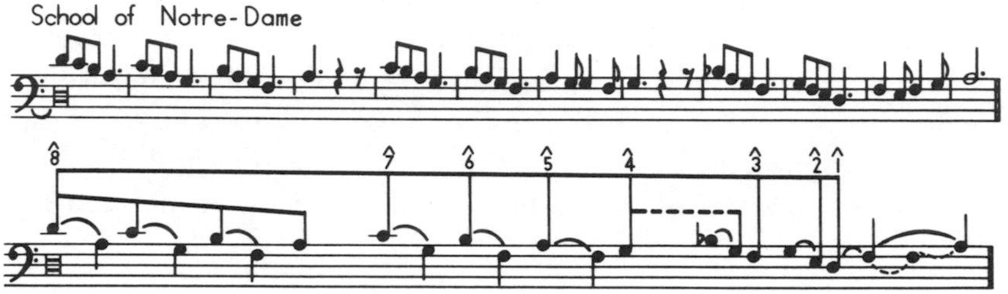

These few examples and observations are sufficient to indicate the presence of triadic tonality in both sacred and secular music well before the fourteenth century, when the expansion of this art into a more sophisticated form took place both in France and in Italy. Perhaps the most important single contribution to the development of tonality by Machaut, Landini, and their contemporaries was the articulation of tonal order within the *formes fixes* that had developed out of poetry. Form is externalized not only by the various repetitions and alternations that typify the rondeau, ballade, virelai, etc., and their Italian counterparts, but through the role played by tonality as well in creating form. A number of published analyses make it unnecessary to consider new ones

6. Only a few facets of early polyphony have been examined. A rich and detailed study continuing to Perotinus is provided by Felix Salzer in "Tonality in Medieval Polyphony," *The Music Forum* 1 (1967), pp. 35–98. In the works of Perotinus, Salzer demonstrates the further development of prolongation through the mutual activity of *two* voices above the tenor. These important examples require careful study.

at this point.[7] Several of these works reveal the principle of interruption as a form-creating device, not only at the *overt* and *clos* of the two main sections, but internally as well in the delineation of subsections. Further, the leading tone, already established as a consistent intensification of tonality, is now frequently aided by the dominant. The latter even enters into the final reduction in a graphic representation.[8] With the arrival of Dunstable, Dufay, and their contemporaries the harmonic tendencies of the past century are secured and strengthened. The leap of the fifth in the bass is well established. Harmonic progressions such as I-IV-V-I (Dunstable, *HAM*, no. 62, mm.38-46) and I-II-V-I (Dufay, *HAM*, no. 65, mm.22-27) occur with increasing frequency. By the beginning of the sixteenth century the harmonic vocabulary had expanded to include the use of the complete diatonic circle of fifths. Thematic concepts developed to the extent of acquiring identifiable motivic character. The unfolding of recognizable design elements, repeated significantly to act as integrative devices, is in itself an important facet of composition. More than that, repetition and tonal direction now worked together, thereby creating inner form, which revealed itself in an endless chain of variety. Musical art had achieved a realization of total tonal triadic organization.

II. THE PROBLEMS

To one versed only in the linear analysis of eighteenth- and nineteenth-century music, the approach to the analysis of pre-Baroque music presents difficulties either due to prejudice or lack of familiarity with the literature, or because of problems inherent in the music of this period. Some of these problems are now examined.

A. Mode

Most general music histories tell us that the Baroque era ushers in the major-minor system of *tonality*, in contrast to the preceding practice of *modality*. This dichotomy, modality vs. tonality, is misleading and unfortunate. On the basis of the evidence we must recognize that the concept of a tonal center in composition was practiced throughout the Middle Ages and Renaissance. Secondly, while Glareanus gave recognition to the Aeolian and Ionian modes in *Dodekachordon* as early as 1547,

---

7. For Machaut, see *Structural Hearing*, vol. 2, examples 528-533. A study by Carl Schachter—"Landini's Treatment of Consonance and Dissonance," *The Music Forum* 2 (1970), pp. 130-186—offers a number of analytical graphs of the Italian trecento master.
8. E.g., see Schachter, ibid., pp. 185-186.

these modes in fact existed long before. The Lydian mode and its plagal form (modes 5 and 6) frequently had a stipulated B♭, thus creating the equivalent of F major. Through both stipulation and *musica ficta*, chromatic changes frequently modified the Dorian and Mixolydian modes to resemble minor and major, respectively. The reasons for the changes were many, governed by melodic or intervallic considerations (*causa necessitatis* or *pulchritudinis*). The only mode which did not lend itself to alteration to resemble either major or minor was the Phrygian (and its plagal form), the retention of the characteristic half-step between the first and second degrees precluding the possibility of a leading tone (the diminished third or augmented sixth with the second degree), and equally important, a perfect fifth above the fifth degree.[9]

The conditions of polyphony were radically different from monophony. The theorists had great difficulty applying the theory of the modes to polyphony. In addition, *musica ficta* and stipulated chromaticism resulted in constant modification. Scholars are becoming increasingly aware of the significance of such practices.[10] With the exception of the Phrygian mode, constant mixture is the rule. Dufay's *Alma Redemptoris Mater* (*HAM*, no. 65) is a characteristic example. The Gregorian melody, paraphrased in the superius, has been transposed from its original Lydian F setting (as in the *Liber Usualis* version, p. 273—a mode 5 chant). This version of the chant possesses a signature of B♭; hence the transposition by Dufay is actually to C Ionian, or major. The presence of B♭ in the signatures in the tenor and contratenor is an example of partial signatures, a complex problem remaining unresolved to the satisfaction of most scholars. It is obvious, however, that the lower voices frequently require B♭ to support an f in the superius, i.e., the necessary perfect fifth. Elsewhere, especially at cadences, there are sometimes strong implications for applying *ficta*, i.e., b♮ in the tenor or contratenor, b♭ in the superius. The result is mixture of the seventh degree within the context of clearly established prolongations of C major, in which the dominant, with or without the leading tone, asserts itself (e.g., in m.34 from the end, where the stipulated f♯ intensifies the motion to the dominant). The implications of the major mode are strong, even though attenuated by the presence of the lowered seventh. The upper voice, in repeated motions throughout,

9. A detailed study is given in Saul Novack, "The Significance of the Phrygian Mode in the History of Tonality," *Miscellanea Musicologica* **9** (1977), pp. 82-127.

10. Edward Lowinsky, *Tonality and Atonality in Sixteenth-Century Music*, Berkeley and Los Angeles: University of California Press, 1961. The cadence and the approach to it are still the most important factors in the evaluation of the tonal characteristics.

definitively outlines various segments of the C major triad, always terminating on the tonic. The plan is as follows:

mm. 1- 22	Ascent of an octave (c^1-c^2); stepwise descent of an octave.
24- 43	Ascent from 5 to 8 (g^1-c^2); with harmonic motion I-II-V-I, followed by descent of an octave.
45- 60	Descent of an octave.
61- 67	Descent from 5 to 3 (g^1-e^1).
68- 81	Descent of an octave.
82- 91	Descent of an octave.
92-104	Ascent from 5 to 8 (g^1-c^2), followed by octave descent.
105-127	Coda: chordal.

In the above references to the ascents and descents, the intervals given are filled in by stepwise motion, various tones being prolonged by neighbor motions, motions to inner voices, and superimposed inner voices. The tonality of C via the major mode is further fortified through the strategic support of G midway in the octave descent in four of the above phrases by an unequivocal V (mm.30, 51, 73, 95), intensified by its own leading tone or dominant. In addition, the termination of five of the phrases is harmonically treated as V-I—in two phrases with a minor V and in one phrase through subtle extension (mm.60-62).

The Dorian mode mixture resembles the minor mode, as in Heinrich Isaac's so-called instrumental canzona reprinted in *HAM* (no. 88). Originally this composition was part of a larger setting to *Salve Regina*. The excerpted portion, originally with text, commences as a paraphrase of the third phrase of the antiphon melody, *a te clamamus*.[11] As a vocal piece there can be no question about the application of *ficta* in performance. While the composition is Dorian transposed, the presence of the E♭, either through *ficta* (especially in m.11) or stipulated (as in m.38, which is not unlike m.11), and the customary use of the leading tone through *ficta*, present us with an actual minor mode setting. (An analysis of a portion of this composition will be given later.) The major-

11. The author is indebted to Edward E. Lerner for calling this to his attention. The *HAM* example, drawn from the *Denkmäler der Tonkunst in Österreich*, is based on *Ms. Florence 59*. Other sources, e.g., *Ms. Berlin 40021*, indicate the presence of text.

minor system as it was practiced up through the nineteenth century thrives on mixture, e.g., the major employing the flatted sixth in various ways, the minor raising and lowering the sixth and seventh degrees. Schenker fully recognized the importance of mixture on various levels, going beyond major-minor mixtures to consider the use of $^{\flat}$II and its $^{6}_{3}$ position as manifestations of Phrygian, particularly in reference to upper-voice motion.[12]

While the Phrygian mode lends its specific character to the minor mode, particularly in later times, it refuses to yield or change its basic qualities. Since there is no diatonic dominant possible, and no leading tone as well, it cannot follow the usual path. The tonic triad, however, can be outlined in the top voice, even though the motion to the first degree is through the half-step above it. In the absence of the necessary dominant to create a basic tonal structure, the Phrygian mode must rely on other contrapuntal techniques. For various reasons the chords within E Phrygian that usually are prolonged within the composition are the A minor triad and the C major triad. Frequently such compositions are referred to as being in A minor and terminating on the dominant. Such a faulty view is the result of failing to understand the inherent properties of the Phrygian mode and to grasp the presence of E as the tonal center. (A number of analyses demonstrating the unique features of the Phrygian mode are available in the literature referred to at the beginning of this essay.)

B. Form

Schenker demonstrated that the study of form is intimately related to the organic tonal process. The large-scale divisions cannot be understood solely through the various ways in which thematic elements are distributed and repeated. It is here that the foreground, middleground, and background levels, in their relationship to the thematic process, best explain the character of the form. When these concepts are applied generally to pre-Baroque composition difficulties are encountered. Such works as Masses, motets, chansons, and madrigals are genres rather than forms. Further, there is no characteristic division of space into two or three parts. Even "inner form," or subdivisions of space, can be difficult to identify when there is an absence of repetitive thematic elements to serve as guides. For example, the characteristic "points of imitation" of many sixteenth-century motets are emphasized

12. See *Free Composition*, translated and edited by Ernst Oster, New York: Longman, 1979, pp. 41 and 71.

to the degree that—in the face of constant overlappings of textual phrases—the motion seems continuous and the spatial divisions blurred. Gombert's *Super flumina* (*HAM*, no. 114) is an example of this procedure. *Vox in Rama* by Clemens non Papa (*HAM*, no. 125) is less problematical because of the restraint of the overlapping, the directed falling line, and the changes in design. Polyphonic settings of the Mass offer problems, particularly those of the fifteenth century. Large-scale divisions are created by the textual units, as are subdivisions, such as *Et incarnatus est*. It is Josquin who first points the way towards the concept of unities going beyond the simple subdivisions or of unities which depend completely on the repetition of a *cantus firmus*.[13]

Elements of repetition joined by tonal motion demonstrate inner unities. The cultivation of the sequence in the late fifteenth and sixteenth centuries reflects the tendencies towards greater emphasis of tonal direction. The previously mentioned example by Isaac (*HAM*, no. 88) is quoted in part (example 6). The articulation of the descent from I to V is provided by the sequential repetition. The use of the voice-leading chords, incidentally creating a complete diatonic circle of fifths, as well as the repetition of the descent through the third in the uppermost voice are noteworthy features of this passage.[14]

Textual organization provides a strong framework for outer form in some cases. Mention already has been made of the *formes fixes*. The virelai *Plus dure* by Machaut (*HAM*, no. 46b) is analyzed in detail in Salzer, *Structural Hearing*, vol. 2, example 532. The shaping forces of the text to which Machaut responds create a two-part composition highly unified through the principle of interruption on various levels. The support of the second degree is provided by a leading-tone chord other than the dominant, but the force of the superius in creating the tonal form is not diminished. The ballade, *Je puis trop bien*, also by

13. For analyses of complete Masses see Saul Novack, "Fusion of Design and Tonal Order in Mass and Motet: Josquin Desprez and Heinrich Isaac," *The Music Forum* 2 (1970), pp. 187–263. For the influence of large-scale thematic repetition, i.e., the cyclic Mass, see Edgar H. Sparks, *Cantus Firmus in Mass and Motet, 1450–1520*, Berkeley and Los Angeles: University of California Press, 1963. The possibly restrictive effect of the *cantus firmus* will be discussed shortly.
14. For additional examples see Saul Novack, "Tonal Tendencies in Josquin's Use of Harmony," *Proceedings of the International Josquin Festival-Conference*, edited by Edward E. Lowinsky, London: Oxford University Press, 1976, pp. 317–333.

Machaut (*HAM*, no. 45), based on a different textual-musical relationship because of the organization of the poem, also reveals a direct structural reflection of that organization, with the principle of interruption playing a primary role. The chanson, in its development throughout the sixteenth century, exhibits an increasing dependence of tonal order on the text, with repetition and interruption fusing to project the features associated with later music. Rhythmic motives contribute to the growing clarity. This occurs in the chanson *Allon, gay, gay* by Costeley (*HAM*, no. 147), which is based on a text-music refrain with alternating stanzas. Not only is interruption present, supported by harmonic motions and dominant, but also mixture in the closing sections of the chanson.

Example 6: Isaac, Instrumental Canzona.

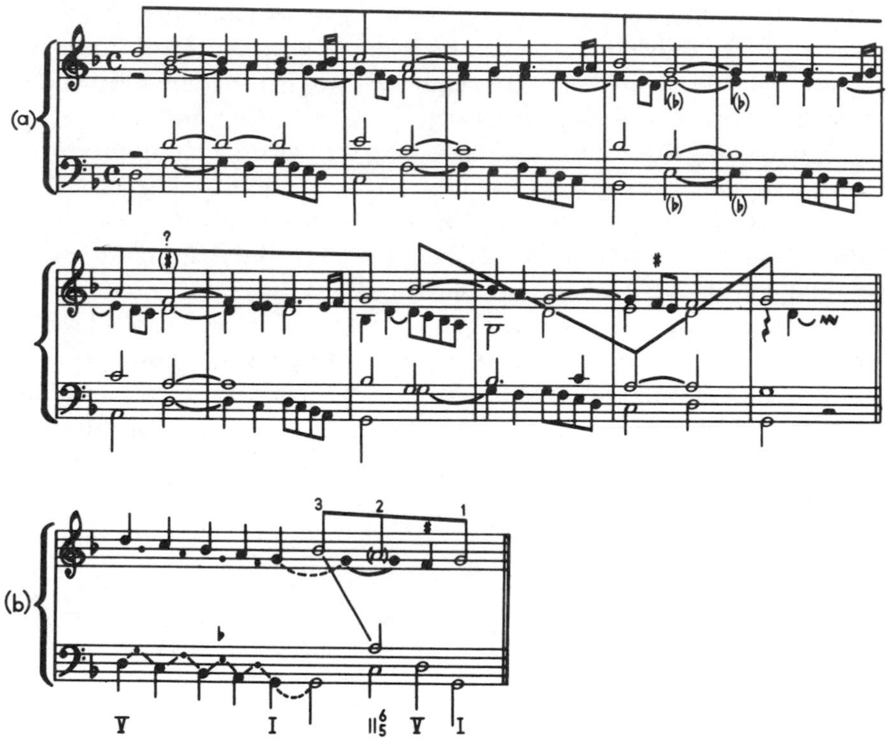

The dance, already clear-cut in its implications as far back as the thirteenth century, continues throughout the Renaissance as a genre in which tonal order and spatial control are emphasized. The regularity of rhythmic grouping, motivated by the dance factor, combines with the already well understood sense of tonality to achieve an unquestionably high degree of articulation of tonal form in the Schenkerian sense. A *Passamezzo antico* by Ammerbach (*HAM*, no. 154), published in 1571 and written as organ tablature (whereby all accidentals are stipulated), illustrates this type of clarity. The uppermost voice descends from $\hat{3}$ into the leading tone as an inner voice of the dominant, hence the structural motion $\hat{3}$ to $\hat{2}$. The phrase is then repeated, this time terminating on $\hat{1}$. As observed before, interruption is utilized to create form, but now a full-fledged harmonic order is present. The strong descending motion of the bass line towards the dominant convincingly strengthens the sense of G minor. This example is a genuine forerunner of the model dances of the early Baroque characterized by descending bass lines moving from tonic to dominant. The effect of the dance on vocal compositions in the late Renaissance is obvious in such works as Morley's *My bonny lass* (*HAM*, no. 159) and Dowland's *What if I never speed* (*HAM*, no. 163).[15]

The Italian madrigal has such a variety of types and poetic shapes that one cannot discuss the implications of its poetic-musical characteristics in a general sense. The dramatic madrigal, however, from Cipriano de Rore to Monteverdi, is a most fascinating genre for the study of tonal structure. Since there are no main divisions, the madrigal must be considered a continuous form. The composers' responses to the sensitivity of text meanings, however, clearly create inner changes which reflect groupings of text meanings and even specific words within groups. Indeed, it is in the madrigals of Monteverdi that we finally witness great masterpieces in the sublime expression of texts through inner tonal form. The representation of the text through the use of chromaticism results in a constant expansion of the tonal palette. It is misleading to regard most of the examples of such chromaticism as experiments which reach out towards atonality. A linear analytical approach will cast aside such misunderstandings.[16]

---

15. For an analysis of the Dowland ayre see Salzer, *Structural Hearing*, vol. 2, example 473.

16. A revealing analysis is provided by William J. Mitchell in his study "The Prologue to Orlando di Lasso's Prophetiae Sibyllarum," *The Music Forum* 2 (1970), pp. 264-273. This work, while not strictly a madrigal, is an example of a highly chromatic representation of the text.

C. Cantus firmus *settings*

Cantus firmus settings of the Mass and motet in the fifteenth and sixteenth centuries offer grave obstacles at times. When the *cantus firmus* is in long extended tones, usually in the tenor (as in the so-called tenor Mass of the fifteenth century), it acts as a controlling force which tends to inhibit tonal direction in the larger sense. Then, too, much depends on the nature of the *cantus firmus*. Thus, a *cantus prius factus "L'Homme armé,"* a popular folk melody which became perhaps the most frequently used single source for *cantus firmus* Masses throughout the Renaissance, has such triadic definition that it sometimes strongly affects the polyphonic setting. (The melody is quoted in *HAM*, no. 66.) Chant melodies often do not offer such possibilities. In the tenor Mass setting the *cantus firmus* is for the most part an inner voice, imposing at least partial restrictions on the polyphony. The constant crossing of voices also tends to obscure the path of the lowest linear motion. Sometimes this can be advantageous, as in the Agnus Dei III of Ockeghem's *"Missa L'Homme armé"* (*HAM*, no. 73b). Commencing at m.16 the tenor crosses below the bass, allowing melody, itself clearly tonal, to provide the foundation for the tonality, including the convincing 5–1 of the melody exploited for a V–I motion.

D. Voces aequales *(equal voices)*

Quasi-fugal beginnings, canonic procedures, and pervading imitation are stylistic features of the Mass and motet composition firmly established during the period of Josquin. This tradition was maintained throughout the century, and the procedures were absorbed by various genres, instrumental as well as vocal. The prevailing view of these procedures is that they constitute a style in which each voice is regarded as equal to all others. In the teaching of counterpoint, Palestrina has been used as the outstanding model, having wrongly been regarded as the representative composer of sixteenth-century counterpoint. Actually, though, the outer voices do become more important than the others by virtue of their double roles of stating thematic design *and* of projecting tonal prolongation and direction. Schenker led us to this understanding through his views on the organic tonal properties of a fugue in his study "Das Organische der Fuge."[17] It is essential that this critical approach be applied as well to the works of the sixteenth century. The bass line is carefully molded to prolong chords and to reach goals. The "style of Palestrina" needs to be revisited. There are bass leaps of fifths that

17. *Das Meisterwerk in der Musik* **II**, pp. 55–96.

repeatedly project harmonic function. The meanings of "contrapuntal" and "harmonic" require careful reconsideration. The condition of multi-linearity is not exclusively contrapuntal, and to view Palestrina thus is incorrect. On the other hand, chordal texture is not necessarily harmonic. A further difficulty is encountered in fourteenth- and fifteenth-century examples in which the attention drawn to the linear activity of each voice tends to obscure the real line of the lowest voice. The contratenor and tenor cross each other, and the lowest voice-leading activity is shared by the two voices. It is necessary to state again that harmonic practices and the various expansions of the I-V-I relationship are strengthened and exploited throughout the sixteenth century.[18] The significant bass arpeggiation in the minor mode, I-III-V-I, appears with regularity in various types of music. Successive fifths, as in example 6, occur frequently. Harmonic prolongations of chords other than the tonic also take place, especially in compositions of relatively greater length. Definition of space by harmonic motion is established as an important contribution to "inner form."

III. SUMMARY

The analytical graphs of pre-Baroque music cover a long period of time, c. 1125-1600, during which there is a diversity of techniques. Therefore, general statements are impossible. On the basis of these graphs, however, some preliminary observations can be made. It is hoped that the foregoing discussion serves as an adequate orientation to these statements in summary. In the end, however, a detailed study of existing graphs and an extended study of the music of these centuries are essential. The statements are not presented in any order of importance.

1. Tonal prolongations are present from the beginnings of true polyphony. Even though the procedure is mosaic (i.e., represented by chains of small units) in each of the units, the triad, major or minor, is horizontalized, thus indicating the almost immediate establishment of the triad as the basic organizing property.

---

18. In various studies Edward E. Lowinsky calls attention to the uses of successive fifths. See especially *The Secret Chromatic Art in the Netherlands Motet*, New York: Columbia University Press, 1946. A number of such types in Josquin are illustrated in Saul Novack, "Tonal Tendencies in Josquin's Use of Harmony," op. cit.

2. The history of musical structure of these almost five hundred years reveals a constant growth in the use of the triad as an organizing force. Its history is continuous as well as gradual, whereas differences in the small details of the immediate foreground, the turf of traditional style analysis, are sometimes marked.

3. Modality and tonality are not opposites. Modes in polyphony are not pure and are constantly altered, with the notable exception of the Phrygian. Through alteration these modes tend to resemble more and more the major or the minor mode. The leading tone, through *ficta* or stipulation, is an early occurrence, resulting in emphasis of the central tone.

4. The leap of a fifth in the bass, a concept which is not linear, evolves from the fourteenth century onwards as a property of tonal relationships. During the fifteenth century the dominant phenomenon is well established. While the dominant sometimes appears internally as a minor triad, thereby lacking the leading tone, its force, though attenuated, still effects harmonically defining motion.

5. Outer form, stemming from the form-creating sources of poetry and dance, fuses with tonal direction, thus creating tonal form. Interruption, an important principle of structure that reflects the overall conditioning force of triadic tonality in creating form, emerges at a relatively early stage.

6. Inner form, or the organization of internal space, becomes identifiable through the techniques of repetition. Motivic elements, both melodic and rhythmic, join with tonal direction to create spatial entities which likewise are frequently interrelated. Interruption often plays a role in the realization of inner form.

7. The *Urlinie* of the top voice makes itself clearly felt at a very early stage, with recurrent motions of direct descent outlining the triad, the octave, or the lower third of the triad repeatedly revealed in examples. Ascending motions to a tone with structural property occur with considerable frequency.

8. Frequently the motion of the *Urlinie* is to the leading tone as a penultimate point before the first degree. The leading tone acts as an inner voice below the second degree, as is characteristic in later musical practice.

9. The lowest voice frequently supports tones of the *Urlinie* contrapuntally rather than harmonically.[19] This takes place in the represen-

19. Felix Salzer uses the term *contrapuntal–structural* (CS) to indicate this function.

tation of the background as well. The emergence of fully harmonic structure is gradual and steady, increasing rapidly in the sixteenth century.

10. Prolongations of chords other than tonic occur with increasing frequency. Such prolongations also apply to chords which are harmonic and so function in the background.

11. The techniques of prolongation are varied, involving many of the same procedures that characterize the music of the eighteenth and nineteenth centuries, e.g., voice exchange, neighbor-motions (complete, incomplete, and combined), passing chords, motion to and from the inner voice, superimposition of the inner voice.

12. The distance between foreground and background varies. It is less so in the early examples, more so in the sixteenth century. The small spatial elements and the general absence of registral shifts prior to the sixteenth century eliminate the need for a number of hierarchical levels. Further, the frequent demonstration of the complete definitive *Urlinie* descent and the total background representation at the last stage of the composition eliminate the didactic need to separate *Ursatz* from middleground.

13. Mode may have no bearing on the final *Ursatz*, i.e., the outer voices would not reflect any condition that is not typical of the *Ursatz* representation in either major or minor. The Phrygian mode is, of course, an exception.

IV. CONCLUSIONS: SCHENKER AND PRE-BAROQUE MUSICAL ANALYSIS

It is not necessary to restate the essential character of Schenker's ideas except to cite again that the concept of the prolongation of a triad in time is based on the activity of the uppermost voice and the bass arpeggiation, the former outlining the triad or the lower segment thereof, the latter unfolding the chord in the most elementary fashion, I-V-I, or in expansions thereof.

The complexity of composition of the Bach-Brahms era is offset partially by conditions of musical time and space. Thematic repetition has a role in outlining space and in making tonal motion, when controlled by spatial boundaries, more easily defined. Further, when thematic repetition is controlled by a tonal boundary (i.e., by a prolongation) that chord prolongation becomes more easily identifiable! For example, a Mozart theme stated at the outset of a sonata movement may be closed, exhibiting within itself the complete basic structural properties that may reflect an entire movement. A development section of a Mozart sonata-allegro movement has a tonal motion that can be recognized and identified. We have learned to expect certain predictable qualities and purposes of various compositions and portions of compositions. Schenker, therefore, was able to demonstrate not only the structure of complete compositions, but simultaneously the portions thereof, pointing out parallelisms and motives in diminution and augmentation. To a large extent, but not always, such parallelisms are missing or considerably less prominent in "early" music. But the essential condition upon which Schenker based his system is not missing. The composition is the unfolding in time of a major or minor triad.

It is true that Schenker regarded most of pre-Bach music as inferior. The question of the comparison of artistic quality is not considered here, though many of us have been deeply moved on hearing a Josquin Mass, a Lassus motet, or a Monteverdi madrigal. The basic principles of Schenker do apply to much of this music, although the resultant styles of the structure are different.

The essential ingredients of the *Urlinie* and the bass line may be there, particularly in the sixteenth century. As for the upper voice, it is there almost from the beginnings of polyphony. The bass line, slower in arriving at the fundamental V–I relationship, offers substitutes which support the top voice, thus realizing tonality but not with the same intensity as through the inherent "natural" background of the V–I relationship.

As musicians, theorists, and musicologists, we have a great desire to understand the history of musical structure. If we are to concern ourselves with the evolution and history of triadic tonality from the earliest prolongations of simple tones, which tools are we to employ? What has traditional musicology offered us? Shall we depend on descriptions of modes, sometimes several operating simultaneously in accordance with the limited views of contemporaneous theorists? Shall we count the cadences and their various ways as the basis for determining the sense of "key"? Shall we yield to the computer to enumerate the statistical status of chords as a determinant of "style"? Shall we be content to talk about the obvious so-called stylistic features that are in effect the small details of the foreground? Etc., etc. Schenker recognized the continuity of music history, which he regarded as the history of musical structure. He proposed the many questions that must be asked in the writing of a history of music.[20] Had Schenker undertaken such a task, he would not have borrowed tools alien to his thought.

The discovery of the prolongation of the triad in polyphony was a momentous historical event. For that reason it may very well be that the era from the School of Compostela to Perotinus is perhaps the most exciting period in the history of Western music. It shaped the future course of musical composition through the nineteenth century. We could not begin to understand the historical process without a Schenkerian approach to triadic tonality. This is the only way we can cut across the boundaries of eras of style that have distorted much of our understanding of the history of the art of music. We have seen the differences in the structure of this music, but we have also seen the many similarities. It is the similarities that explain to us the continuity of the historical evolution, that give us insight into the conceptual imagination of the ear in selecting and organizing sound. We have no other recourse for understanding the music of the past but to rely upon what Schenker has taught us. Its validity is unquestionable; its limitations, none.

---

20. *Der Tonwille* 2, pp. 3–4.

Heinrich Schenker and Historical Research: Monteverdi's Madrigal *Oimè, se tanto amate*

FELIX SALZER

As is well known, Schenker's entire work is concentrated on the music of the eighteenth and nineteenth centuries. The masterworks of this period were close to his heart and mind and completely absorbed his interest. In our obsession with specialization he is still considered by many as a specialist in this period only, with the implication that his conceptions of tonal construction, coherence, and continuity apply solely to this particular period in the history of music. One also encounters the view that meaningful analysis depends on temporal proximity between composer and analyst or on the absolute correspondence between a composer's theoretical outlook and the type of analysis presented.

Such views, I believe, overlook an important distinction, the distinction between style and content in a work of musical art. Our histories of music do not concern themselves with the development of musical content; rather, they are concerned with the development and the history of ever-changing styles of contrasting musical expression. This type of history has resulted from a painstaking description and categorization of the musical surface of compositions from chant to the music of our times. Without questioning the validity of such a history of styles and forms, one should recognize what these historical researches have achieved and what they cannot achieve.

A number of the traits or characteristics of any composition will undoubtedly lend themselves to description. Consequently, descriptive methods and systems of categorization have arisen, upon which many invaluable works about the historical development of music are based. These vast stylistic investigations employ analytic methods or procedures and thus, quite justifiably, use the term "style analysis." As everyone knows, the analysis of style is an important branch of historical musicology.

The knowledge acquired through style analysis will, however, remain fragmentary if it is not followed by a different type of analytical investigation, now frequently called "structural analysis." It is my belief that one kind of analysis without the other leads only to partial and even misleading knowledge. Music cannot be analyzed in an historic void. Although I am well aware that one cannot suggest a rigid schedule as to which branch of analysis should be studied first, it is my personal conviction that any structural analysis of a work from the "historic" past must be preceded by a study of the stylistic-historical properties of the period to which a particular work belongs. Only then will the analytic study of the musical content prove meaningful.

Another factor often overlooked is that Schenker—even beyond his deep penetration of the music he dealt with—has presented us with a concept of tonality, not as a style but as a language, a language with its intricacies of construction and its capability to create musical sentences, paragraphs, and chapters, that is, wide arches of tonal continuity which transcend stylistic divisions. Thus Schenker focused on the language of a climactic late period within a continuous development that began many centuries earlier.

In order to recognize and evaluate properly Schenker's work, one has to free oneself from what are, in my view, dated assumptions. Only then will one realize that behind or beyond the facade of constant stylistic change there occurred the steady development of a single language which expressed a particularly Western thought—the development of tonality as tonal coherence and consequently the development of composition as a stratified organism.[1]

Structural analysis may thus serve to uncover such development in works of different historical periods. With this in mind, we now offer an analysis of a work of the very early seventeenth century, Monteverdi's madrigal *Oimè, se tanto amate*. This work, which is from the fourth book of madrigals (1603)[2] and thus written well before the famous *stile concitato* compositions, is an example of the composer's supreme power of lyrical as well as dramatic expressiveness. Since such works often display a definite word-tone relationship, musical understanding depends on a full grasp not only of the meaning of the words but also of the significance of the sentence structure.

1. See also Felix Salzer, "Tonality in Early Medieval Polyphony: Towards a History of Tonality," *The Music Forum* 1 (1967), pp. 35–98.
2. This madrigal appears as No. 188 in volume 2 of the *Historical Anthology of Music* (*HAM*), edited by Archibald T. Davison and Willi Apel, Cambridge: Harvard University Press, 1950, pp. 9–10, and in *Tutte le Opere di Claudio Monteverdi*, edited by G. Francesco Malipiero, Asolo: Nel Vittoriale degli Italiani, 1927, vol. 4, pp. 54–58. In the preparation of the new Monteverdi edition to be issued by *Les Editions Renaissantes* (under the general editorship of Bernard de Surcy), Harry Saltzman has made some slight changes in the above versions; he kindly made his reading available to me.

Monteverdi set the following text by Guarini, which is given here with its translation:[3]

First sentence:	Oimè, se tanto amate di sentir dir, oimè, deh perche fate chi dice, oimè, morire?
Second sentence:	S'io moro, un sol potrete languido e doloroso oimè sentire;
Third sentence:	ma se, cor mio, vorrete che vita abb'io da voi, e voi da me, n'avrete mille e mille dolci oimè.
First sentence:	Alas, if it pleases you so much to hear the word alas, why do you cause him, who says alas, to die?
Second sentence:	If I die, you will be able to hear but a single languid and sad alas;
Third sentence:	but if, my heart, you wish that I have life from you, and you from me, then you will have thousands and thousands of sweet alas's.

Before embarking on an analysis, one should be cognizant of several basic factors regarding the textual as well as the musical construction of this poignant, but at the same time whimsical, expression of a conflict between two lovers.

The poem, which (as we have seen) consists of three sentences, is set to music within a two-part form: Part A, the conflict (bars 1–38); Part B, the suggested resolution (bars 39–67). Part A is the musical setting of two sentences, the first beginning with *Oimè, se tanto amate* and ending with *morire* (bar 19); the second beginning with *S'io moro* and ending with *sentire* (bar 38). This entire section is dramatic and brooding. Part B presents the third sentence; it expresses the wish and hope for reconciliation; it is tender, even playful—a change to a more lighthearted mood.

Note that all three sentences of the poem open with conditional clauses, each beginning with "if" (*se*): (1) Oimè, *se* tanto . . . ; (2) *S'io* moro, . . . ; and (3) ma *se* . . . . It will be interesting to discover how the composer deals with the division of the sentences into conditional and principal clauses.[4]

3. The text of the poem is given as in Nino Pirrotta, "Scelte Poetiche di Monteverdi," *Nuova Rivista Musicale Italiana* 2, p. 26. I am grateful for Ellen Rosand's assistance in preparing the translation, which differs somewhat from that given in *HAM*, vol. 2, pp. 295–96.

4. During the ensuing detailed analysis the reader may wish to view certain details in relation to the whole. The total tonal organization comprised by this work is presented in the final graph, example 10.

In our analytic approach to bars 1–19, the musical setting of the first sentence, we shall concentrate first on bars 1–8 (see examples 1 and 2). Monteverdi presents the opening *oimè* motive in 2 + 2 bars (example 1, part (a)). The four *oimè* enter like calls from the distance; their striking effect is heightened by expressive dissonances. We hear so-called free entering dissonances (perfect and augmented fourths in bars 2 and 4); moreover, the dissonant character of these four bars is enhanced by two leaps of a ninth (example 2).[5] The thirds serve as a kind of mournful motto; they pervade the texture of the entire madrigal. *Oimè* is a meaningful exclamation in the text and thus is equally meaningful in the music.

Example 1

Example 2

We might now consider whether one should interpret these opening statements of the motto as an isolated event or as the beginning of a larger progression leading to bar 8. If one does in fact hear the repeated motto as a self-contained unit, one could state only that the tonic is followed by the dominant, this procedure being repeated a third higher on the mediant. We believe, however, that this "harmonic" analysis,

5. Monteverdi's progression is based on a 10–5 10–5 progression whereby each top voice tone is preceded by an ornamental upper third. The dissonances of the foreground are arrived at by suspension of the bass tones G and B♭ together with a transfer of register from the main tone to the following ornamental tone.

though correct as far as it goes, would ignore the meaningful direction developing between bars 1 and 8. For there seems to be no doubt—provided one examines the voice leading—that the F chord of bars 4-5 is a pivotal sonority in the motion from the tonic G chord of bar 1 to that of bar 8. Since we consider these eight bars to be of great significance for the entire work we shall now offer an analysis of them, proceeding in stages from the basic underlying progression to the bold and so very impressive foreground.

Example 3, part (a), presents the basic progression underlying bars 1-8; the F chord is a neighbor-passing chord. Part (b) indicates the division of this progression into two subprogressions and shows that the main ascending third of the top voice creates the prolonging thirds B♭-D and C-E♭. Part (c) includes the *oimè* calls of the bass, which in bars 1-4 form an expressive ascending seventh (G-F), an inversion of the descending second of the underlying progression.[6] Finally, part (d) indicates the actual registers of the composition, which create additional sevenths in the top voice: B♭-A and D-C in bars 1-2 and 3-4 (as already shown in example 2). We thus realize that the *oimè* opening is in fact connected with the subsequent imitative *se tanto amate*, the conditional clause of the first sentence. Music and words grow, so to speak, out of the weird *oimè* exclamations of bars 1-4; the entire clause begins and ends with the word *oimè*.

Example 3

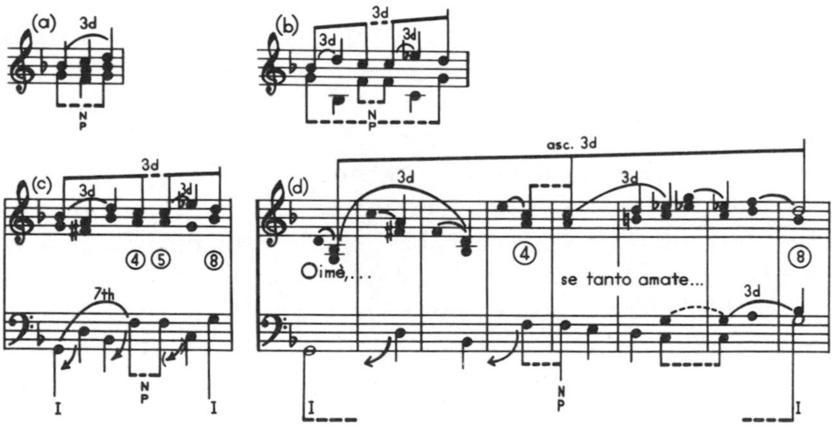

6. Although the C chord could function as a back-relating dominant, its appearance as a minor chord practically nullifies that function; thus the arrow (↙) has been placed in parentheses.

The impressionistic beauty of the widely dispersed thirds of the *oimè* motive set over sustained bass tones, the effect of the dissonances, the wide skips, and (last but not least) the sudden agitation of the entering eighth notes that create a rhythmic acceleration and intensification—all these events and effects are in no way diminished, but rather enhanced if one understands them as emanating from the basic tonal continuity shown in the voice-leading graphs. The progression from bar 1 to bar 8 is highly original and immediately establishes a somber and dejected mood, which prevails until the end of the second sentence.

In bar 8 the third entrance of the eighth-note motive of *se tanto amate* is about to begin in the alto when it is interrupted in the canto by the sudden, almost impatient entrance of the challenging *deh perché fate* motive (a descending fifth and an ascending second resulting in an overall descending fourth). This motive marks the beginning of the principal clause of the first sentence. The dramatic insistence of the *deh perché fate* which now dominates is emphasized by several consecutive appearances of the motive. The principal clause then concludes with the mournful *chi dice, oimè, morire* (bars 16–19) sung by all five voices without any imitation. Before presenting the voice-leading graph of the music for the entire first sentence (example 4) we should point out that the *se tanto amate* motive is the beginning of a phrase (bars 5–8) consisting of a stepwise ascending third and two *oimè* motives. In the graph, the ascending third together with both *oimè* motives are marked by a bracket. The phrase, which spans four bars, appears three times (bars 5–8, 6–9, 8–11).

In spite of the premature entrance of *deh perché fate* in bar 8, the music follows the poem's division of the sentence into a conditional and a principal clause. The musical setting, of course, can do here what cannot be done in a reading or recitation of the poem; an excited and challenging statement can be made to enter prematurely, as if one person's statement were interrupted by another's. Thus (as was indicated earlier) Monteverdi lets the musical setting of the conditional clause and that of the principal clause overlap (bars $^{1-8}_{8-19}$).

The first entrance of *deh perché fate* (the motive is indicated on the graph by means of connecting lines) coincides with the change from the contrapuntally prolonged I (bars 1–8) to the ensuing harmonic prolongation of the V (I–III–V–I of V). This I–III–V–I is the harmonic progression that underlies the principal clause of the first sentence. The top voice and the voice leading above the bass tones of the III–V–I (of V) are of great interest and significance (see especially part (b) of example 4).

Example 4

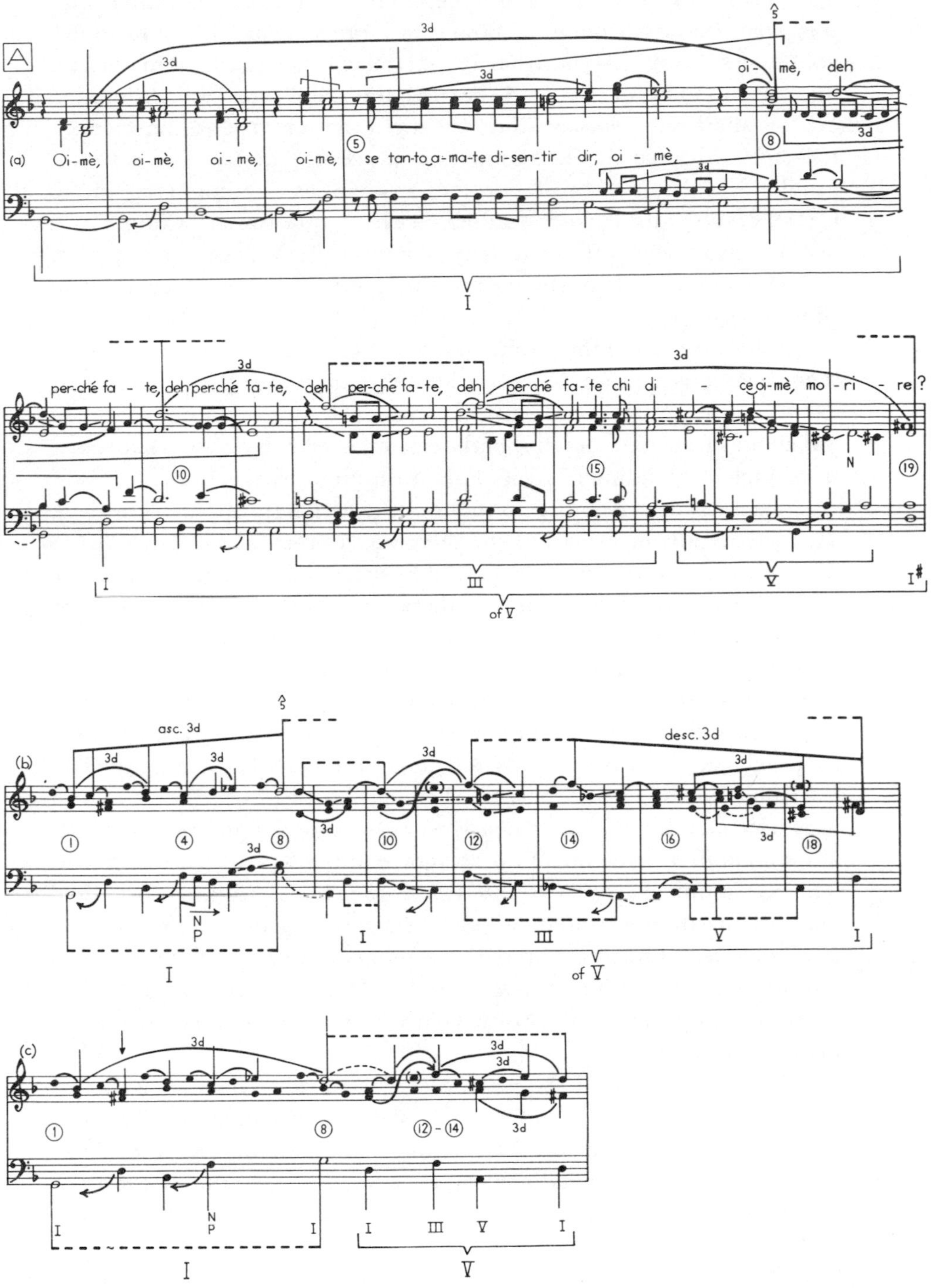
A
(a) Oi-mè, oi-mè, oi-mè, oi-mè, se tan-to a-ma-te di-sen-tir dir, oi - mè,
oi- mè, deh
perché fa - te, deh perché fa-te, deh perché fa-te, deh perché fa-te chi di - ce oi-mè, mo - ri - re?
3d
5̂
N
I
III
V
I#
of V
(b)
asc. 3d
desc. 3d
N P
I
III
V
I
of V
(c)
3d
N P
I
I
I
III
V
I
V

Following the top voice's upward move from D (bar 10) to F (bars 12–14), a broad melodic descent of a third begins to unfold, causing rather complex voice leading: from F—followed by motions to and from the inner-voice tones C and C♯—via E (bar 18) to D (bar 19). Thus the D in bar 17 is a passing tone between the C♯ (bar 16) and the E (bar 18); this motion creates another, now ascending, third. In the foreground, however, E has been "displaced"; it outlines an expressive descending seventh. Finally, yet another third becomes evident as the counterpoint to C♯–D–E. This dense voice leading, with its quasi-interlocking thirds occurring together with the descent of a seventh, expressively illustrates the tense atmosphere of the poem's first sentence, which culminates in the word *morire*.

Of course, all of these tonal motions are governed by the main descent mentioned above, F–E–D, which dominates the top voice of bars 14–19. These measures constitute the musical setting of the entire principal clause of the first sentence of the poem. Thus this clause is expressed by a single descending third, F–E–D, supported by III–V–I.

Concerning the numerous motions through a third—short or long, used motivically or as part of the thematic process, moving upward or downward, in the top voice or the middle voice—they all originate in the *oimè* thirds and in the first large-scale ascent of a third in bars 1–8. They dominate the voice leading of the entire work, be it on the foreground or middleground level. And—as we shall soon realize—motions through a sixth, as inversions of thirds, may act as enlarged variations of thirds.

Whereas, from the overall structural point of view, the music for the first sentence of the poem leads us from a prolonged I to a prolonged V, the music for the second sentence (bars 20–38) begins with a large prolongation of V followed by a nearly equally extended prolongation of I. We should first take note of the structure of the second sentence itself. The conditional clause is extremely short (*S'io moro*) while the principal clause is an extended statement (*un sol potrete languido e doloroso oimè sentire*). The composer follows this sentence division exactly: just two chords in half notes for the *S'io moro* but (after a rest) eight bars for a most expressive musical illustration of the remainder of the sentence (see example 5).

The foreground of the new prolongation of V (bars 20–29) is, of course, completely different from the preceding prolongation of the V in the first sentence, although both employ the same harmonic progression, I–III–V–I. In fact, the contrast between the contrapuntal (and also the rhythmic) foregrounds of two harmonic prolongations of the V, both

Example 5

using I–III–V–I, could not be greater, a point to which we shall return later on. Bars 20–29 show a three-voice setting; this is followed (bars 30–38) by a repetition of the text with a nearly identical musical setting, but now in five voices, with the entire harmonic and contrapuntal middle- and foreground shifted upward(!). This latter compositional procedure, as well as the change from a three- to a five-voice setting, creates the heightened emphasis that is characteristic of a warning reiterated in a raised voice. If one mentions only the sequential relationship between bars 20–29 and bars 30–38, one ignores several important facts: First, the increase in musical expressiveness achieved through the change to a five-voice setting; second, the fact that the succeeding phrase (bars 30–38) is now based on a I–III–V–I prolongation of I (not of V!); and third, that the total ascent is now that of a sixth (see part (b) of example 5).

In the musical foreground of bars 20–38 we find that the word-tone relationship is again most impressive. This relationship can best be defined by comparing the music of the first sentence with the contrasting musical setting of the second sentence. These contrasts are to a great extent achieved by the strong rhythmic differences between the two settings. In the first sentence, the opening dispersed *oimè* calls with their rests and half notes are abruptly followed by the agitated eighth-note passage, *se tanto amate. . . .* This clause, in turn, is interrupted by the rhythmically contrasting *deh perché fate* (𝅗𝅥|♩ ♫ 𝅗𝅥|𝅗𝅥) and its skip of a descending fifth followed by an ascending second. Both motives are expressed in imitative counterpoint. The second sentence, however, deals with the possible consequences of the conflict expressed in the first sentence. In great contrast to the previous musical excitement, a sorrowful and eerie calmness is now expressed in the music and is made all the more impressive by the repetition of the text and the music, though—as was stated earlier—with some changes and on a different tonal plane (see example 5).

As to the foreground, we hear that the upward motion of the top voice is broken off, or rather, interrupted after the second half note of *S'io moro*, as if to let the emotional weight of these words sink in. Immediately, however, the motion resumes with a stepwise progression rising out of the inner voice and the bass in a quasi-funeral march rhythm (♩|♩. ♪♩ ♩), set to the text *un sol potrete languido e doloroso. . . .* At last, in bar 25 (and bar 35), the ascending motions reach A (and D), completing the ascending third of the top voice (*e doloroso* is repeated). Even after the third has been completed the stepwise progressions are continued as counterpoints to the now descending thirds: A–G–F♯ (bars 25–29) and D–C–B♮ (bars 35–38) set to the words *e doloroso oimè sentire*. These descending thirds are, of course, further examples of *oimè* calls in what is truly "slow motion."

At this point a short provisional summary may be helpful. The entire reproachful conflict, expressed in two sentences, begins musically with a *contrapuntal* prolongation of the I and ends (after two harmonic prolongations of the V) with a *harmonic* prolongation of the I. Thus one large harmonic framework

I–V	V–I
first sentence	second sentence

serves as the musical illustration of one specific human situation. At the same time each of these harmonies is, when it reappears, prolonged in a completely different way, although—with the exception of the opening contrapuntal prolongation of the I—both the V and the final I are based on I–III–V–I progressions as their main harmonic prolongations.

Example 6 is presented now. It shows not only the musical structure of the first two sentences, which form a single organic whole ending at bar 38 (Part A), but also—as a kind of preview—the position of the large I within the succeeding events of Part B.

Example 6

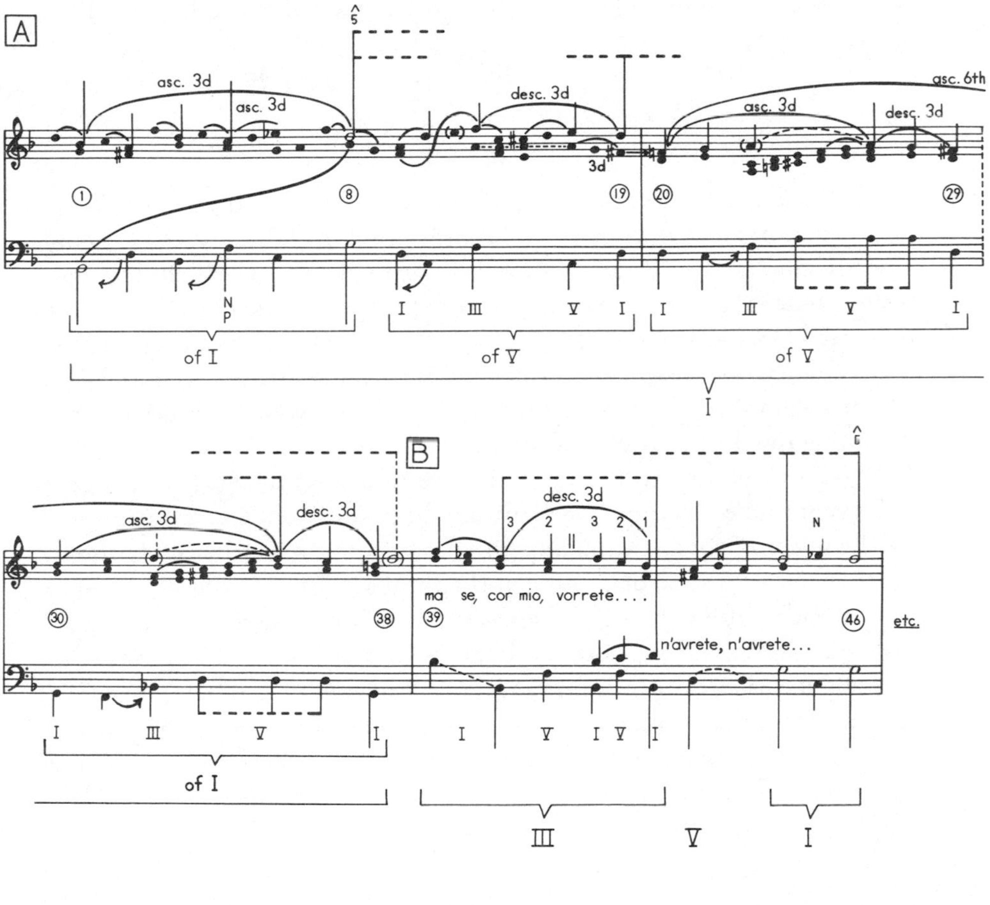

Part B, beginning at bar 39, opens with the setting of the conditional clause of the poem's third and final sentence. This clause suggests a possible solution to the foregoing conflict: *ma se, cor mio, vorrete che vita abb'io da voi, e voi da me*. Monteverdi, in a single stroke, beautifully expresses the change from despair to hope. Whereas the beginnings of the previous sentences were dark and somber, both beginning on tonic chords (I of G and I of D), this third sentence begins on III, the $B^\flat$ major chord. The significant effect of the prolonged $B^\flat$ sonority stems also from its particular function: it follows the large-scale I (bars 1-38) as a harmony of equal structural order.

The bright sound of the III becomes even more meaningful when we realize that Monteverdi depicts the developing change of atmosphere through a playful variation of one of the somber *oimè* calls (see part (c) of example 7). This variation now gives expression to a tender lyricism, which dominates the entire five-bar phrase that musically illustrates the text (given above the graph at (a) in example 7). One will notice that these five bars (bars 39-43) practically form a self-contained unit; this is the only phrase or section of the entire madrigal based on the technique of interruption:

$$\begin{matrix} & \mathrm{D} & \mathrm{C} & & \mathrm{D} & \mathrm{C} & \mathrm{B}^\flat & \\ (& \hat{3} & \hat{2} & // & \hat{3} & \hat{2} & \hat{1} &). \\ & \mathrm{I} & \mathrm{V} & & \mathrm{I} & \mathrm{V} & \mathrm{I} & \end{matrix}$$

Special notice must be taken of the tenor part, which—after functioning as the bass in bar 39—moves up through the third $B^\flat$-C-D, the D being specifically stressed by another motion through a third (which, incidentally, contains the only sixteenth-note figuration in the entire piece; see part (d) of example 7). This tenor part should be heard as a most significant counterpoint expressing (quasi-independently from the top voice) the motion of an ascending third, while the top voice outlines the descending third with interruption.

This ascending third may make one reflect on the very contrasting effects produced by the "same" third, which functioned as the top voice of the opening bars 1-8 and appeared as an equally somber variation in bars 30-35. With the beginning of the final section, various allusions to the music of the opening sentence seem to occur; however, they now express exactly the opposite sentiment. Although we will have more to say about this later on, a few examples will be mentioned here. There is, for instance, the reappearance of eighth notes in bars 39-43. They are used here in a completely different manner from those in the opening section (see *se tanto amate* . . .). The same applies to the *deh perché fate* motive and its variation at the beginning of the music for the second sentence (a skip of a descending fifth followed by a stepwise ascent). This motive reappears in bar 39 of the final section, in stretto (tenor, bass, alto), and now expressing neither challenge nor despair, but becoming a convincing part of a changed atmosphere.

Example 7

With the completion of the five-bar prolongation of III, a V–I ending of the large-scale harmonic progression is due. The B♭ major prolongation, however, represents the musical setting of the entire conditional clause of the last sentence of the poem, leaving no words to be supported by the cadential V–I of G. This brings us to the only "interference" on the part of Monteverdi with Guarini's poem. Monteverdi, in a bold gesture, twice uses *n'avrete* with its promising implication, thus anticipating and even magnifying the first word of the imminent principal clause. This magnified anticipation, set in half notes and lasting three bars, elevates the straightforward *n'avrete* to a veritable promise:

n'avrete, n'avrete: n'avrete mille e mille dolci oimè.
V I

We now realize that the "promise" (*n'avrete, n'avrete*), which is supported by V–I, represents both an ending and a beginning. It is the end of the preceding large-scale progression of I–III–V–I under the widely prolonged and structurally retained top-voice tone D. The same tonic, however, is also the beginning of the final part of the B section, the musical setting of the principal clause of the last sentence of the poem. This overlapping of the end and beginning of the two phrases ties the "promise" clearly to the "reward" of the "thousand little *oimè*," which is announced in bars 46–52. However, the somewhat grandiosely announced promise is not followed by any kind of solemn statement, but instead by a rather playfully composed "reward." This makes the entire ending all the more sensitive and tender, while coupled with a tinge of irony.

This brings us to the inspired musical setting of the "reward." After taking note that the top voice of the opening bars 46–52 shows a variation of the preceding bars 40–43, one comes to the realization that the melodic descending fifth is part of a larger octave descent, from the structural D of bar 46 to the D of the tenor in bar 52, D–G–D. This descent prepares the ear for the specific characteristics of the now ensuing structural descent: the appearance of the structural tones D–C –B♭–A–G in different registers. Furthermore, what is so remarkable about this final section is the slow unfolding of the structural descent while all the many *oimè* motives prolong, embellish, and retard it, thus effecting a gradual rather than a rapid release of accumulated tension (see example 8).

After the octave descent of the opening structural D (bars 46–52) the structural progression of the top voice descends first via C (bar 56) to the B♭ of bar 57; this motion is prolonged by two melodic fourths, the broad DCB♭A and the short FC. The motion of the melodic structure shows the continued significance of the interval of a third, since it clearly marks a division of a fifth into progressions through two thirds, DCB♭AG. The progression through the first third is clearly marked off by its ending on the word *n'avrete* (bars 56–57), again using the longer note values already encountered in the previous setting of this word (bars 44–46). This temporary end of the descent leads immediately to the extended prolongation of the structural V that supports the structural top-voice tone A; notice the two prolonging descending sixths, which, as most effective melodic prolongations, "take care" of the many,

Example 8

many *dolci oimè*. The voice leading here, especially the four-voice setting above the pedal point of the V, is particularly effective (see bars 62–66), allowing the final tonic G of the top voice to arrive only in the last measure. It is also of interest that the melodic prolongations—apart from their programmatic effect—seem to force the structural tones to appear in the different registers mentioned earlier.

In looking back now and comparing the graphs of examples 4 and 5 with those of examples 7 and 8, it appears most remarkable that the voice leading of the "conflict" (bars 1–38) is definitely more dense and complex than the voice-leading texture of the proposed "solution." This is another example of Monteverdi's genius for characterizing a mood through purely musical means. In this connection another interesting musical factor comes to mind. In Part A predominantly ascending motions of the top voice occur: from B♭ via C to D (bars 1–8), and the broad ascent of a sixth from the inner-voice tone F to the retained D (bars 20–37/38). In Part B, on the other hand, we find that almost exclusively descending progressions unfold in the top voice. These motions seem, somehow, to complement each other and create a certain symmetry which nevertheless allows each section to express its sharply contrasting mood and character.

It may now seem that we have come to the end of our analytical discourse. I believe, however, that an analysis of this work would be incomplete if mention were not made of a tonal event that, on first hearing, hardly seems to have any deeper meaning: the exact correspondence of the bass of bars 52–56 (G–D B♭–F) with that of bars 1–4, both showing the same ascending seventh from G to F. This correspondence may become more meaningful when one realizes that the bass set under the structural descending fifth of the top voice (D–C–B♭–A–G) is as follows: G–F–B♭–D–G. This latter bass is the retrograde of the bass of bars 1–8 (with the sole elimination of C). See example 9.

It seems, therefore, that the probable purpose of the quotation in bars 52–56 of the bass of bars 1–4 in its original form (with its ascending seventh) is to alert the listener that something is about to happen to this particular progression of an ascending seventh. For within the total structural descent it becomes a foreground detail of the now reversed bass pattern (see example 8, part (b)). One thus hears the original bass of bars 1–4 and its retrograde quasi-simultaneously, within one large bass progression. As a whole, this progression expresses a harmonic bass, in contrast to the contrapuntal bass of bars 1–4. At the same time, of course, the now descending line of the top voice reverses the top voice's initial ascending third; B♭–C–D (bars 1–8) becomes D–C–B♭ in bars 52–57.

Example 9

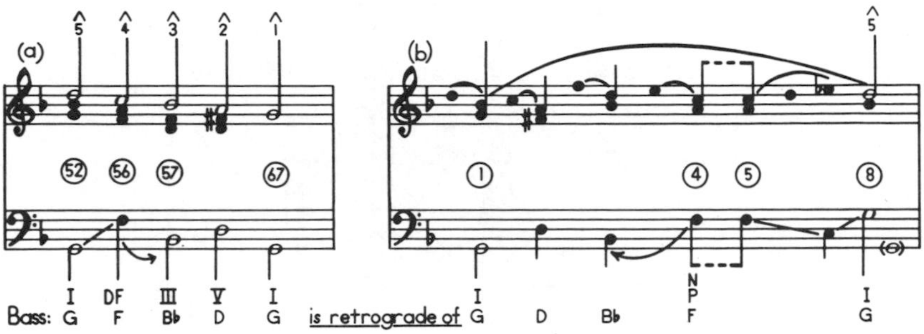

In comparing parts (a) and (b) of example 9 one could conclude on musical grounds alone that no greater contrast between the beginning and ending of a work could occur than the contrast created here by Monteverdi. However, when viewed in relation to the contents of the poem, these events seem to have a deeper meaning, which a less purposeful manipulation of tones could never have conveyed. Are not the first eight bars, with their weird *oimè* calls, the perfect musical illustration of the underlying dejected mood depicted in the beginning of the poem? And—in this particular instance—could not the retrograde of the original bass be interpreted as a musical symbol of the "reversal" or change of mood? The initial situation between the two lovers appears to have changed, and so has the direction of the initial bass.

In conclusion, and as a final survey, I offer a graph depicting, in condensed form, the entire contents of this imaginative work (see example 10). This graph points clearly to the economy of Monteverdi's tonal language, which nevertheless gives the impression of great variety. Of course, we must distinguish here between chord progressions resulting from basic harmonic relationships and those that result from contrapuntal texture, such as the sonorities in bars 1-8 and the various progressions of passing chords illustrated in the previous graphs. Of the harmonic progressions I-V-I and I-III-V-I, only the latter can be found on all structural levels, appearing either as I-III-V-I or as I-III-V-I of V. And, of course, the overall harmonic structure is also I-III-V-I. Nevertheless, the usage of these sonorities and their surroundings are so different that the impression is one of variety and never one of monotony.

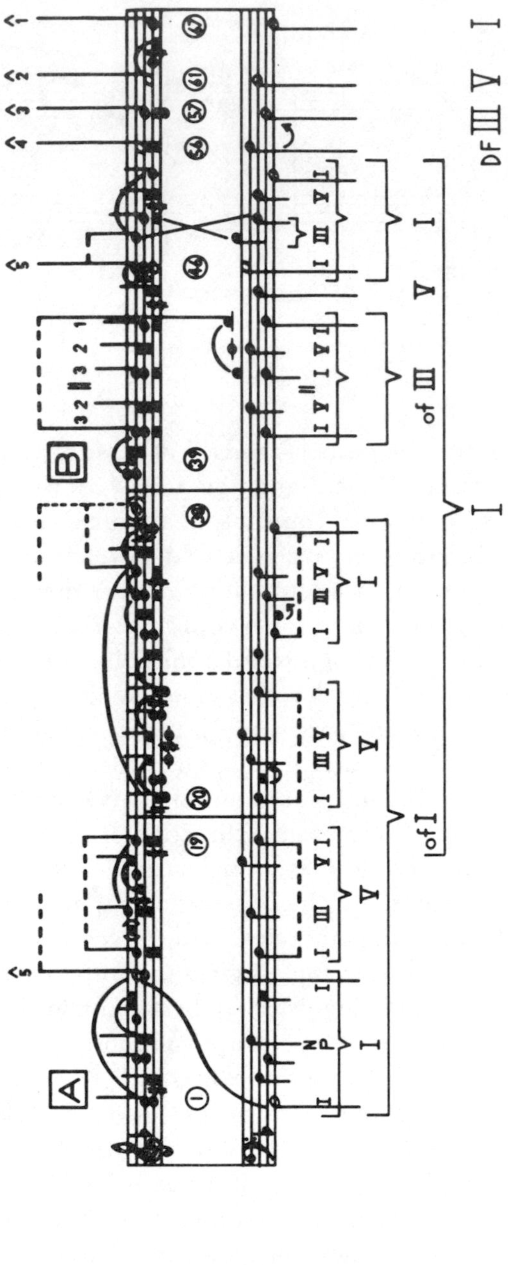

Example 10

Schenkerian Analysis and Post-Tonal Music

JAMES M. BAKER

It is no secret that Heinrich Schenker valued most highly those compositions whose structures conform to the principles of tonal organization set forth in his *Der freie Satz* and other writings. Schenker believed that this "tonal" music—comprised almost exclusively of masterpieces of the eighteenth and nineteenth centuries—manifests an organic structural coherence which surpasses in strength and effect the organization of any other music of any era. He found this type of coherence particularly lacking in contemporary music, which for him (as is well known) meant anything after Brahms. Despite Schenker's own conservatism, more recent theorists have sought to extend his principles of structural levels and prolongation to the analysis of post-tonal music. This work has not always been successful. Some theorists have made a conscientious effort to emulate Schenker's analytical approach, attempting to deal systematically with contemporary works as holistically unified structures. Others, however, have failed to comprehend fully Schenker's theoretical requisites for hierarchical structure. In this essay I shall provide a survey and critique of some of the more important and influential efforts to apply Schenker's theories to twentieth-century music. The question of analyzing works which lie on the borderline between tonality and atonality will also be explored. On this latter subject I shall propose an analytical approach and demonstrate it in an analysis of a problematic composition by Scriabin.

Not all theorists following in the tradition of Schenker's teachings have accepted the possibility of applying his techniques of analysis to compositions whose structures differ to some degree from those of the music which Schenker recognized as tonal. Ernst Oster has stated that

> . . . in non-triadic music we will occasionally find lines and simple progressions that resemble certain lines and progressions in tonal music. However, in tonal music, their deepest meaning and their very existence originate from the triad which they help to "unfold through time" and which they interpret in an endless variety of ways. If this basic premise, this originating principle of tonal music is lost in non-triadic music, any apparent similarity between tonal and non-triadic music cannot be considered a true analogy.[1]

---

1. Ernst Oster, "Re: A New Concept of Tonality (?), "*Journal of Music Theory* 4 (1960), p. 96.

For Oster, any modifications of the Schenkerian principles which might be necessary in order to extend them to analysis of post-tonal music would break open the closed system which they comprise, rendering the analysis meaningless.

Adele Katz, in the later chapters of *Challenge to Musical Tradition* (1945), deals with music of Debussy, Stravinsky, and Schoenberg, and attempts to evaluate the adequacy of Schenker's tonal principles for dealing with their post-tonal works.[2] She finds that *Verklärte Nacht* "discloses a concept of tonality having little in common with [Schoenberg's own] theoretical approach to the problems of harmony and counterpoint" (p. 367). In this work, Katz finds that tonal unity is achieved through the prolongation of a tonic triad, in spite of the fact that Schoenberg never treated the subject of prolongation in his theoretical writings. She establishes that a passage from *Petrushka* which has been almost universally considered to be "polytonal" in fact possesses a single underlying tonality to which the other "polytonalities" relate as neighbor harmonies (p. 304). However, Katz generally finds Schenkerian analytical techniques ineffectual in dealing with post-tonal music. This is the case even in a passage from the "Lullaby" of Stravinsky's *Firebird*, which can be shown to prolong a tonic triad. For in this work ". . . the prolongations, instead of intensifying the structural motion by giving it greater force and momentum, enervate its inherent strength and attenuate its tonal implications" (p. 301).

In general, Katz assumes that in post-tonal music principles of coherence and unity associated with triadic tonality have been replaced by totally new techniques which make the analytical application of any of the former principles a futile pursuit. After establishing that Debussy's "Voiles" is based on an augmented triad which is expanded (not prolonged!) by means of horizontalization and repetition of melodic motives, Katz evaluates the implications of this finding for attempts at analyzing such a piece as a tonal structure:

> It is possible that the whole-tone scale, in its substitution of an augmented for a perfect fifth, does not provide the same kind of structural coherence that is inherent in the older system. If this be true, we cannot apply the same form of analysis to the prelude that we used in connection with compositions that emerged out of the tonal concept [pp. 286-87].

---

2. Adele T. Katz, *Challenge to Musical Tradition: A New Concept of Tonality*, New York: Alfred A. Knopf, Inc., 1945; New York: Da Capo, 1972.

She finally concludes that

> . . . as both harmonic analysis and the Schenker method were evolved out of tonal techniques, it is probable that a new system of analysis is needed to understand the new concepts defined by the whole-tone, polytonal, and twelve-tone systems and the new and different techniques they disclose [p. 293].

She herself offers no such new system. Katz and Oster, among others, reject the possibility of applying Schenkerian techniques in the analysis of post-tonal music—no doubt because of the high value they place on musical structures as the tautly organized products of closed musical systems. These theorists would warn that, in analyzing music not within the tonal system, one must not invoke principles of tonality merely for the sake of expediency. Rather, one must incorporate all aspects of the music—including progressions and configurations resembling those found in tonality—into as systematic a view as possible.

In opposition to the views of Oster and Katz, Felix Salzer, in his *Structural Hearing* (1952), offers a more generalized definition of tonality as "prolonged motion within the framework of a single key-determining progression."[3] In contemporary music, according to Salzer, the tonic-dominant axis is no longer the only framework within which directed motion can take place. Rather, "contrapuntal progressions . . . can be key defining and capable of assuming structural significance" (p. 204). In music of the twentieth century "the distinction between consonance and dissonance appears replaced by a distinction between dissonances of lesser and greater intensity" (p. 192). Salzer interprets works of Stravinsky, Hindemith, Bartók, and others as fundamentally tonal in structure (although presumably he does not believe that all music by these composers and their contemporaries is based on expansions of tonal procedures). In most cases, he finds a traditional triadic component prolonged by means of an embellishing "contrapuntal-structural chord" which serves as the central member of the structural axis in the background of the piece. (See, for example, his analysis of the beginning of Hindemith's Piano Sonata No. 3, example X.)

Very few of Salzer's analyses, in fact only his examples 415–17, point to basic structures dependent on prolongations of dissonant chords, and his remarks justifying these analyses are sketchy. In general, Salzer seems to rely on locating tonal-like bass progressions and voice-leading motions as the bases for prolongational structures in post-tonal works. In Ravel's

3. Felix Salzer, *Structural Hearing: Tonal Coherence in Music*, New York: Dover, 1962, p. 227. All references to pages of this work refer to the first volume. Musical examples are found in the second volume.

"Jeux d'eau" he finds that "the triad, as an architectonic factor of structure as well as of prolongation, is replaced by seventh chords and altered chords" (p. 194). In the first movement of Copland's Piano Sonata, the fundamental structure shown by Salzer is a polychord fusing together what would be dominant and tonic functions in traditional tonality. However, Salzer infers the prolongation of a simple tonic triad in this situation, "for the chord built on the bass will always be the stronger one, and it is the bass and its chord which will determine the chord grammatical status of the whole chord cluster" (pp. 192–94). In general, whenever possible Salzer isolates as elements of a fundamental tonal sonority only those belonging to a triad. Other pitches which might legitimately be heard as integral parts of a nontraditional, dissonant fundamental component are interpreted by Salzer as serving purposes of coloristic inflection as opposed to voice-leading or structural functions, and are therefore "reduced out" before reaching deeper levels of structure. Such analytical procedures, which depend on reference to traditional tonality, ignore the possibility that these "tonic triads with alterations or added dissonances" might themselves constitute basic components of a nontriadic structure. It is quite possibly not as easy to distinguish between coloristic harmonic devices and structural chords as Salzer would have us believe, for example, in his examples 418–419 (p. 195) or in no. 504 (p. 248), where a final major-minor chord is interpreted simply as the tonic harmony.

Roy Travis has continued the work of Salzer in exploring the "structural problem of creating a large-scale tonal entity out of nontriadic materials."[4] His definition of tonality is accordingly broad: "Music is tonal when its motion unfolds through time a particular tone, interval, or chord."[5] Travis admits that

> . . . the music of atonality and serialism does not readily yield to analysis from the standpoint of directed motion. Such an approach implies not only the possibility of recognizing clearly established origins and goals of motion, but the concomitant possibility of understanding the details of such motions as elaborations on various levels . . . of a primordial progression or structure which can be assumed to underlie the entire composition and to unfold through time some sort of tonic sonority, triadic or otherwise.[6]

4. Roy Travis, "Tonal Coherence in the First Movement of Bartók's Fourth String Quartet," *The Music Forum* 2 (1970), p. 298.
5. Roy Travis, "Toward a New Concept of Tonality," *Journal of Music Theory* 3 (1959), p. 261.
6. Roy Travis, "Directed Motion in Schoenberg and Webern," *Perspectives of New Music* 4 (1966), p. 85.

Despite these difficulties, Travis proceeds more boldly than Salzer, analyzing such pieces as Schoenberg's Op. 19, No. 2, the second movement of Webern's Op. 27, No. 124 of Bartók's *Mikrokosmos*, and the beginning of Stravinsky's *Rite of Spring*.[7] In general, his analyses suffer from the failure to specify the operations of the systems governing the structures of these compositions. He indicates voice leadings and, especially, bass progressions resembling those of tonality; however, he is at a loss to explain the basis for his determination of the fundamental, prolonged sonority of each structure. The closest he can come to stating a rule whereby the basic sonority is articulated is as follows: "It is almost a general principle of musical coherence that those chords which mark the beginning or end of a given procedure of motion tend to serve in a structurally more important capacity than the chords in the midst of that motion."[8] He generally relies on musical intuition and a good ear to determine a single prevailing characteristic sonority, which is assumed to be the structural "tonic" (e.g., his analysis of the opening of the *Rite of Spring*). In this sense, his "tonal" structures are hardly related to those tonal structures of the nineteenth century, where the true tonic is seldom encountered at the surface of the music.

Travis's work is concerned more explicitly than Salzer's studies with the question of the extent to which twentieth-century works which exhibit a number of tonally related procedures represent, at the same time, a break with the past. In his article, "The String Quartets of Bartók," Milton Babbitt deals with the same problem. He states that Bartók achieved "an assimilated balance" between two opposing systems—traditional tonal functionality versus a contextual structure-defining process. Relating the two systems to musical spans of time, Babbitt notes that the former "is most dangerously explicit in the small," while the latter is "least structurally explicit in the large."[9] Therefore, Bartok determines structures on local levels according to new contextual procedures which are analogous (but not equivalent) to those of tonal harmony, while the background is more conventional. Travis was probably influenced (as perhaps was Salzer) by Babbitt's observations. He uncovers a conventional tonal *Ursatz* at the background of the first movement of Bartók's Fourth Quartet, admitting the difficulty of reconciling this analysis with the "equally definite—and even systematic—use of chro-

7. The analyses of pieces by Schoenberg and Webern are found in "Directed Motion," and the works by Bartók and Stravinsky are analyzed in "New Concept."
8. Travis, "New Concept," p. 266.
9. Milton Babbitt, "The String Quartets of Bartók," *Musical Quarterly* 35 (1949), pp. 377–78.

matic and whole-tone clusters, melodic doublings of the second and ninth, glissandi, etc., elements commonly associated with the vocabulary of atonality."[10] (Salzer notes no such discrepancy when analyzing the second movement of Bartók's Fifth Quartet as his example 452.) The problems with Travis's analyses of these surface features in terms of directed motion are, of course, no different from those encountered in his dealings with thoroughly nontraditional pieces. Beyond this, the fact that ostensibly opposing systems are seen to operate at different levels of structure in these analyses is at odds with the very concept of structural coherence as established by structuralists (including Schenker). Neither Babbitt nor Travis explains the relationships between these systems—if any—nor do they specify the operations whereby a structural balance between them is achieved.[11]

In his article, "Dissonant Prolongations: Theoretical and Compositional Precedents," Robert P. Morgan addresses the subject of prolongation of dissonant chords.[12] He sets forth the theory that types of dissonant prolongations evolved within the tonal system, progressively assuming positions of greater prominence and scope in overall forms until, at the end of the nineteenth century, such dissonances were prolonged throughout entire compositions, thus serving as "tonics." Morgan offers occurrences of prolonged dominant-seventh chords, as shown in Schenker's analyses, as precedents for the prolongations of other dissonances over greater time-spans in romantic music.[13] In the early nineteenth century, composers began to prolong dominant sevenths

10. Travis, "Tonal Coherence," p. 299.

11. In my Ph.D. dissertation, "Alexander Scriabin: The Transition from Tonality to Atonality," Yale University, 1977, I show that Scriabin devised a method whereby novel sonorities with interesting non-tonal properties can be generated at the surface of a fundamentally tonal composition. To my knowledge, my work provides the first thorough explanation of the operations of both tonal and atonal procedures within integral musical structures.

12. Robert P. Morgan, "Dissonant Prolongations: Theoretical and Compositional Precedents," *Journal of Music Theory* **20** (1976), pp. 49-91.

13. Ibid., pp. 53-54. Morgan's example 2 (p. 55) shows a portion of Schenker's analysis of the Prelude in C major from Bach's *Well-Tempered Clavier*, book I, which involves the prolongation of a dominant-seventh chord. He takes this example as a contradiction of Schenker's statement that "an interval that is itself passing in character cannot at the same time provide the first tone [*Kopfton*] of a prolongation, which must always be consonant." Morgan apparently does not realize that, in the largest context supplied by the background of the example he cites, the dissonant seventh is in fact a passing note in an inner voice of a prolonged V supporting $\hat{2}$. (See Heinrich Schenker, *Five Graphic Music Analyses*, New York: Dover, 1969, pp. 36-37.) Morgan's misreadings of Schenker's analyses here and elsewhere in the article considerably weaken his argument.

throughout sections of compositions formerly associated with formal stability (p. 56). Morgan admits, however, that "the tonal sense of these passages depends upon the presence of an implied tonic" (p. 57). However, other dissonances in music of about this time were prolonged, according to Morgan, without reference to the overall tonality of the composition. These were typically the augmented triad or diminished-seventh chord (because they are the only triadically structured dissonances within the system). He cites the prolongations of a diminished-seventh chord in sections of Schubert's "Die Stadt" (including the final section of the piece where the return to the tonic is only implied) as being contextually defined, declaring that "within the context of its dissonant 'tonic,' this section seems almost completely stable" (p. 58). This highly debatable subjective conclusion is refuted by the relationship of the diminished-seventh chord as auxiliary chord to the tonic of the piece.[14]

Since the diminished-seventh chord in "Die Stadt" remains unembellished, it represents for Morgan the simplest form of contextual dissonant prolongation. A famous example of a more complicated type is the opening section of Liszt's *Faust Symphony* (1855), where, according to Morgan, an augmented triad C–E–A♭ is the referential sonority, and other harmonies, some of them consonant, are secondary to it (p. 60 ff.). However, in the context provided by the structure of the entire first movement or by the entire symphony, this prolonged augmented triad is not a stable chord but rather resolves to the tonic triad C–E–G. Neither the considerable duration of the opening section nor its melody, which contains all twelve tones, negates the role of A♭ as $\flat\hat{6}$ which ultimately resolves to $\hat{5}$ in the key of C.

Morgan's concrete contextual criterion for determining the prolongations of dissonant chords within tonal frameworks, as discussed above, appears to be duration — and duration more in an absolute than a relative sense. Morgan himself admits that "only in the case of complete

---

14. One might well question whether "Die Stadt" is a totally independent structure. The ultimate resolution of the diminished-seventh chord occurs at the beginning of "Am Meer," another of the six songs (including "Die Stadt") which Schubert composed in August 1828 for a projected cycle on poems from Heinrich Heine's *Buch der Lieder* (1827). The compilers of Schubert's *Schwanengesang*, a posthumous collection of disparate songs, appropriately placed "Am Meer" immediately following "Die Stadt."

Morgan's reading of "Die Stadt" shown in his example 5, p. 59, which is clearly geared to his interpretation of the diminished-seventh chord as a stable harmony, is in conflict with the tonal structure demonstrated by Schenker's analysis. (See Heinrich Schenker, *Free Composition*, translated and edited by Ernst Oster, New York: Longman, 1979, vol. 2, figure 103, 4.)

pieces . . . is the dissonance absolute," and he offers Liszt's "Die Trauer-Gondel I" (composed 1882, published 1916) as an example of one of the first "independent compositions organized entirely by means of dissonant prolongations" (p. 74). Even here a tonal context is possibly provided by "Die Trauer-Gondel II," composed at the same time, which allows Morgan's referential sonority, an augmented triad E-A♭-C, to resolve to an F minor triad. A more convincing example of a complete composition prolonging a dissonant chord is Liszt's "Bagatelle ohne Tonart" (1885), which, in Morgan's analysis, prolongs a diminished-seventh chord. A final stage in the evolution of dissonant prolongations postulated by Morgan was reached in the first decade of the twentieth century, when composers adopted synthetic chords as the bases for prolongational structures (p. 79). Morgan cites Debussy's "Voiles" (1910) as an example of one of the new systems. In this work a whole-tone scale serves as the fundamental sonority. However, in Scriabin's "Enigme" Op. 52, No. 2 (composed in 1906), Morgan finds a "much less restricted" use of the whole-tone formation, incorporating a "considerable degree of dissonant inflection" (p. 79).

In music of these later stages in the evolution of dissonant prolongations, it becomes increasingly difficult to determine the basic harmonies underlying the highly chromatic musical surface. In one instance, his analysis of a passage from Liszt's "Bagatelle ohne Tonart," Morgan cites a version of Travis's rule that endpoints of gestures possess greatest structural weight: "The passage essentially consists of a series of parallel diminished sevenths moving up by half-step, but the question of which chords are referential is settled unequivocally only when the last chord of the series—the 'tonic' seventh—is reached . . ." (p. 76). Beyond the rule implied here, Morgan can only offer the glib advice that one should "look for the simplest possible solution consistent with the actualities of the piece . . ." (p. 67). In dealing with compositions whose structures he alleges to be nontriadic, Morgan does not succeed in relating their prolongational procedures to those of tonality. Rather, in Scriabin's "Enigme" he shows that the elaboration of the "tonic" sonority is achieved by treating it as an unordered set of pitches which may be transformed by means of certain operations (p. 84). However, the operations he demonstrates do not provide the means for determining with certainty a basic referential chord. (At the end of this essay I shall offer an alternative analysis of "Enigme.") In concentrating on dissonant components which, on the largest levels of structure, are embellishments of consonant tonic triads—and in discussing in detail only two examples of musical structures possibly based on dissonant chords—Morgan never comes to grips with important questions concerning the relationships between two fundamentally different types of musical structure.

A much more systematic approach toward contextual analysis than Morgan's was offered by Allen Forte in his *Contemporary Tone Structures* (1955), where he "attempts to discover the structural premises and postulates of individual compositions without recourse to pre-established theory."[15] The basic assumption of Forte's study is that "an individual musical structure is a complete system and, as such, reflects a larger, logically complete concept" (p. 13). Therefore, his analyses consistently avoid isolating passages from the context of the unified whole. Forte states here his belief that the only ties between contemporary musical structures and traditional tonal music are that individual contemporary compositions may be based partially on postulates equivalent or related to postulates underlying the tonal system: e.g., (1) the tonic-dominant functional relationship, or (2) tonal identity and octave equivalence. Forte finds that most contemporary composers have adopted modified versions of the latter postulates, but have generally rejected the tonic-dominant function in favor of other functional relationships (p. 15). Another connection between tonal and post-tonal music is that both depend on pitch as the primary determinant of structure, and that pitch relations vary in structural weight and exist over varying time-spans. Thus Forte offers a version of Schenker's method of analytic reduction to deal with the hierarchical structures of contemporary music (pp. 20–23). At no time does he carry over techniques of analysis of tonal music simply by identifying configurations similar to those found in traditional structures. Rather, for Forte each new work must be approached on its own terms with nothing taken for granted. He does not offer a theory of contemporary music, but he demonstrates analytical procedures, formulates general types of characteristic events, and lists typical factors which might determine structural value in contemporary music. The chief drawback of the method offered here—or indeed of any type of contextual analysis where a piece is assumed to be a self-sufficient reflection of the system by which it was composed—is encountered in dealing with the phenomenon which Schoenberg called "*schwebende Tonalität*" ("hovering tonality").[16] For in highly chromatic tonal pieces where the axis of tonality is difficult to discern—where it

15. Allen Forte, *Contemporary Tone Structures*, New York: Bureau of Publications, Teacher's College, Columbia University, 1955, p. 4.

16. See the section entitled "Über schwebende und aufgehobende Tonalität" in Arnold Schoenberg, *Harmonielehre*, 3d. ed. revised and enlarged, Vienna: Universal Edition, 1922, pp. 459–60.

may not appear near the surface of the music at all or may exist only implicitly—methods of contextual analysis would in all likelihood be incapable of disclosing the referential tonal structure.

In his dissertation "Tonal Cohesion in Schoenberg's Twelve-Tone Music," Robert Suderburg evaluates the literature in which this music is analyzed in terms of serial procedures—including the studies by Leibowitz, Rufer, and Perle—and concludes that "pitch emphasis in Schoenberg's serial music is not adequately summarized by reference to its set-structure."[17] Rather, Suderburg feels that the structure of this music results less from inherent properties of the set than from procedures and functions related to the principles of tonal coherence discussed in Schoenberg's *Harmonielehre* (Suderburg, p. 171). These include: the functional relationship based on the melodic tendency of the half-step, the supremacy of one tone of an interval over the other, emphasis of pitches through procedures involving pitch retention, principles of root progression, voice leading as possibly the sole determinant of harmonic progression, the dominant functions of whole-tone chords and fourth chords, and modulation by means of chord alteration (pp. 30 ff. and 79–81).

Conspicuously absent from Schoenberg's teachings are concepts of prolongation and structural levels in tonal music. Suderburg, however, bases his analyses to a certain extent on the formation of structural hierarchies, although the extent of his debt to Schenker is never made clear. Further, Suderburg expands Schoenberg's notions of harmony to include the concept of multi-regional or multi-functional combinations as the structural bases for large dissonant sonorities (p. 85). As evidence for this principle, Suderburg offers Schoenberg's own discussion of an eleven-note chord from *Erwartung*, where he refers to the individual groups (differentiated by means of register and orchestration) comprising the chord as being derived from traditional components which each imply their own particular tonal resolutions.[18] Suderburg conveniently fails to cite the remainder of Schoenberg's discussion: "But such a derivation will not always be correct; the return to older forms is not always successful or is managed only by means of a very broad interpretation. For at

17. Robert C. Suderburg, "Tonal Cohesion in Schoenberg's Twelve-Tone Music," Ph.D. diss., University of Pennsylvania, 1966, p. 249.

18. Suderburg, p. 106 ff.; Schoenberg, pp. 502–03.

another time I might write such a chord in much closer position."[19] In fact, determining the individual functional components of large dissonant chords is usually necessarily an arbitrary procedure, and Suderburg's analyses are weak to the extent that they depend upon the concept of polytonality.[20]

Suderburg differentiates three stages in the development of Schoenberg's nontriadic music: (1) "the extraction of basic cohesive relationships from the traditional tonal framework"; (2) "the refusion of these cohesive relationships into a new context without direct reference to the tonal framework"; and (3) "the compositional solidification of this new and expanded context in the serial technique and the return to more frequent use of earlier voice-leading principles" (p. 46). He maintains that even outside of the tonal system traditional intervallic and chordal components retain the qualities associated with their use in tonality because these qualities are inherent in the intervals themselves.[21] These traditional components may therefore be used within a post-tonal context to create "points of focus" which are goals of directed motion (pp. 6 and 176).

Suderburg states that within Schoenberg's later systems, dissonant chords are the fundamental components; they do not resolve, yet nevertheless their expressive potential is dependent upon the implicit resolutions these chords would receive in the tonal system (p. 104). In the later music, effects approximating those of traditional consonance-dissonance treatment are achieved by means of orchestration and registral distribution (p. 108). Suderburg also points out that compositional unfolding is the process underlying both modulation in tonal

19. Schoenberg, p. 503: "Aber eine solche Ableitung wird nicht immer zutreffen, die Rückführung auf ältere Formen nicht immer oder nur bei sehr weiter Auffassung gelingen. Denn ein anderes Mal schreibe ich einen solchen Akkord in viel engerer Lage."

20. The concept of "polytonality" has been questioned and even dismissed as a viable auditory possibility by many theorists, including such varied figures as Paul Hindemith and Milton Babbitt, who has called polytonality a "self-contradictory expression which, if it is to possess any meaning at all, can be used only to designate a certain degree of expansion of the individual elements of a well-defined harmonic or voice-leading unit." See Paul Hindemith, *The Craft of Musical Composition*, translated by Arthur Mendel, New York: Associated Music Publishers, 1942, vol. 1, p. 156; and Babbitt, "Quartets of Bartók," p. 380.

21. This aspect of Suderberg's theory reflects the influence of Paul Hindemith. In the *Craft of Musical Composition*, Hindemith states: "We cannot escape the relationship of tones. Whenever two tones sound, either simultaneously or successively, they create a certain interval value; whenever chords or intervals are connected, they enter into a more or less close relationship. And whenever the relationships of tones are played off one against another, tonal coherence appears. It is thus quite impossible to devise groups of tones without tonal coherence" (p. 152).

music and transposition of set-forms in Schoenberg's post-tonal music (p. 246). Beyond these remarks, he does not manage to relate the two musical systems. Since the tonal structural components which Suderburg points out in Schoenberg's post-tonal music seldom if ever appear in isolation, but rather usually are not differentiated from a dense, highly chromatic texture, the process of extracting tonal gestures becomes a somewhat arbitrary procedure which Suderburg fails to systematize. In light of Schoenberg's striving after control of highly particularized sonorities, Suderburg's frequent use of terms such as "dominant-like" and "tonic-like" is imprecise. Suderburg discounts the possibility that these foreground sonorities, which are related structurally to the basic set, play a part in determining structures at other levels, a thesis related to the conclusions of Babbitt and Travis. As mentioned previously, the lack of correspondence between determinants of structure at various levels poses problems with regard to establishing overall compositional coherence.

Joel Lester, in his dissertation, "A Theory of Atonal Prolongations as Used in an Analysis of the *Serenade* Op. 24 by Arnold Schoenberg," presents an "analytic method . . . based on the links between the tonal and atonal styles."[22] He characterizes tonality as a closed system in which all elements and properties are derived from a single set of related axiomatic operations: passing and neighbor-notes, and the "systematic differentiation between simultaneity interval and connecting interval" (p. 1). He extends to the atonal system the tonal principles of division (achieved by skips) and proximity (steps). However, he stipulates that in atonality any interval may be divided by any tone contained within its bounds (but is most often divided symmetrically), while a tone may be embellished only if displaced by an auxiliary tone a half-step or at most a whole-step away (p. 4). Through these primary operations the pitch content for atonal structures is generated. Lester considers operations related to duration, register, etc. to be secondary in that they involve simply the presentation of elements generated by the primary operations (pp. 7-8). It follows from the extension of these tonal principles to the atonal system that atonal structures are hierarchical, since they entail the distinction between prior and derived elements (p. 106).

The primary difference between tonal and atonal systems is that the atonal system is open—that is, "the properties of the system are not derivable from a single set of closely related axioms" (p. 107). Unlike the

22. Joel Lester, "A Theory of Atonal Prolongations as Used in an Analysis of the *Serenade* Op. 24 by Arnold Schoenberg," Ph.D. diss., Princeton, 1970, p. 112.

tonal system, in which melodic and harmonic intervals are differentiated and harmonic structures are governed by rules for the treatment of consonance and dissonance, the atonal system does not relate the harmonic and melodic dimensions, nor are the harmonies used at various levels necessarily related (p. 108). Indeed, "at the foreground and middleground, and generally at the background, all simultaneities are the result of voice leading operations" (p. 14). The atonal system as formulated by Lester contains an inherent contradiction; for, in a system where all harmonies are determined by the interaction of melodic lines which may be structurally independent of one another, how can these lines be said to prolong a pre-established basic sonority? At best such a sonority could be characterized only as the accidental sum of pitches prolonged by the individual voices. But if no verticality is basic to the structure, what is the basis for the polyphony of the composition? Lester acknowledges that "the atonal system presented here is more a method of analysis than a tight theoretical system" (p. 5). The method itself is applied only to Schoenberg's Op. 24. Lester admits that his method "does not appear to apply equally well to all atonal music" and that, even in the work analyzed, "returns or repetitions of sections often cannot be analyzed the same as the model" (p. 114).

Two other important theoretical studies of atonal music deserve mention, although the systems they advance do not explicitly involve prolongational procedures or hierarchical structures as found in the tonal system. The first of these is George Perle's *Serial Composition and Atonality*.[23] Like Lester, Perle finds that "the 'free' atonality that preceded dodecaphony precludes by definition the possibility of self-consistent, generally applicable compositional procedures" (p. 9). However, like Oster and Katz, he finds it impossible to extend any properties of the closed tonal system to atonality, maintaining: "the abandonment of the concept of a root-generator of the individual chord is a radical development that renders futile any attempt at a systematic formulation of chord structure and progression in atonal music along the lines of traditional harmonic theory" (p. 31). Indeed, he believes that atonal procedures and properties "are not reducible to a set of foundational assumptions in terms of which the compositions that are collectively designated by the expression 'atonal music' can be said to represent 'a system' of composition" (p. 1). Rather, unique structural problems and their solutions are presented in each individual atonal composition, and may be analyzed only in terms of that particular context.

23. George Perle, *Serial Composition and Atonality,* Berkeley and Los Angeles: University of California Press, 1962; fourth edition, 1977.

Perle rejects the contention (of Suderburg, among others) that intervals, when used in atonal music, retain inherently the qualities they evince in tonality (p. 30). He also rejects at least implicitly the concept of structural levels in atonal music, thus receiving Lester's criticism that "most of the analyses presented by George Perle would fall into the category of foreground elaboration."[24] Perle in turn states that, although the harmonic dimension of atonal music is often difficult to analyze, views (such as Lester's) that atonal harmony is determined solely by voice leading are "an evasion of the problem and . . . an overstatement"; for, while harmony is not usually systematically treated in atonality, "in atonal works not based upon rigorous contrapuntal procedures there is in general a total interpenetration of harmonic and melodic elements" (p. 24).

According to Perle, structural coherence in atonal music is obtained most often by means of operations on intervallic cells, including permutation, transposition, and even free association with independent elements (pp. 9–10). Perle summarizes the potential functions of the cell as follows:

> It may operate as a kind of microcosmic set of fixed intervallic content, statable either as a chord or as a melodic figure or as a combination of both. Its components may be fixed with regard to order, in which event it may be employed, like the twelve-tone set, in its literal transformations. . . . Individual notes may function as pivotal elements, to permit overlapping statements of a basic cell or the linking of two or more basic cells [pp. 9–10].

Symmetrical structures are particularly important in the atonal literature, frequently occurring at points of relative stability (p. 26). Often a pitch or set of pitches serves as a point of focus for parts or all of a composition; Perle refers to this phenomenon as "centricity" (p. 34). Rarely in atonal music does centricity achieve the effect of tonicization, a notable exception being in the works of Bartók (p. 27).

The second non-Schenkerian study of atonal music deserving mention here is Allen Forte's *The Structure of Atonal Music* (1973), which supersedes the approach of his earlier *Contemporary Tone Structures*.[25] This later work differs from Perle's study in at least two important respects. Like Perle, Forte offers a set-theoretical framework for the systematic description of atonal structures. Moreover, he does not describe

---

24. Lester, pp. 16–17.
25. Allen Forte, *The Structure of Atonal Music*, New Haven: Yale University Press, 1973; second printing, 1977.

the relationship of atonal structural procedures to those of the tonal system. However, although not explicitly treated, structural hierarchies and prolongational procedures are occasionally implicit in the analytical segmentations found in his examples. Secondly, Forte's catalog of the basic set-forms with accompanying nomenclature, as well as his systematic classification of possible relations among sets, permits a much more precise and thorough accounting of particular sonorities and their interrelationships than has been previously possible. For example, properties of invariance of pitch-classes under transposition of a set, considered in terms of a few particular sets by Perle and others, are systematically described for all sets in Forte's listing of interval vectors.[26]

To sum up this survey: Theorists who have dealt to any extent with the question of the applicability of Schenkerian analytical techniques to post-tonal music have generally subscribed to one of two rather extreme positions. On the one hand, certain "strict constructionists"—among them Oster and Katz—would consider as tonal only those works whose structures conform exactly to Schenker's formulations. Further, these theorists would consider invalid any attempts to disclose structural hierarchies or prolongations in works whose structures deviate to any extent from tonal structural norms. On the other hand, a larger group of theorists—including Travis, Morgan, and Lester—have adopted a much more liberal approach, finding prolongations and stratified structure even in the absence of a tonic-dominant tonal axis. Some of these analysts have sought to establish the existence of prolongations of triads and even of tonal functional progressions in nontriadic music. Others

26. Forte's method of reducing sets to normal-order forms greatly facilitates the recognition of significant relationships among ostensibly unrelated sonorities (pp. 3–5). He points out, for instance, that Perle does not recognize the identity of the "primary referential chord" of *Wozzeck* with Scriabin's *Prometheus* chord (p. 28 n.). Lester refers to lines in Schoenberg's Op. 24 which "feature a symmetrical, often whole-tone scale, motion with a semitone at the end" (p. 16), but these lines (which are also related to the *Prometheus* set—and undoubtedly to other sets in Op. 24 itself) might be more effectively and elegantly related by means of set-complex nomenclature. Travis's analyses often miss the point of particular relationships which are revealed as a matter of course upon application of Forte's method. Travis determines that the tonic sonority of Bartók's "Syncopation" (No. 133 from *Mikrokosmos*) is the set which Forte calls 5-21. Travis states that this chord returns later with "a few more inner voices . . . thrown in," not realizing that the larger chord is Forte's 7-21 (not including the F♮ shown in parentheses by Travis) and that the relationship between the larger and smaller forms of the sonority is one of (nonliteral) complementation (see Travis, "New Concept," p. 276). This relationship does not solve the problem of whether 5-21/7-21 acts as a tonic in the piece, but it does establish a structural basis for the use of the "extra" pitches together with the original set.

have gone further, attempting to disclose the prolongations of dissonant chords. In my estimation, the analyses of those subscribing to these liberal positions, especially of those who accept the possibility of dissonant prolongations, are invariably somewhat arbitrarily based.

The issues involved in extending Schenkerian concepts of structure to the analysis of post-tonal music become most complex when considering compositions which lie on the borderline between tonality and atonality. This body of music, which I shall call "transitional" music, includes works by Liszt, Scriabin, and Schoenberg, and certainly many others. In the past, most theorists who have dealt with transitional compositions have concentrated on innovative aspects of their structures, without paying close attention to the ways in which these structures are related to those of conventional tonality. This is understandable, since the tonal foundations of many transitional works are only implicit or are concealed beneath an intricate chromatic web. Yet in many cases theorists have been too eager to classify as atonal compositions which, under closest scrutiny, would prove to be grounded in tonality, even in the strictest Schenkerian sense. It is my conviction that the important question concerning a composition on the borderline between tonality and atonality is *not*: Is it tonal or atonal? Rather, one must ask: In what way is this piece tonal? To what extent and how do atonal procedures also determine its structure? Moreover, if one is to discover the extent to which a piece is tonal, one must begin as a "strict constructionist," examining every possibility for interpreting the structure in conventional terms. In the absence of any such possibility, the analyst must nevertheless compare the structure of the problematic piece to structures found in conventional tonality. He may then ascertain whether it may be interpreted as a deviation from or an extension of a normal tonal structure, or whether it projects a conventional tonal structure implicitly. If no relation to traditional tonal structures is discovered, then the composition should not be considered tonal. Further, since prolongations are effected by means of operations on functions of varying structural weights, the analyst must establish the existence of a closed system of such operations and functions in order to be able to posit a multi-leveled structure. To date, no closed system has been disclosed for any corpus of post-tonal music.

In the final pages of this essay, I would like to demonstrate this analytical approach by providing an analysis of Scriabin's "Enigme" Op. 52, No. 2. This is an especially problematic transitional work. While it may appear that Scriabin broke entirely new harmonic ground with this piece, nevertheless "Enigme" can be shown to be constructed upon a framework closely related to fundamental structures of conventional tonality. In his article, "Dissonant Prolongations: Theoretical and Compositional Precedents," Robert P. Morgan states that this work is "on the borderline between nonordered serialism and . . . extended tonality" (p. 86). The type of extended tonality which Morgan finds operative here, however, is based on the prolongation of a dissonant *tonic* sonority which is in fact a five-note subset of the whole-tone scale (Forte's set 5-33 [6, 8, 10, 0, 2]) with A♭ in the bass.[27] Morgan recognizes none of the aspects of conventional tonality which shall be disclosed in the present analysis. Thus, there is no systematic basis for the analytical determination of the prolongation-like configurations he points out—although in certain cases these configurations resemble those in the sketches presented here, perhaps because he recognizes intuitively the tonality of the piece. Moreover, Morgan is apparently not even aware of many of the important extra-tonal relations in the piece, such as those involving complementation.

"Enigme" is perhaps the most unconventional of Scriabin's late tonal works, which is surprising since it was composed in 1906 at a time when most of Scriabin's compositions were still fairly explicitly tonal. (For complete analytical sketches along with a score annotated for pitch-class set content, see pp. 180-185.) This piece is Scriabin's first to close with a dissonant nontriadic harmony. In fact, the final chord is none other than the complete whole-tone aggregate (6-35). Although this is only the second statement of the entire whole-tone scale in the composition, this sonority is appropriate since in the most important sets in "Enigme" the majority of elements belong to a single whole-tone scale. (I shall refer to these elements in the majority as "whole-tone elements" and to those in the minority as "nonwhole-tone elements.")

"Enigme" has a simple A B A form, with the contrasting sections taking place on different whole-tone planes—that is, the two complementary whole-tone scales predominate in either main section of the

27. Throughout the following discussion I shall indicate pitch classes (henceforth abbreviated "pcs") by the conventional integers, with B♯, C♮, and D♭♭ as 0; C♯ and D♭ as 1, etc. Members of a single set are enclosed within square brackets. For convenience, Allen Forte's set nomenclature (as set forth in *The Structure of Atonal Music*) will be indicated where appropriate. The name of a pc set, according to this nomenclature, is comprised of two numbers separated by a hyphen. The first indicates the number of elements in the set, while the second shows the position of the set in Forte's listing. N.B.—Morgan does not apply Forte's set nomenclature nor, indeed, any systematic theory of set relations.

piece.[28] The A section (marked "*Etrange, capricieusement*") is highly fragmented, with essentially four disparate events occurring in succession. The form of the A section, as determined by these events, may be outlined as follows:

A (mm.1-22)		
1 (mm.1-3)		
2 (mm.4-5)		11 mm.
3 (mm.6-8)		
4 (mm.9-11)		
1 (mm.12-14)		
2 (mm.15-16)	8 mm.	
3 (m.17)		
4 (mm.18-19)		11 mm.
3 (m.20)	3 mm.	
4 (mm.21-22)		

In content, the B section (marked "*Voluptueux, charmé*") is more through-composed, with essentially two types of events: (1) a highly melodic upper voice (based on the melody in A3) with a descending arpeggiation in the left hand, alternating with (2) a nonmelodic statement of a five-note subset of the whole-tone scale (5-33) depending for its interest on the rhythmic activation of some of the elements of this chord in registrally and dynamically differentiated parts. The form of the B section may be summarized as below:

B (mm.23-46)		
1 (mm.23-25)	See A3.	6 mm.
2 (mm.26-28)		
1 (mm.29-31)		6 mm.
2 (mm.32-34)		
3 (m.35)	See A1.	
1 (mm.36-37)		6 mm.
2 (mm.38-40)		
1 (mm.41-43)		6 mm.
2 (mm.44-66)		

The A section then returns in shortened form:

A (mm.47-62)	
1 (mm.47-52)	expanded by octave transfers
2 (mm.53-54)	
3 (mm.55-57)	
4 (mm.58-60)	
5 (mm.61-62)	final whole-tone chord

28. In this discussion all references to complementation will denote literal complementation, whereby the entire chromatic aggregate is contained in the union of a set and its complement, which have no elements in common. In other words, the complement of a set contains all pitch classes not in the set itself.

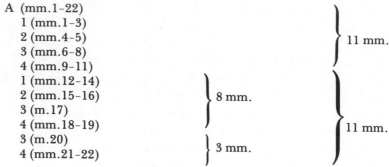

The principal voice-leading procedure of "Enigme" involves voice-leading patterns of ascending parallel sixths. These patterns appear in both the A and B sections, with a more complex interrelationship among patterns found in the latter. In both sections the patterns break down at significant points in the structure.

The retention of whole-tone elements is a main structural determinate in both sections of the piece (this process will also be called "whole-tone invariance"); yet at the surface of the music—particularly in the A section—a rich harmonic variety is achieved through extensive use of non whole-tone elements. The piece actually opens with a diatonic component, 7-35, which contains all seven pitch-classes of the D♭ major scale. In mm.9-11, the six-element set formed by all pcs is 6-Z19, which contains an equal number of even- and odd-numbered pcs. A similar distribution of even- and odd-numbered elements is found in 8-28, which is the basis for each of two similar sections in mm.18-19 and 20-22.[29] While the even-numbered whole-tone scale (i.e., [0, 2, 4, 6, 8, 10]) is predominant at the beginning of the A section, in the course of the entire section all pcs of the complementary whole-tone set are introduced. At first these odd-numbered pcs occur for the most part in an obviously passing or auxiliary capacity (as in 7-35, 6-34, and 6-21, heard in the first few measures), but later they attain a balance with those of the original 6-35 (as in the statements of 6-Z19 and 8-28 cited above). Ultimately, a transition to the B section, where the odd-numbered whole-tone scale prevails, is effected by shifting weight toward these complementary elements.

"Enigme" opens in such a way as to suggest the key of D♭. Not only do all of the pcs in the first measure form the D♭ major scale, but also the key signature assigned by Scriabin to this work indicates this tonality. Moreover, the initial verticality (on the downbeat of m.1) would appear to function as V^{4}_{2} in this key. In the course of the first eight measures A♭ is firmly established in the bass by means of a descending arpeggiation of $V^{7}_{\flat 5}$ of D♭. Note that the lowered fifth of this chord is indicated by the spelling of E♭♭ in m.4.[30] When this pitch is respelled as D♮ in m.7, the relationship to the harmony on A♭ is somewhat obscured. Nevertheless, the tritone bass progression thus delineated serves to prolong the

29. The balance between even- and odd-numbered pcs is not a property peculiar to 6-Z19 and 8-28. (Indeed, seventeen eight-element sets and twenty-two six-element sets manifest this distribution.) These sets, however, are ideally structured for effecting a transition between complementary whole-tone planes.

30. The dominant-seventh chord with lowered fifth is a characteristic component in Scriabin's late tonal harmony.

harmony on A♭. This is particularly evident because the pcs held invariant between the two different forms of 6-21 found in mm.5-9 form 4-25 [0, 2, 6, 8] (a whole-tone subset)—the same 4-25 which occurs prominently in mm.4-5 and which is the set of all elements belonging to the V $^{7}_{\flat 5}$ harmony.

Before the completion of this bass arpeggiation to A♭, the voice leading in the upper registers departs from elements of the V7 harmony: For the sixth formed between the high A♭ and the C below in m.1 progresses to the sixth a whole-step above—B♭-E♭♭—in mm.2-4. In these and subsequent measures through m.11, the augmented triad D♮-G♭-B♭ (a subset of the underlying whole-tone scale) is the predominant component in the upper registers. (The A♭ ostensibly remains effective through these measures in the bass.) In mm.4-6, the G♭-B♭ third is connected by a stepwise motion in the upper register. This third also appears prominently an octave lower at the beginning of the piece. Further, in mm.4-10 a descending motion fills in the G♭-D♮ third in the uppermost register in the middleground.

Note that in this analysis the E♭ in m.10 is interpreted as a chromatic passing tone connecting E♮ in m.7 with D♮ immediately following. This interpretation is subject to a certain amount of question. Whereas in previous measures nonwhole-tone elements may be relegated to auxiliary status without serious difficulties, this E♭ may appear to be more important than D♮. The set formed by the elements of mm.9-11 is 6-Z19, which contains an equal number of even- and odd-numbered pcs. Thus weight is already being shifted toward the elements of the complementary whole-tone scale at this point. However, since the original whole-tone scale underlies the material of m.12 ff., this E♭ does ultimately yield in favor of a whole-tone element. The D♮ in m.10 occurs in the same register in m.12, confirming the analysis of a resolution to D♮ in m.10. Further, the D♮ in m.10 may take precedence over E♭ on the basis of its beginning a restatement of the pattern initiated by the D♮ an octave lower at the end of m.8.

Only the G♭ of the D♮-G♭-B♭ augmented triad qualifies as an element of the V7/D♭ harmony which possibly underlies the opening measures of the piece. The B♭-D♮ sixth, though important over a proportionately large span of time, is, as mentioned above, involved in a patterned voice leading and in m.12 proceeds to the sixth a whole-step above—C-E♮. The material of mm.12-17 is equivalent to that of mm.1-6 transposed up four half-steps. Thus the pattern of ascending parallel sixths continues in these measures, reaching the D♮-G♭ sixth in mm.13-15. (Note that this sixth also belongs to the D♮-G♭-B♭ augmented triad!) Instead of duplicating (at the new level of transposition) the material of mm.7-8 in mm.18-19, new material is introduced. An important effect of this unexpected event is the avoidance of the low bass register in which A♭ was established in m.8. Thus the bass C in m.17 is denied the structural weight of this A♭, which has yet to be strongly displaced. The new material in mm.18-19 closely resembles the passage in mm.10-11, but involves a completely unrelated set, 8-28. Here again there is an equal distribution of even- and odd-numbered pcs. This distribution is structurally exploited in this passage, for the four-note subset of one whole-tone scale is alternated with that of the complementary whole-tone set. Significantly, both four-note subsets are 4-25—the important set formed by $V\,^{7}_{\flat 5}$ at the beginning of the piece. Set 8-28 is the complement of the diminished-seventh chord, which is itself formed by the prominent pcs in either outer voice and in general by the successive transpositions up three half-steps. Note that the upper voice in mm.18-19 consists of interlocking forms of the diminished-seventh chord (annotated in the score by means of stems in opposite directions). This contrasts with the melody in mm.9-11, where two forms of the minor triad are dovetailed. The later (8-28) statement of the A4 idea (in m.18 ff.) appears to be more unstable than the earlier (6-Z19) presentation in m.9 ff. for several reasons: (1) set 8-28 contains four pcs of the complementary 6-35 instead of the three found in the earlier version (6-Z19); and (2) it employs forms of the diminished-seventh chord, which probably connote greater instability than do the minor triads intermeshed in mm.9-11.

In spite of the fact that the voice leading of mm.18-19 involves mainly arpeggiation, underlying linear connections may be demonstrated here, at least for the compound parts of the upper voice. Most important, at m.20 we return to a clear statement of the D-F♯ sixth first reached in m.13-15. This coincides with a transposed repetition of m.17 up two half-steps. (Note that the chord connection between the final chord of m.19 and the chord in m.20 resembles a tonal cadence.) The D-F♯ sixth then proceeds up a whole-step to E♮-G♯ in m.20, whereupon the material of mm.18-19 is interjected (transposed up two half-steps) in mm.21-22. The sixth expected to occur next is almost attained by the end of the A section—but not quite. The E♮ does progress to G♭ in the upper voice, but the lower voice moves no further than G♯, which is now spelled A♭ and occurs only an octave lower than the G in m.20. This constitutes the first interruption of the pattern of parallel sixths—but the pattern is broken for an important structural purpose. For a voice exchange between outer voices—$\substack{A^{\flat} \\ G^{\flat}} \times \substack{G^{\flat} \\ A^{\flat}}$—is thereby accomplished across the span of the entire A section. (Note that the main melodic progression throughout the A section forms an entire whole-tone scale, ascending from $A^{\flat}$ to $G^{\flat}$.)

There is further evidence that this section is unified. First, the final chord of the section, in m.22, is 4-25—the same 4-25 (with the same pcs) which is heard at the beginning of the piece in mm.4-5 and which is formed by all pcs held invariant in mm.6-8. Further, this 4-25 is also found in m.20, which replicates exactly the material of m.7 an octave higher. The disclosure of this fact leads to the discovery that the events of mm.20-22 constitute an expansion of the progression of mm.6-8. In both cases the same 4-25 is held invariant throughout. The main difference is that in mm.20-22 the whole-tone invariance is accomplished in a more complicated fashion, for here pcs from the complementary whole-tone scale separate the elements of the underlying whole-tone set. (Note that only four elements [0, 2, 6, 8] of this whole-tone scale are contained in mm.20-22, but in mm.17-19, where whole-tone invariance is obtained in precisely the same manner, another 4-25 [10, 0, 4, 6] is retained throughout. Together these 4-25's, which are transpositional equivalents separated by two half-steps, comprise the entire whole-tone aggregate.) Of course, the latter passage entails an ascent into upper registers in contrast to the corresponding passage in mm.6-8, where the descent to the low bass $A^{\flat}$ is effected. As demonstrated in the sketches, the $D^{\natural}$ in the lowest part of m.20 links up with $D^{\natural}$ in the same register in m.8. The only intervening element in this register (none occur in lower registers) is $C^{\natural}$ in m.17, which functions as an auxiliary note to the $D^{\natural}$'s. By the end of the section, $D^{\natural}$, which divides the $A^{\flat}$ octave symmetrically, progresses via arpeggiation back to $A^{\flat}$, which is thus prolonged in the bass throughout the section.

We have determined, then, that a whole-tone tetrachord, 4-25, has been prolonged throughout the section over $A^{\flat}$ in the bass. This sonority possesses at least implicitly the function of $V^{7}_{\flat 5}$ in the key of $D^{\flat}$, due to the tonal expectations set up in the opening measures of the piece. The prolongation is especially artful here since it is accomplished by means of the retention of whole-tone elements throughout a succession of highly varied, ostensibly unrelated sonorities.

The gesture in mm.18-19 ends with a 4-25 which is a subset of the odd-numbered whole-tone scale (which is the underlying sonority of the B section of the piece and, of course, the complement of the whole-tone set basic to the A section). This 4-25 also contains the highest pitch heard thus far—G♮. This pitch appears to resolve to the high G♭ in m.22—indeed, the entire 4-25 in the latter half of m.19 seems to be an auxiliary chord to the final 4-25 of the A section—but G♮ also points ahead to events in the B section.

The B section begins with a shift to the complementary whole-tone plane. This shift is dramatized by an important instance of complementation: For the 4-25 formed in the left-hand arpeggiation in mm.23-24 is the complement of the 8-25 formed among all elements in mm.6-8 (where another 4-25 was held invariant throughout)! This arpeggiation sets up the lowest pitch heard thus far. (This low register will be consistently exploited only in the B section.) The melody in mm.23-26 forms the same set (6-21) as the melodic figure in m.6, and both presentations of these elements entail the same ordering and contour. Here, of course, these elements are differentiated rhythmically and comprise a significant melodic segment extended over several measures.

As mentioned earlier, the B section also is structured by a patterned progression of ascending parallel intervals. Here, three different pairs of sixths are involved, along with a pair of voices proceeding in parallel sevenths in the lowest register. Each sixth or seventh is clearly associated with a particular motivic role. For instance, the seventh is always formed by the two lowest pcs of a verticality (as in m.26), and the uppermost sixth of the pattern is formed by the fourth and fifth pcs of the melodic fragment, as in m.25. The motivic roles of various intervals are differentiated in the sketch according to the directions of stems. One complete progression of the pattern entails the ascent by one whole-step of each interval. In fact, only one complete progression (the minimum necessary to establish the pattern) takes place before the pattern is broken: For at m.35 the material from the very beginning of the piece suddenly recurs, followed by the material associated with the B section—but transposed up six half-steps from m.29 ff. instead of the expected two. The effect of this level of transposition is that some of the intervals which would have occurred had the pattern continued as expected are still attained, but they occur in other roles than those with which they had previously been associated. Another effect is that the sixths involved with the moving parts in mm.33-34 exchange roles in mm.39-40. Only at m.41 (when the material is transposed down four half-steps from the corresponding material in m.38 ff.) are these intervals presented in connection with their original roles as would have been expected in m.35 ff.—with the exception that no 6-21 melody occurs here.

The break in the voice-leading pattern at m.35 serves a definite structural purpose, however. It makes possible the exploitation of the extreme upper register in such a way as to link with the high G♭ at the end of the A section. (Had the G♮–B♮ sixth occurred in its expected role, it would not have been transferred to the extreme upper register.) This high G♮, the highest pitch in the B section, is used on the largest level as a passing note from G♭ at the end of the A section to A♭ which occurs in m.49 with the return of the A section. (The successive octave transpositions of the material of m.47 are responsible for attaining the extreme high register.) The other crucial event coincident with the breakdown of the pattern at m.35 is the establishment in this measure of the lowest pitch heard thus far in the piece—A♮, which is doubled an octave higher. This low A♮ is also involved in a large-scale connection, for it "resolves" to the A♭ in m.47, the lowest pitch of the entire piece. The material of m.47, which is very similar to that in m.35 (it is in precisely the same register but has an added chord in the right hand), marks the return of the A section. The reference to material of the A section in m.35 ff. in the middle of the B section is more than just a common factor unifying the contrasting sections of the composition, for the correspondence of subject matter in mm.35 and 47 insures that the large-scale linear connections between elements at these two points will be perceived.

In the B section retention of whole-tone elements is accomplished in a much more straightforward manner than in the A section. Five of the six possible forms of the five-note subset of the underlying (odd-numbered) whole-tone scale are found in the B section: m.23 [11, 1, 3, 5, 7], which will be considered the original level of transposition (T_0) in this listing; m.26, transposed up four half-steps (T_4); m.29, T_{10}; m.31, T_8; m.32, T_6; m.38, T_0; m.41, T_8. No attempt to provide a transition back to the A section by balancing odd- and even-numbered pcs is evident in the B section (as was evident in the A section). In fact, the B section contains only four elements of the even-numbered whole-tone scale—pcs 2, 4, 6, and 10.

There are, however, important connections between the A and B sections on the basis of complementation. One instance, involving 4-25 at the beginning of the B section, has already been cited. The other important occurrences involve sets formed with elements of m.31, the exact midpoint of the composition. Although whole-tone invariance is a basic procedure throughout, the entire whole-tone scale (6-35) appears as a unified segment at the surface of the music only twice—once in m.31 and again as the final chord of the piece. These two 6-35's are complements (although this fact probably comes as no great surprise, given the fact that the two sections of the piece operate on complementary whole-tone planes). More compelling is the fact that the 7-33 found in m.31 is the complement of the 5-33 which is the set of all whole-tone elements occurring in the first eleven measures of the piece. However, even more astonishing, Scriabin's mystic chord, 6-34, is formed by the upbeat to m.31 (pc 4) plus the 5-33 on the downbeat of m.31. This chord is in fact the complement of the 6-34 presented so teasingly in mm.4-5 of the piece! This complement relation, involving forms of the mystic chord—a sonority to which we can be sure Scriabin was quite sensitive—can hardly be dismissed as coincidental, especially since this chord occurs at only one other point in the piece. (The other occurrence is at m.15, transposed up four half-steps from the 6-34 in mm.4-5. This level of transposition produces the maximum of four pcs held invariant between the two set-forms.) There is thus every indication that Scriabin regarded m.31 as an important point for the symmetry of the structure—even though this measure does not coincide with a significant point in the phrasing of the work. The important set-forms which occur here are no doubt primarily responsible for changes in the treatment of the accompaniment which occur in mm.29-32 (cf. mm.23-26).

In terms of the structure of "Enigme" as a whole, the purpose of the B section appears to be to connect and/or embellish the more important elements of the A sections which frame it. These functions are most conspicuously served by the extreme outer voices: For A♮ introduced in the bass in m.35 clearly serves in an auxiliary capacity to A♭ in m.47. (The pitch A♭ is also established as the effective bass tone for the A section, but an octave higher.) And the high G♮ (m.40) connects G♭ (m.22) with A♭ (m.49). (Note that the high G♮ is respelled F𝄪 in m.41 ff. This respelling produces the interval of the augmented sixth between the low A♮ effective in the bass and the high F𝄪, and this interval then expands outward in resolving to the A♭ octave formed between the main outer voices in m.47 ff. The minor seventh formed between the bass A♮ and G♮ would have demanded an inward resolution to a smaller interval.) By the end of the piece, this primary linear succession progresses up to B♭.

The most important question concerning "Enigme" is whether the piece is Scriabin's first atonal work (and, thus, one of the first atonal works by any composer). As has been seen, the piece is not without tonal implications. A whole-tone chord supported by A♭ in the bass is prolonged throughout the A section—not simply by means of retention of elements of this chord but also through the special tonal-contrapuntal device of an exchange of elements in the outer voices at the beginning and end of the section. In view of the D♭ major key signature and the presentation of the sum of all elements from the D♭ major scale as the first main segment of the composition, this whole-tone sonority is very likely perceived as having a dominant function in this key. Moreover, this chord is actually allowed to "cadence" to a chord on D♭ (albeit a whole-tone sonority, not a consonant triad) at the beginning of the B section. Ultimately, of course, the chord on A♭ returns with and is prolonged throughout the second A section. However, in spite of the fact that a V-I cadence in D♭ is implicit, the reversal of the usual tonal functional associations found in connection with A B A form (that is, the tonic is typically prolonged throughout the A sections while another function, possibly the dominant, is prolonged throughout the B section) prevents this cadence from exerting its full tonal effect. In terms of the structure as a whole, one would have to conclude that the whole-tone dominant chord on A♭ is prolonged throughout (since this chord frames the possible tonic in the B section). The ultimate cadence to D♭ must be assumed to take place, if at all, after the piece has ended. (This is a step beyond other compositions by Scriabin such as the "Feuillet d'album" Op. 58, which ends with the dominant harmony suspended over the tonic note in the bass.)

It is important to note that in this piece the tonality hinges on the fundamental activity in the bass register. Without the bass as an organizing force, little tonal sense may be made of the upper voices. In "Enigme" the overall upper-voice motion, which spans a major ninth from A♭ to B♭ via ascent by whole-step, appears to conflict with the A♭ prolonged in the bass. The ending of the piece is of course deliberately inconclusive. If one considers that with the return of the A section in m.47 ff. an unfolding from one A♭ to another an octave higher is completed in the upper voice, then the remainder of the piece occurring after the completion of this octave-span might be interpreted to begin another cycle in a structure which could continue ad infinitum. This aspect of perpetual motion is of course enhanced by the ability of the whole-tone scale to avoid tonal gravitation. Significantly, the piece ends in the extreme upper register at the greatest possible distance from the tonal influence of the bass. Thus a tonal structure is implicitly contained within the piece (specifically in the first forty-nine measures), at least to the extent that a dominant function is prolonged. But the tonal forces here are deliberately attenuated by the commencement of another cycle of the structure and the avoidance of a cadence from the prolonged dominant to a tonic at the close of the piece.

A final consideration must be the larger context provided by Op. 52 in its entirety, where "Enigme" occurs as the second of three pieces. The whole-tone scale is an important sonority in the other pieces of the opus as well, both of which are tonal in a more conventional sense. (The Poem Op. 52, No. 1 is in C major, and the "Poème languide" Op. 52, No. 3 is in B major.) In general, the whole-tone components function as dominants or as dominant preparations in these two pieces. In particular, the "Poème languide" appears to contain references to events in "Enigme." It begins with the even-numbered whole-tone scale (with which "Enigme" ends) functioning as ♭II in B major. At the end of the piece, a whole-tone dominant cadences to the tonic, and there are definite links between this event and the preceding composition. (These are illustrated at the end of the analytical sketches of "Enigme.") It may be that the links between "Enigme" and the other pieces in Op. 52 occur only because Scriabin sought a rationale for the most avant-garde work he had composed up to that time. Later, however, he did perform "Enigme" without the other pieces of the opus as legitimating frames. Clearly, the varied functions of the whole-tone components in Op. 52, No. 1 and No. 3 (in C and B respectively) establish that the whole-tone scale is subject to many harmonic interpretations. Neither C major nor B major are indicated to any extent in "Enigme" itself.

Although "Enigme" Op. 52, No. 2 constitutes perhaps Scriabin's furthest extension of implicit tonality in the music of his transitional period (1903–10), tonal forces are nevertheless responsible in large part for the overall coherence of the work. At the same time, the retention of whole-tone elements participates in the prolongation of the dominant function, while other nontonal relationships, in particular those based on complementation, are important in establishing structural bonds between the contrasting sections of the piece.

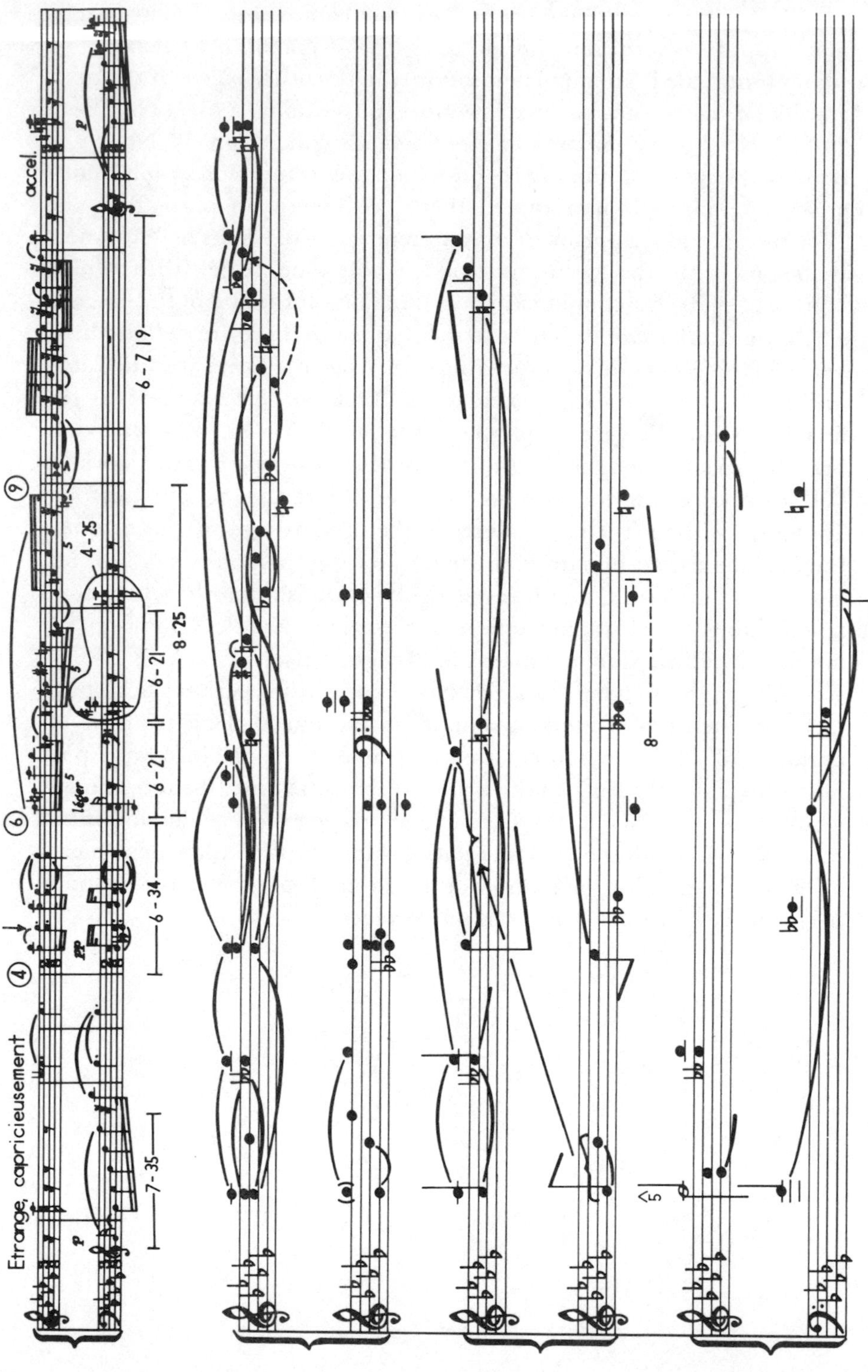
Etrange, capricieusement
accel.
4-25
7-35
6-34
6-21
6-21
8-25
6-Z19
4-25

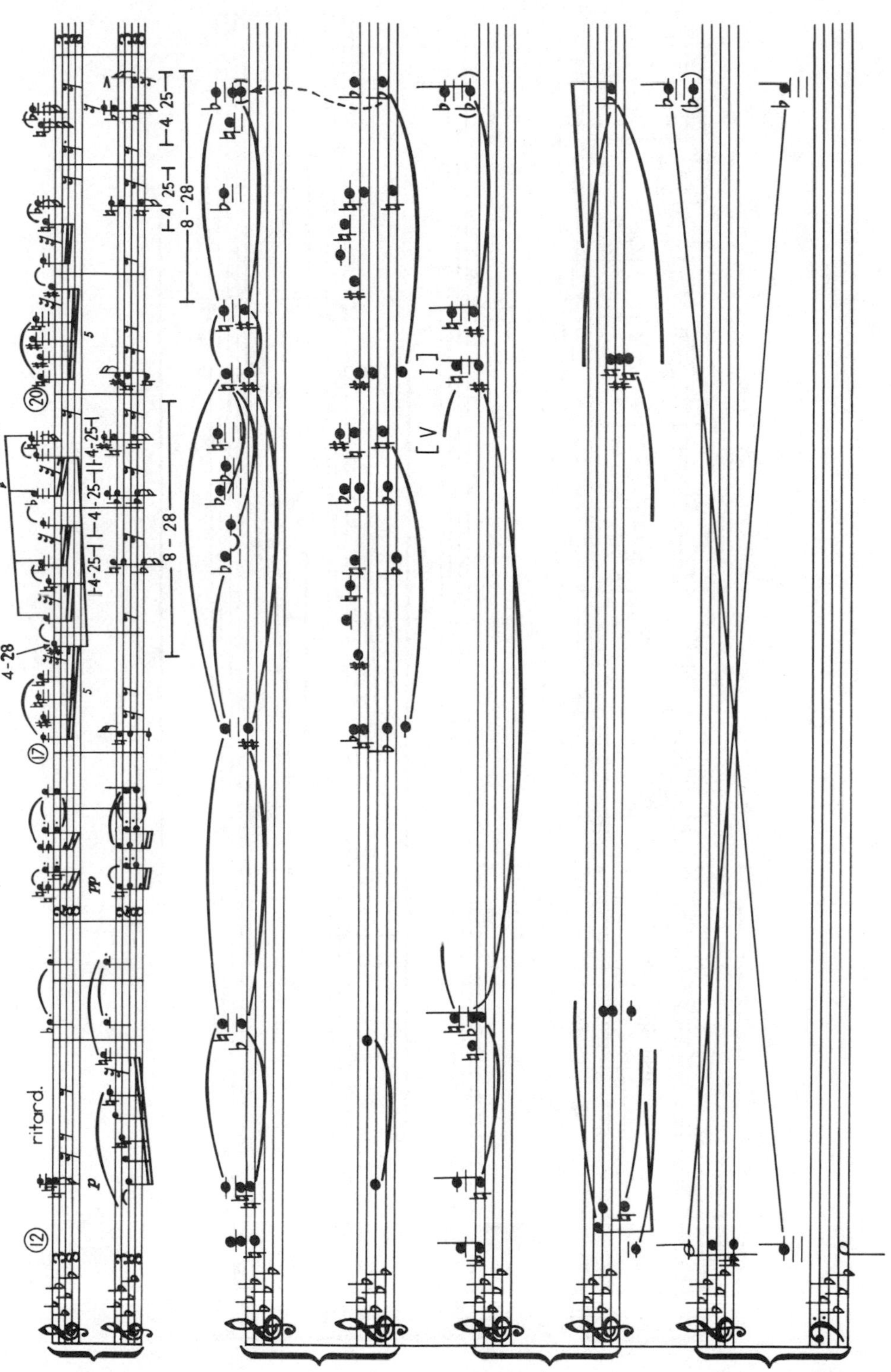
12
ritard.
p
pp
17
4-28
4-28
20
4-25
8 – 28
[V I]

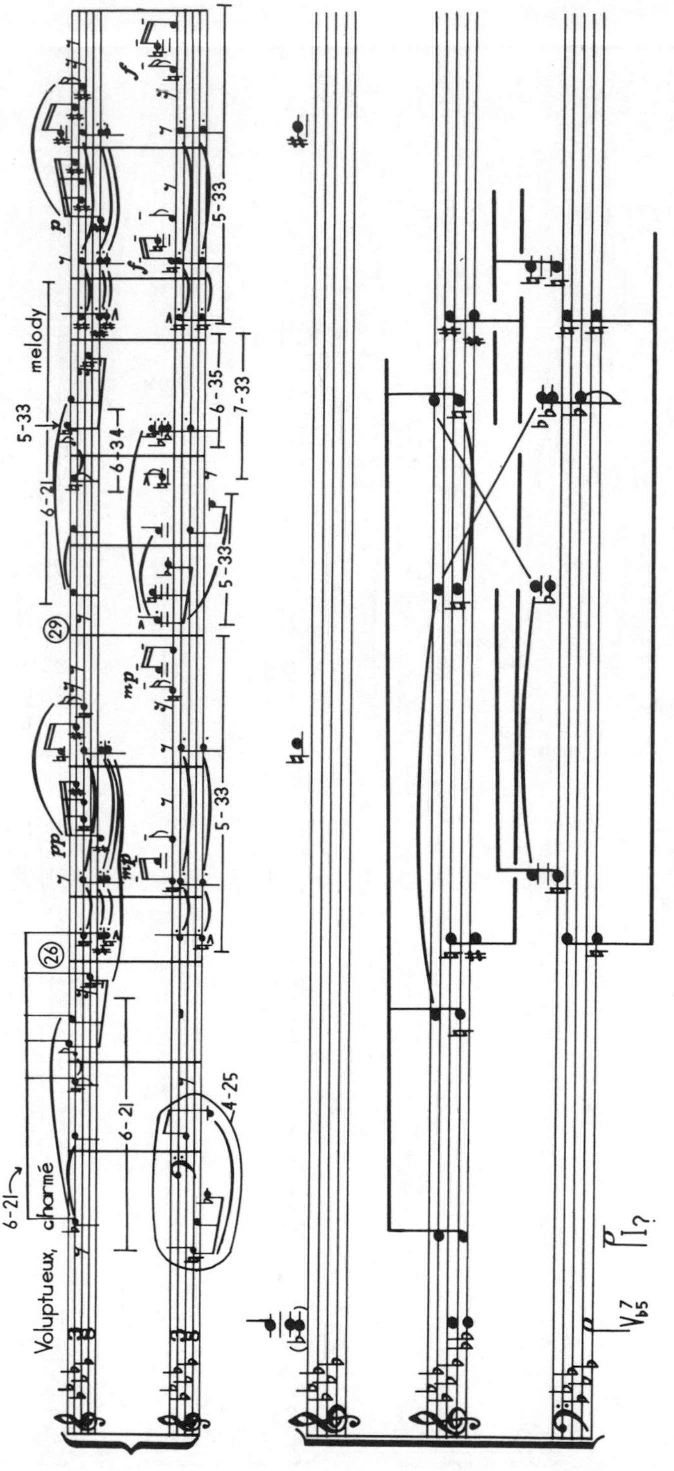
Voluptueux, charmé
6-21
26
29
melody
5-33
6-34
6-35
7-33
4-25
V$^{7}_{b5}$
I?

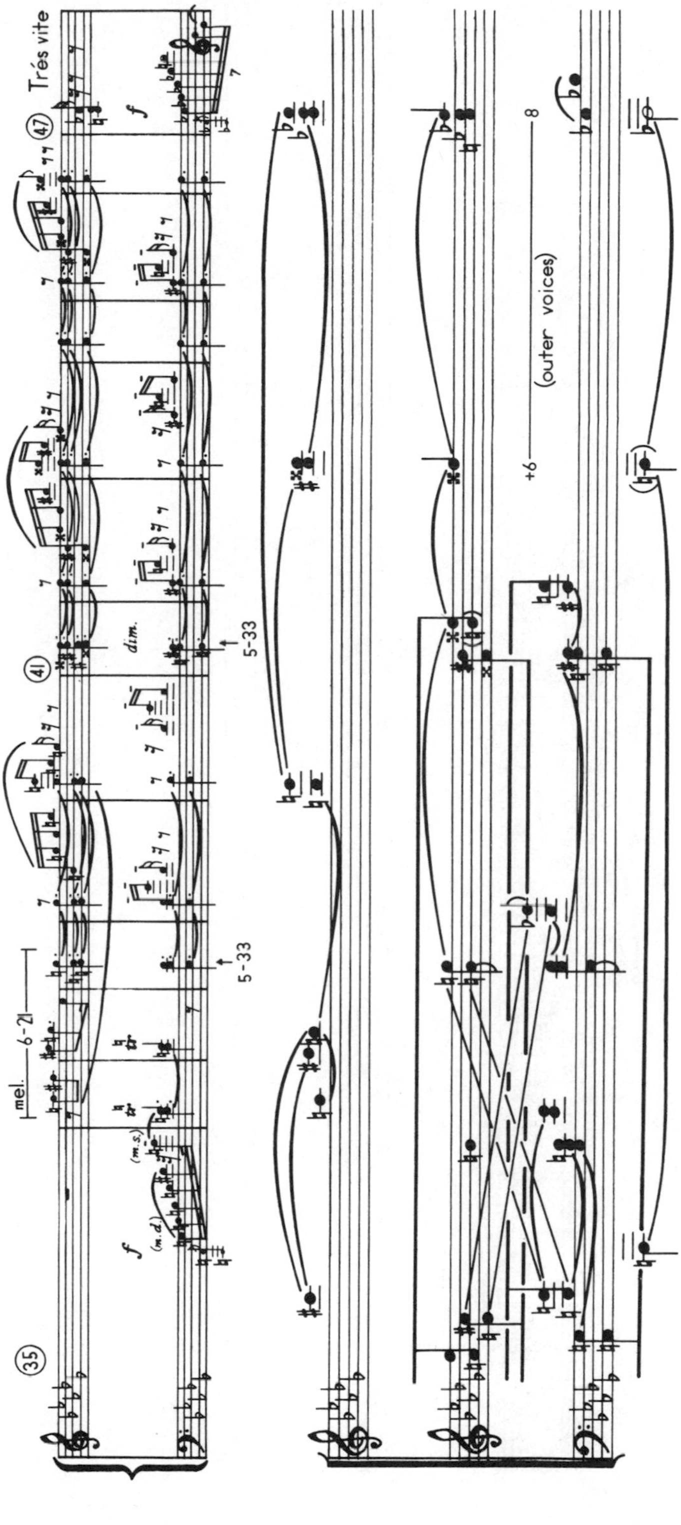
35
mel.
6-21
f
(m.d.)
(m.s.)
5-33
41
dim.
5-33
47
Trés vite
f
+6
(outer voices)
8

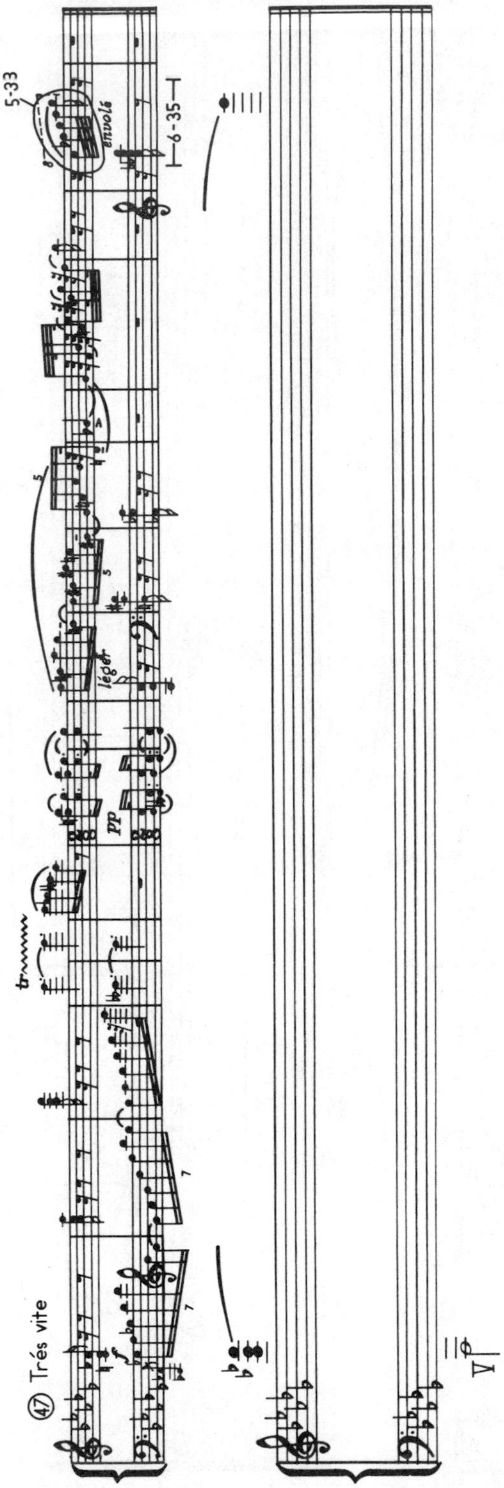
47
Trés vite
5-33
envolé
6-35
léger
pp

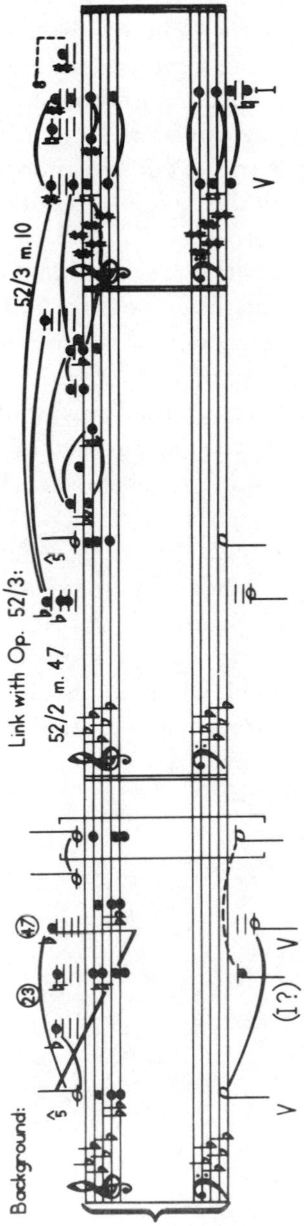
Background:
23
47
(I?)
V
Link with Op. 52/3:
52/2 m. 47
52/3 m. 10
I

In closing, I wish to stress the danger of analyzing a single transitional work without understanding its place in the chronology of the composer's work as a whole. Many composers, like Scriabin, were experimenting independently with innovative compositional procedures during the early years of this century, often adopting highly idiosyncratic methods bearing little relation to those employed by others. In order to realize the structural significance of an unusual device or procedure, one must look beyond the context of the composition at hand, and examine an adequate sample of the composer's work which represents every stage and aspect of his growth.

It is crucial to analyze a transitional composition thoroughly not only in terms of innovative components and procedures but also in terms of its relation to conventional tonal structures. As Schenker demonstrated, tonal compositions are integral entities possessing a unique organic coherence resulting from relationships among levels of structure. Therefore, if one is to analyze the tonal aspects of a transitional work, one must deal with this work (insofar as possible) as a holistically unified structure. Judgments concerning parts of compositions are not sufficient since they do not come to grips with the essential factor in tonal organization—structural coherence. Under no circumstances does the mere pointing out of tonal-like configurations, gestures, or progressions constitute a valid analysis establishing the tonality of a composition. Rather, in order to demonstrate that such components fulfill tonal functions, their precise roles within a conventional hierarchical tonal structure must always be specified. If no such explanation is possible, a basis in another type of structure must be sought.

Two Articles by Ernst Oster

The *Fantaisie-Impromptu*: A Tribute to Beethoven

ERNST OSTER

The *Fantaisie-Impromptu*, now one of Chopin's most frequently performed and popular compositions, was not published by Chopin himself. This was done by his friend Jules Fontana, who edited the work—along with numerous other unpublished pieces—after Chopin's death. He thus acted contrary to Chopin's expressed desire never to bring these compositions before the public. And indeed, when examining them critically, we find that very few of them are comparable in musical value to Chopin's other works. A great number of them were written at an early age; others, like the well-known waltzes in B minor and E minor, are comparatively primitive with regard to their form and whole conception. Only two of the mazurkas, Op. 67, No. 2 in G minor and Op. 68, No. 4 in F minor, which Chopin wrote in the year of his death, 1849, might have been published by him if he had lived longer.

The *Fantaisie-Impromptu*, however, was written in 1834, together with the Four Mazurkas, Op. 17, and the great E♭ major Waltz, Op. 18, compositions that show Chopin at the height of his mastery. What might have been his reasons for keeping the *Fantaisie-Impromptu* from being published? There can hardly be any doubt that it possesses high musical value. This is proven not so much by its great popularity, but by the fact that at all times it was to be found in the repertoire of the greatest artists. Niecks, Chopin's foremost biographer, writes:

> Whatever Fontana says to the contrary in the preface to his collection of Chopin's posthumous works, the composer unequivocably expressed the wish that his manuscripts should not be published. Indeed, no one acquainted with the artistic character of the master, and the nature of the works published by himself, could for a moment imagine that the latter would at any time or in any circumstances have given his consent to the publication of insignificant and imperfect compositions such as most of those presented to the world by his ill-advised friend are. Still, besides the *Fantaisie-Impromptu*, which one would not like to have lost, and one or two mazurkas, which cannot but be prized, . . .[1]

1. Frederick Niecks, *Frederick Chopin as a Man and Musician*, London and New York: Novello, Ewer and Co., 1888, vol. 2, pp. 270-271.

In another article he uses expressions like "artistically unimportant," "imperfect, in every respect inferior trifles" for the posthumous works, and says about the waltzes, Opp. 69 and 70, in particular:

> The non-publication of these waltzes by the composer proves to me what an excellent judge he was of his own works—a rare gift in authors.[2]

Yet of the *Fantaisie-Impromptu* he writes:

> [The *Fantaisie-Impromptu*] is the most valuable of the compositions published by Fontana; indeed it has become one of the favorites of the pianoforte-playing world . . . According to Fontana, Chopin composed this piece about 1834. Why did he keep it in his portfolio? I suspect he missed in it, more especially in the middle section, that degree of distinction and perfection of detail which alone satisfied his fastidious taste.[3]

And Huneker:

> The *Fantaisie-Impromptu* . . . is one of the few posthumous works of Chopin worthy of consideration . . . Its involuted first phrases suggest the Bellini-an fioriture so dear to Chopin, but the D-flat part is without nobility. Here is the same kind of saccharine melody that makes mawkish the trio in the "Marche Funèbre."[4]

Huneker's opinion about the middle section cannot necessarily be shared. The fact that it is often played in a cloying manner does not mean that it actually is sweetish. With the same right one might as well call the D-flat major Prelude sugary, to take another composition in the same key. We shall see later on what a poor judge Huneker is when we examine the "Bellini-an fioriture" of the first measures. But it should be said at this point that we shall not get anywhere using aesthetic generalities like "without nobility" and "mawkish." At least they are much too indefinite to supply a satisfactory answer to the question why Chopin did not publish the composition.

The only procedure which can help us is a technical exploration and thorough investigation of its tonal life and content.

To be sure, music theory as it is commonly taught will not be of great help for our purpose: It confines itself chiefly to a "harmonic analysis" and is unable to give account of the real life and deeper problems of a composition. The only musical approach that brings to light the most obscure details, which under ordinary processes of analysis would go unobserved, is that of Heinrich Schenker.

---

2. Frederick Niecks, "A Critical Commentary on the Pianoforte Works of Frederick Chopin," *The Monthly Musical Record* **9** (1879), p. 179.
3. Niecks, *Frederick Chopin*, vol. 2, p. 261.
4. James Huneker, *Chopin: The Man and His Music*, New York: Charles Scribner's Sons, 1901, p. 241.

It is deeply regretted that today, more than ten years after Schenker's death, none of the books of this great musician has been translated into English, nor anything exhaustive written on his work. It is the author's intention to demonstrate what surprising results can be achieved by using Schenker's principles, and to prove what unexplored regions of music, generally considered to be well-known, still await actual discovery.

An exact investigation by the author into the tonal content of the *Fantaisie-Impromptu* resulted in the startling fact that it had been inspired and strongly influenced by another renowned composition: Beethoven's "Sonata quasi una Fantasia" in C♯ minor, Op. 27, No. 2, the so-called Moonlight Sonata. (This title does not originate from Beethoven, just as the name "Fantaisie-Impromptu" is not Chopin's.)

It is necessary to anticipate this finding, and then, in order to prove it, to provide an analysis of both compositions. For the sake of economy we will discuss the common features through which their close relationship is expressed.

Of the three movements of Beethoven's sonata, it was mainly the finale which inspired Chopin to write the *Fantaisie-Impromptu*, and it shall therefore be dealt with first.

In the first two measures the two chord strokes marked "sforzato" and "pedal" by Beethoven stand out most strongly. The same is true of measures 4, 6, and so on. From measure 9 on the picture changes for a short time: the bass, having arrived at the dominant G♯, is sustained, and it is as if measures 9 to 14 represented one large fermata. To be sure it is not an ordinary fermata, the tones of which are struck only once. Instead it is prolonged and exquisitely elaborated, the motion of the preceding measures still vibrating within it.

After the close of the fermata, Beethoven carries on the initial idea with renewed and intensified vigor. The outward picture alone, the uniformity of the motivic material, indicates that the prolonged fermata was but an interruption, like someone standing still to catch a new breath.

The chord strokes continue after the fermata to the entrance of the second subject, and condensation of their motion from the beginning reveals that their highest tones ascend from $g\sharp^2$ over $c\sharp^3$ to e^3. This same motion occurs in the first two measures: The quarter notes of the right hand again reveal $g\sharp$-$c\sharp$-e^1, $g\sharp^1$-$c\sharp^2$-e^2, and even the first three sixteenth notes repeat the idea. [See example 1.]

Example 1

Astonishing as this may be, we must go still further and ask: What is the meaning of all this, what is the significance of the elaboration, the expansion of this simple motive? The answer is as wonderful as it is simple: The first three tones of the entire sonata present the same motive. It is, in other words, the main motive of the "Sonata quasi una Fantasia," the motive on which Beethoven improvises.

Beethoven also uses this motive as the basis for his "phantasy" in the first and the second movements, in the first movement perhaps in an even more ingenious manner than in the finale. Since, however, it was mainly the finale which influenced Chopin, we shall now proceed with its discussion, and comment briefly on the other movements later.

It may be asked how the tones $g\sharp^2$-$c\sharp^3$-e^3 in measures 2 to 16 can be understood as one motive, as a simple arpeggio of the C♯ minor chord, without taking into consideration the many different harmonies between measures 2 and 15. The similarity of the first measures to measures 15 to 20 is, in fact, an indication that an inner relation, an actual connection, exists between them. For in all truly great works of art, repetitions, similarities, and associations of sound are never just accidental—they are always indicative of a connection in content or form.

The harmonies of measures 3 to 8 can be explained in a very simple manner: While the top voice states the first two tones, $g\sharp^2$ and $c\sharp^3$, of the large arpeggio, the bass moves stepwise downward to the dominant G♯. The bass tones between C♯ and G♯ are merely passing tones, and Beethoven's harmonies result almost automatically from the vertical coincidence of the two horizontal movements.

The harmonic meaning of the written-out fermata, which interrupts the large arpeggio motive in such a drastic manner, is somewhat more difficult to understand. Not only is the dominant *per se* much stronger than the preceding passing harmonies, but the interrupting fermata also uses a considerable amount of time. However, if we realize that measures 1 to 15 have no meaning other than their being a large-scale motion from tonic (measure 1) to tonic (measure 15) with an inserted dominant, and if we then hear a similar insertion in the top voice between $c^{\sharp 3}$ and e^3, there exists no discrepancy between the large arpeggio of the top voice and the motion to the dominant in the bass. [See example 2.]

Example 2

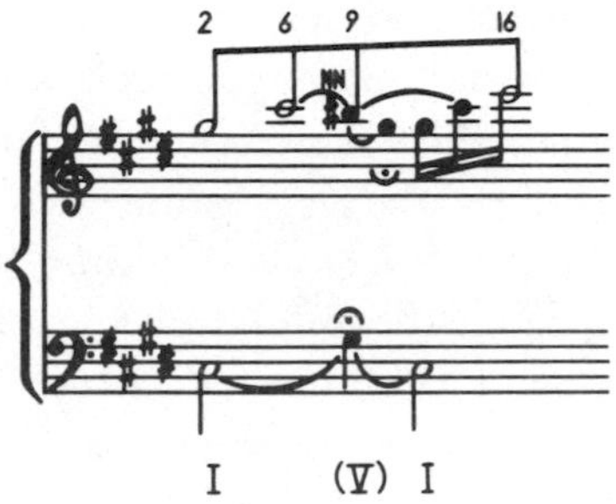

As the bass moves from the tonic to its fifth and back, $c^{\sharp 3}$ moves to its neighbor note (NN) $b^{\sharp 2}$ (measure 9) and back to $c^{\sharp 3}$. The second $c^{\sharp 3}$ does not appear as part of the actual melodic line, however. It is as if the composer, with a sudden spurt, reaches out and grasps toward the last tone, e^3, having no time to repeat $c^{\sharp 3}$ expressly.

The purpose of this interpolated dominant is that it isolates and delays the entrance of the high point e^3, whereby the striking power of e^3 is considerably heightened. Before its entrance Beethoven repeats the entire arpeggio $g^{\sharp 2}$-$c^{\sharp 3}$-e^3 once more in sixteenths, thus summarizing measures 1-16 (example 2).

The second subject and the development are of lesser interest for our particular purpose. It must be mentioned, however, that the first motive of the second theme is derived from the main motive: it answers the upward arpeggio with one in the opposite direction. [See example 3.]

Example 3

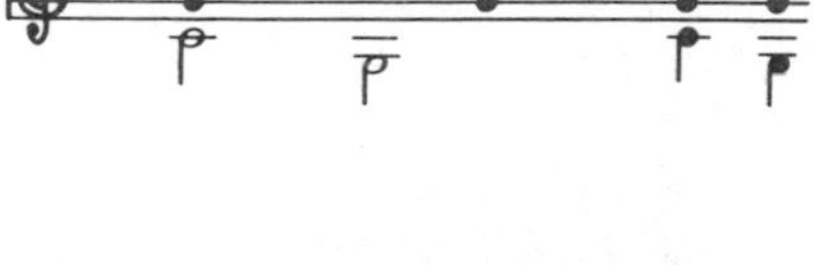

In all its simplicity, this is an incomparably great idea. And only if we are aware of the connection of the two motives can we fully comprehend the disparity between the first and the second "theme," and the true character of the latter: after the energetic ascending arpeggio, which was extended over the first 20 measures; the quasi-tired sinking down of the opening of the second subject; the harsh staccato strokes followed by a smooth legato; the sforzati, followed by the piano. It is a striking musical picture, testimony of Beethoven's greatness.

The manner in which Beethoven interrupted the large arpeggio in measure 9 and yet continued it, so that we cannot fail hearing measures 1-20 as an entity and as this same arpeggio, was the achievement of a master in composition. The interruption presents such a difficult problem that a composer inferior to Beethoven would have failed to solve it—perhaps he would never even have tried to tackle it.

Yet Beethoven does not content himself with this great achievement. In order to build up the last and greatest climax in the recapitulation and coda he employs the very same idea of the interruption, although on a much larger scale, still more imposing.

At the beginning of the recapitulation we realize immediately that Beethoven does not ascend to e³; instead, after c♯³ and the written-out fermata, he continues at once with the second theme. Beethoven brings this second theme, the leading melody tone of which is g♯, to its close as in the exposition, and then goes into the coda. He does all this in order to save e³ for the coda and thus to state the complete uninterrupted arpeggio there for the first time. [Example 4] shows the general idea; and example 5 demonstrates the execution of the arpeggio in detail:

Example 4

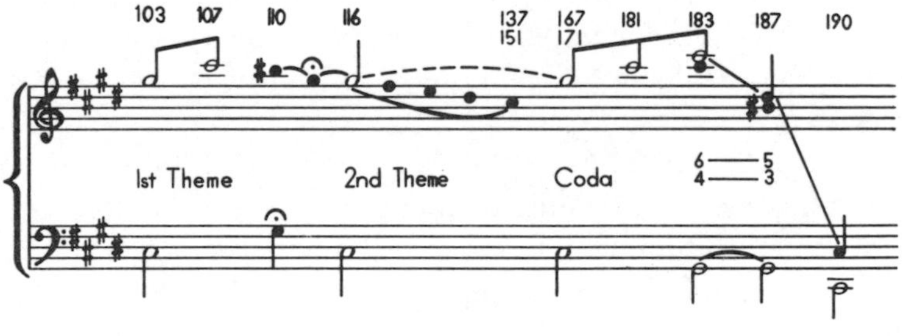

After g♯² in measures 171-176 Beethoven inserts the neighbor note a² (mainly because of the bass line) and then goes to c♯³ and e³, the latter being reached only in the $\frac{6}{4}$ chord on the dominant. Then, following the "adagio" measures, the motive appears for the last time, uninterrupted and based entirely upon the tonic harmony, as at the beginning of the first movement of the entire sonata.

Example 5

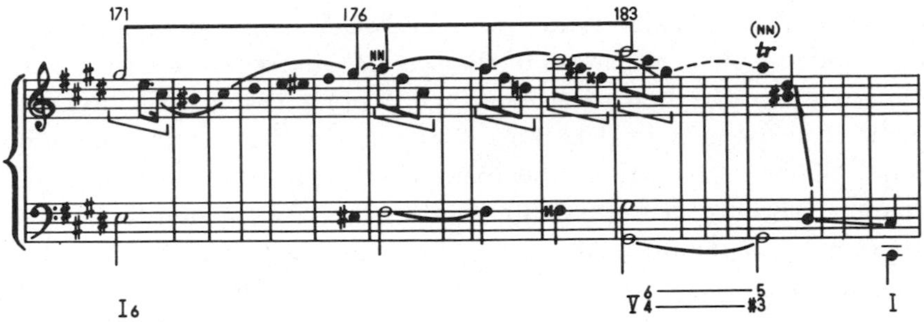

Having arrived at the climax on the $\frac{6}{4}$ chord, Beethoven has the truly magnificent idea of introducing the inversion of the motive. The entrance of the inversion stops the impetuous upsurge, and makes the ascending arpeggio flow back over its original course, as it were, indicating that we are at the end of the composition. And how Beethoven's genius has carried out this idea! At first we encounter the inversion three times in eighths, not triplets, without doubt a reference to the beginning of the first movement. In other words these triplets are an inversion of the beginning of the *entire* composition. After this, Beethoven continues in sixteenth notes—an inversion of the beginning of the finale. And just as the beginning of the finale contained the motive in quarter-note rhythm (example 1), so the inversion of the sixteenth notes contains the inverted arpeggio motive (see the down-stemmed quarter notes and the brackets in example 6). As if this were not enough, the three measures quoted in example 6 also express the inverted motive on a large scale: The first measure has as first and last tone e, transferring the high e^3 to the lower octave (see the dotted slurs). The second measure expresses in the same manner c♯, and in the third measure we have arrived at G♯, the last three notes being e–c♯–G♯ again, this time in sixteenth notes. It is of an unparalleled ingenuity the manner in which Beethoven has compressed

Example 6

the motive in all these different sizes into hardly more than two measures. Without any doubt this passage has to be regarded as the high point of the entire sonata.

Furthermore the rhythmic variety Beethoven brings to the motive is noteworthy. In the triplets the first tone e is emphasized, in the succeeding first group of quarter notes the accent lies on $c\sharp^1$, and in the last group the final G♯ falls on the strong beat. Seven or even eight times, if we count the sixteenth notes in the second quarter in measure 2, the motive appears in these short measures. It is like the downfall into hell, depicted in paintings of the Last Judgment by Rubens and other Baroque painters. Just as the bodies of men in the paintings are seemingly in chaotic disorder, the motives tumble down toward the depths (G♯) that are to embrace them all. At first they descend slowly, in eighth-note triplets, then accelerate in their plunge, in sixteenths. The two quarter-note motives, standing metrically at different places of the measure, seem to be flung into the general downfall, and, as if powerless, are dashed down along with the others.

The huge concentration of the inverted motives at this point forms a kind of counterweight to all the preceding places where the motive had appeared ascending, starting from the first movement. It is as though the equilibrium were restored; after this the motive appears only once more in the last five measures of the movement, ascending as well as descending in quarter notes.

Incidentally, Beethoven introduces the inversion masterfully. He precedes it by the second subject (measure 171), the beginning of which is a free inversion of the arpeggio motive, as was mentioned previously (example 3). Subsequently, as further preparation, the inversion also appears at the neighbor note a^2 (measure 177) and at $c\sharp^3$ (measure 181), then in its fullest development at e^3 on the $\frac{6}{4}$ chord, as we have just described (see the brackets in example 5).

The first and second movements of the sonata shall be touched upon only briefly, since they are of minor importance for this comparison with the *Fantaisie-Impromptu*.

The first movement is a free phantasy. As if to improvise, the composer wanders aimlessly from key to key, without any definite melody or theme crystallizing. It seems purely accidental that at e^2, the highest tone of the first section (measure 27), the C♯ minor harmony is again reached. And yet it is no mere accident. For in the whole first section of the first movement the idea of the arpeggio motive, with which we are already familiar from the last movement, was present in Beethoven's mind. With g$\sharp^1$ the "melody" enters in measure 5, c$\sharp^2$ in measure 23 is earmarked by the return of the dotted motive, and the drive towards and attainment of the climax at e^2 are brought into relief by the "crescendo" and "piano" (according to Beethoven's manuscript), the first dynamic marks of real significance after the pianissimo of the beginning. [See example 7.]

Example 7

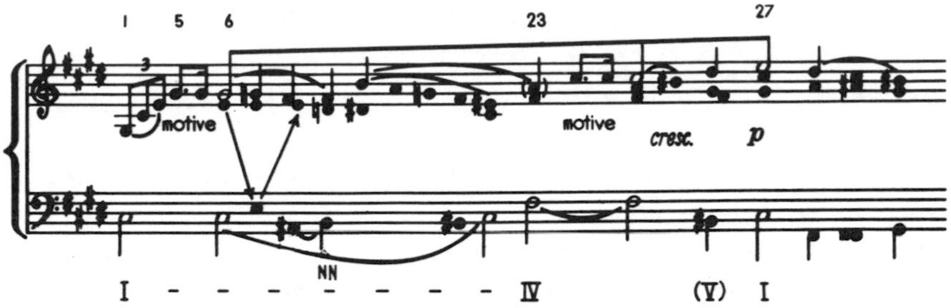

We cannot go into the details of construction, but this short sketch will give an approximate idea of the connections. It is hardly necessary to mention that this sketch and the following one (example 8) are derived from thorough detailed analyses.

Only now do we understand the true meaning of the movement. It does not show an aimless drifting around, not an arbitrary improvisation. As if by a hidden bond all the musical motions are held together by the motive. Now we also recognize what Beethoven understood by the title "quasi una Fantasia": It was his intention to give the impression, the *semblance* of an entirely free phantasy. Yet there exists in art, as in life, no unbridled freedom, no freedom without law. Thus even the freest phantasy—provided that it is meant to be a work of art—must be logically coherent. The coherence may be of a purely contrapuntal and harmonic nature, or it can be strengthened by melodic or motivic ideas which are apt to give the composition a somewhat programmatic character. An example of the second one, in addition to the first movement of the C♯ minor Sonata, is Mozart's Piano Phantasy in D minor. The fact that very few composers were able to write true phantasies is testimony to the difficulty of writing such a composition, where it is necessary never to lose sight of the guiding idea, maintaining, however, the semblance of arbitrariness. Really productive in this field were perhaps only Johann Sebastian Bach and his son Carl Philipp Emanuel, whose works, incomprehensibly enough, are still as good as unknown. In Mozart, Haydn, and Beethoven this form is found much more rarely, and probably the only great composer of the later period who wrote free phantasies in larger number is Chopin. Some of his compositions, the Ballades or the F♯ major Impromptu, are phantasies of the freest kind, although they are not as greatly conceived as those of their predecessors. The *Fantaisie-Impromptu*, however, is written in too outspoken a form to be pronounced a free phantasy.

This, then, is the secret of the first movement of the Moonlight Sonata. With all the "technical" mastership which is revealed in it, it is filled with an indescribable mood of longing. However, this mood originates in turn from the manner in which the three tones of the motive are drawn apart and separated from each other by wide spaces. To be sure, this has very little to do with moonlight—rather with the enlightened spirit of a genius.

The following simple sketch (example 8) shows the execution of the basic motive in the second movement. It is obvious that the key of D♭ major stands for C♯ major. Therefore our motive, here turned to Major, is a♭-d♭-f (instead of g♯-c♯-e♯). Apparently it was Beethoven's idea to employ the motive in its original form in the trio only; for the trio, the middle section of the movement, is also its center of gravity from a standpoint of sound. Only here Beethoven takes up the low fifth C♯-G♯ of the left hand which he had relinquished at the end of the first movement, and which later opens the finale.

Example 8

Beethoven also uses the motive in the main section. But in order not to anticipate the effect of its entrance in the trio, he deflects it and brings f in the lower octave (measure 23). This again is an extraordinary idea, which, by the way, resembles somewhat the saving in the last movement of the e³ for the coda, omitting it in the recapitulation.

In our analysis of the *Fantaisie-Impromptu* let us start with the "Bellini-an fioriture" of measure 5, as Huneker called the sixteenth-note figures of the right hand. The main mistake one can make here is to read the third quarter as twice d♯²-c♯². The actual meaning is shown at (a) in example 9: The second half of the measure is a repetition of the first one, only in a different position of the chord. Consequently d♯² on the third quarter is an accented passing tone connecting e^2, the last tone of the first group, with $c\sharp^2$, the first tone of the second group.

The first group consists of a turn on $g\sharp^1$ followed by the broken chord $g\sharp^1$-$c\sharp^2$-e^2. Or to describe it more correctly: the first half of the measure reveals the arpeggio $g\sharp^1$-$c\sharp^2$-e^2, the first tone of which is embellished by a turn. The meaning of the whole measure is represented at (b) in example 9.

Example 9

Consequently, the relation between the right hand and the first measures of the left hand now becomes clear. The piece starts like a real phantasy: The left hand, as if improvising, plays broken chords, whose highest tones are g♯, $c\sharp^1$ and e^1; the right hand takes them over and molds them in its own way. Here we clearly see the motive g♯-c♯-e; and, just as at the beginning of the Beethoven work, the motive appears at first in triplets, although otherwise of quite different character.

In the further course of the analysis we shall discover more similarities. At present let us consider the middle section of the composition.

Like the middle movement of the sonata it is written in D♭ major. If we transcribe it from D♭ major to C♯ major and compare its first measures with the opening of the entire composition, we see that it is nothing but a transformation of this opening. And here it becomes even more clear that Chopin's intention was to express the motive $g\sharp^1$-$c\sharp^2$-$e\sharp^2$—he even inverts it in measures 5-6. [See example 10.]

Example 10

But Chopin goes far beyond what is shown at (b) in example 10: He bases the entire first part of the Major section on the motive. The following sketch of measures 11–18 [example 11] may make this clear. It should be noted here that the > mark in measure 17 serves to emphasize f², the goal of the arpeggio motion.

Example 11

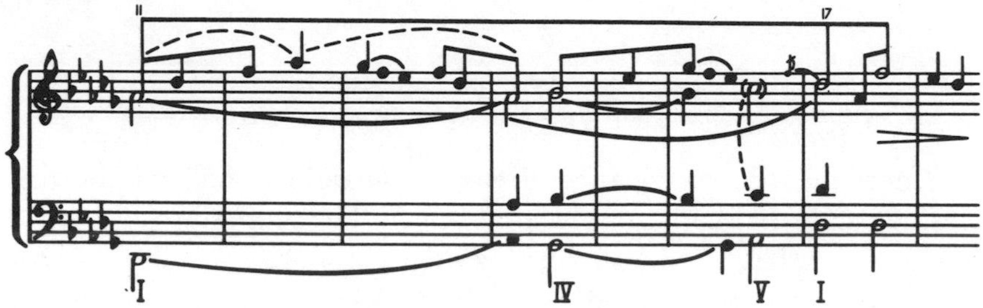

Returning to the C♯ minor section, we find that its middle part (measure 13) starts with an enlargement of the turn motive, after measure 12 has ended with the same motive in the original position. [See example 12.] The arpeggio motive plays a rather subordinate role in this

Example 12

part. In the concluding part, however, it is developed all the more powerfully: In measure 33 we find the turn on g♯², and then on e³, marked with an accent, both an octave higher than at the opening of the composition. In measure 35 Chopin starts again, still higher, with g♯³, and after the two measure chromatic passage he superimposes even e⁴, so that the result is again g♯³–e⁴. Surely g♯–e is not the complete motive, but it obviously stands for it. The succeeding measures make this even clearer. For now, having arrived at the climax e⁴ on the 6 chord, the composer rushes downward from these extreme heights, three times using the inversion of the motive e–c♯–g♯—almost exactly as Beethoven did at the end of the coda of the finale. And, just as Beethoven introduced the inversion by means of the second subject, in the Chopin the inverted motive is contained already in the end of the chromatic passage preceding the climax (see the brackets in example 13 (b)).

Example 13

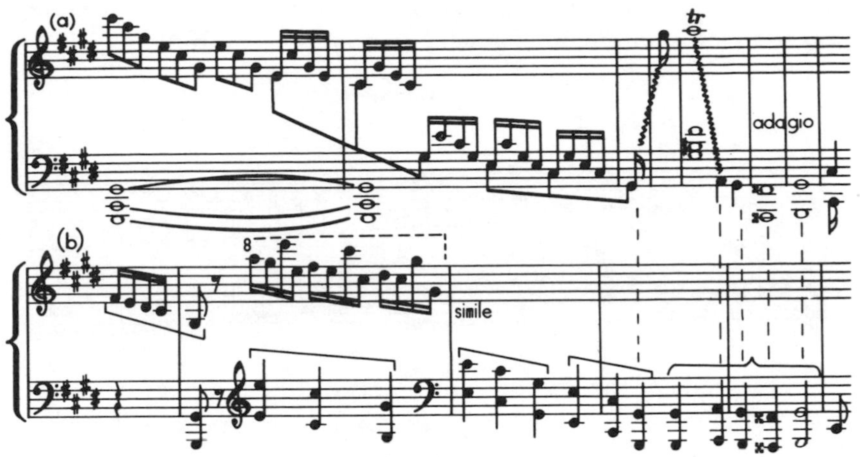

It was Chopin's own particular idea to succeed the inversion immediately with the turn motive (see the brace). The ending (inverted arpeggio and turn) shows the same tones as the beginning of the right hand in measure 5, only almost exactly in reverse order. [See example 14.]

Example 14

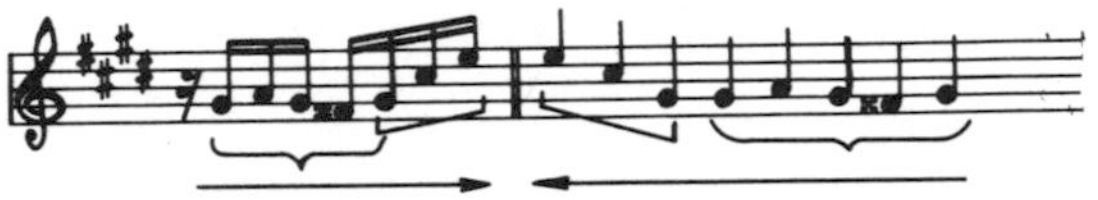

Certainly it was a reminiscence or a conscious imitation of Beethoven that led Chopin to employ the inversion of the motive after the arrival at the climax e^4. But the use of the turn at the conclusion is an idea which, in a limited way, goes beyond the model of Beethoven's sonata. And, although it was Beethoven's idea to invert the opening of the composition toward the end of the movement, Chopin understood this idea, made use of it, and amplified it in a completely personal and magnificent manner.

The strangest phenomenon in the *Fantaisie-Impromptu*, however, is the fact that the imposing thought of concluding the first section with an almost exact "crab" of the beginning owes its existence to a quite ordinary reminiscence of Beethoven. A comparison of parts (a) and (b) of example 13 will show that at once. The significance of this reminiscence shall be discussed later. At any rate, example 13 makes it clear beyond any doubt that a close relation exists between the two compositions.

And, as if the *Fantaisie-Impromptu* were marked by a brand indicating the spiritual proprietor, a passage taken literally from Beethoven's coda has been left standing in measures 7 and 8. [See example 15.]

Example 15

The coda of the *Fantaisie-Impromptu* (the last page of the whole composition) is dominated by the inversion of the arpeggio motive. The left hand plays it constantly in eighth notes and in this way prepares the low register of the concluding C♯ major melody, which contains the motive in both directions (see part (b) of example 10). And the right hand states it several times in different forms, the first time as shown in example 16.

Example 16

If we draw together the threads of our musical discoveries they weave a pattern which reveals the close relation between these two compositions:

1. Identical keys: C♯ minor, D♭ major, C♯ minor;
2. Identical motive: g♯–c♯–e;
3. Both compositions open with triplets;
4. Climax on the $^6_4$ chord on G♯ (example 13), followed by
5. Inversion of the motive at the end of the coda of the sonata as well as at the end of the first section of the *Fantaisie-Impromptu* (example 13);
6. Chopin's reminiscence of the "adagio" of the close of Beethoven's finale (example 13); and
7. The literal quotation of the passage shown in example 15.

Moreover, it is interesting that Chopin's principal biographers disclose the fact that Chopin regarded the sonata very highly, and that his pupils studied it with him.

Niecks speaks of Chopin's "high opinion" and admiration for Beethoven and quotes Liszt as saying:

> However great his admiration for the works of Beethoven might be, certain parts of them seemed to him too rudely fashioned. Their structure was too athletic to please him; their wraths seemed to him too violent . . .[5]

Niecks then continues:

> Chopin said that Beethoven raised him one moment up to the heavens and the next moment precipitated him to the earth, nay, into the very mire. Such a fall Chopin experienced always at the commencement of the last movement of the C minor Symphony.[6] Gutmann, who informed me of this, added that pieces such as the first movement of the Moonlight Sonata (C♯ minor) were most highly appreciated by his master.

Later on Niecks quotes Lenz:

> He did not take a very serious interest in Beethoven; he knew only his principal compositions, the last works not at all [II, p. 111].

This being so, it is especially interesting that the C♯ minor sonata was in his "teaching repertoire" (according to Gutmann, one of his favorite pupils)[7]:

> Beethoven he seemed to like less. He appreciated such pieces as the first movement of the Moonlight Sonata (C-sharp minor, Op. 27, No. 2).

And, also according to Niecks, Madame Dubois studied with him:

> of Beethoven, the concertos and several sonatas (the Moonlight, Op. 27, No. 2; the one with the Funeral March, Op. 26; and the Appassionata, Op. 57).

The fact that the first movement has been mentioned twice does not mean that Chopin did not approve of the finale. It is quite obvious that the first movement, in its ethereal dreamy vein, very closely approached Chopin's character. But it would be wrong to assume that the last movement was too tempestuous, too robust or too "rude" for him. In this respect Chopin himself goes even farther in some of his compositions, as for example at the opening of the recapitulation of the B minor Scherzo, Op. 20, written only one year after the *Fantaisie-Impromptu*. Furthermore, it is extremely improbable that he had his pupil, Madame Dubois, study only the first movement instead of the whole sonata. And if Niecks said (after Lenz):

> He did not take a very serious interest in Beethoven; he knew only his principal compositions,

5. Niecks, *Frederick Chopin*, vol. 2, p. 110.
6. Niecks probably means the sudden forte entrance of the horns at the beginning of the scherzo.
7. Niecks, *Frederick Chopin*, vol. 2, p. 189.

and if, on the other hand, the C♯ minor Sonata is mentioned three times, this proves that the C♯ minor Sonata was one of those compositions with which he was thoroughly familiar. In other words, he must have found it in some respect interesting and remarkable.

To the seven similarities between the *Fantaisie-Impromptu* and Beethoven's C♯ minor Sonata we can therefore add an eighth point corroborating our thesis: According to the biographers, Chopin took a particular interest in the sonata. No other one of Beethoven's compositions is mentioned so often in the biographies.

We now have to deal with an extremely difficult question: Of what particular nature is the relation between the two compositions? At first one is inclined to consider it a reminiscence of unusual proportions. Yet a true reminiscence always has some of the characteristics of the following examples [example 17].

Example 17

Schubert, Sonata in G Major, Op. 78

Brahms, Rhapsody in B Minor, Op. 79, No. 1

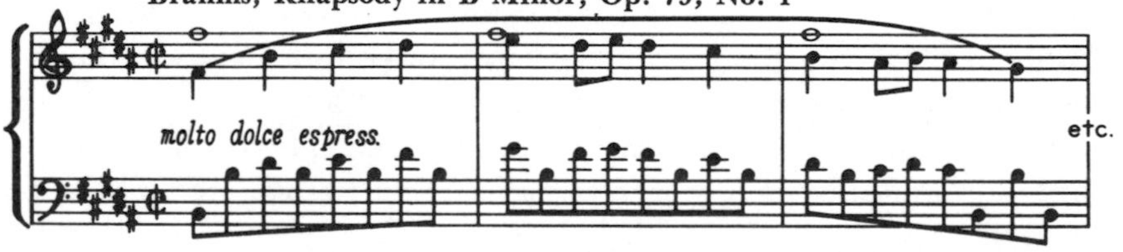

The composer has a faint recollection of a musical idea or a sound which remained in his ear from another composition. Without being conscious of its origin he uses it in his own composition, although completely reshaped in his personal style. The quotation of Brahms, for example, has an entirely different musical content than the one of Schubert, of which it no doubt is a reminiscence.

Can we really see an unconscious reminiscence in the *Fantaisie-Impromptu*, which follows Beethoven's finale in so many essential points? Perhaps one could assume this of the passage given in example 15, which might have flowed from Chopin's pen without his being aware of the "plagiarism." But if we remember the glorious plan of Beethoven's coda with its inversion of the motive, which Chopin follows exactly, it is inconceivable that he should have done this unconsciously too. We must rather conclude that he was so impressed by the idea of the last movement and the coda that he consciously followed it.

We can therefore say: The fact that the *Fantaisie-Impromptu* consciously redraws—one might almost say copies—some of the main features of Beethoven's finale is the reason why Chopin kept it from publication. Surely he did not have to fear that the "plagiarism" would be discovered. More than 90 years have passed since Fontana published the piece, and innumerable artists and music-lovers have played and studied it without anyone's realizing the state of affairs. People have racked their brains about what might be "wrong" with the composition, but all that storming did not lead them to a deeper understanding. Rather they took refuge in the vague explanation that the piece was simply "no good" or even showed lack of taste—an explanation that certainly does not withstand the test.

The real explanation is that Chopin possessed the modesty of a truly great man, and a feeling of responsibility toward art that did not permit him to publish the *Fantaisie-Impromptu*. To him it was not an authentic, not an independently wrought composition. And even if it were entirely obscure, for Chopin it was only a kind of study after Beethoven, and he made his decision accordingly.

Certainly it is a study worthy of the genius of a Chopin. Aside from the coda with its inversion of the motive, it is a rather autonomous composition, having in common with the Beethoven only the basic motive g♯–c♯–e and a few minor features. It differs from Beethoven, among other points, insofar as it uses two motives, the turn and the arpeggio, whereas Beethoven confines himself to one. But how inconspicuously Chopin introduces the motive of a turn (example 9), presenting it at first just as an embellishment of the first tone of the arpeggio motive! Only from measure 13 on it becomes independent and grows to an almost tragic greatness in the coda, where it concludes the "crab" and the whole first section.

And yet we must say that Beethoven's composition is still more powerful. The interruption of the big arpeggio in measure 9, and in the recapitulation the saving of e^3 for the coda, are truly titanic deeds, the like of which Chopin's genius, smaller as it was, could not accomplish.[8]

One point still remains to be clarified: How is it possible that the turn at the end of Chopin's coda is of such an eminent motivic significance, although it seems to owe its existence just to a superficial reminiscence of Beethoven's bass line (example 13)? If we want to answer this question also, it must be clear to us that by so doing we must leave the firm ground of provable facts and enter the uncertain field of conjecture.

We have not yet mentioned one obvious circumstance, the fact that most similarities between the two compositions originate from Beethoven's coda. Not only do we see the striking correlation of parts (a) and (b) of example 13, but the passage in example 15 is also taken from the coda, connecting the trill with the low bass notes A and G♯. This looks exactly as if Beethoven's coda had especially interested Chopin and had almost fascinated him.

Is it too daring to assume then that Chopin proceeded in the following way when he wrote the *Fantaisie-Impromptu*? He heard in the Beethoven that the inversion of the arpeggio motive was followed by something like a turn. That gave him the idea to use the arpeggio and turn motives to create the beginning of a new piece, by re-inverting the inverted motive and placing them in reverse order (example 14)—just as in the Beethoven the downward arpeggio motive was the inversion of the beginning. Described in other words, our assumption is that in composing Chopin started out with the coda and derived the opening from it as a kind of a "crab"—that he did not proceed the other way around as the finished composition would indicate.

This interpretation of the resemblance of parts (a) and (b) of example 13 and of the meaning of the turn in the Chopin in contrast to the same tones in Beethoven may appear rather audacious. The generally accepted picture of Chopin does not portray him as a speculative composer who produces his ideas by the process of intellectual construction.

However, we must not forget how much mere brainwork has to go into even the simplest piece of music (not to mention very complicated compositions), as every composer knows from his own experience. Furthermore, we must be cautious in rejecting this interpretation simply because nothing of all that we have found in the two compositions was known until now. Since we but faintly see the horizon of the world of art

8. A comparison of both composers' inversion of the motive (examples 6 and 13) throws an interesting light on their individual talents.

of which Chopin and Beethoven were masters, our humility prevents us from categorically denying a theory like the one brought forth.

However it may be—whether the *Fantaisie-Impromptu* is something in the middle of the road between a reminiscence and an imitation, or is quite consciously a study after Beethoven, or if Chopin developed or constructed his opening from Beethoven's coda—one thing is clear beyond doubt: Chopin understood Beethoven! He understood him, despite the fact that some of Beethoven's compositions did not suit his taste. Reports by his contemporaries to this effect are probably true to fact. But our comparison of the two compositions proves that there are quite different things in music that are at least as interesting to a great artist as questions of mere taste. We still know next to nothing about them, and it is very uncertain whether circumstances will ever be altered. But with the aid of the *Fantaisie-Impromptu* we can at least recognize what particular features of the C♯ minor Sonata struck fire in Chopin. We can actually regard Chopin as our teacher as he points to the coda and says: "Look here, this is great. Take heed of this example!"

Chopin understood Beethoven to a degree that no one who has written on the C♯ minor Sonata or the *Fantaisie Impromptu* has ever understood him. It is true that an understanding as penetrating as his goes far beyond what can be expected from a theoretician and a writer on music; and, as we said at the beginning of this article, we owe it only to Heinrich Schenker and his profound ideas on music that we were able to follow Beethoven and Chopin in their musical ideas to a point that has hitherto been inaccessible.

Chopin understood precisely what Beethoven expressed, but it is doubtful if anyone else after him understood Beethoven in this sonata. We may assume though that men like Mendelssohn and Brahms were able to follow Beethoven. But they were composers, not writers on music, and therefore they did not explain in what way they listened to Beethoven's music. The *Fantaisie-Impromptu* is perhaps the only instance where one genius discloses to us—if only by means of a composition of his own—what he actually hears in the work of another genius. And if we realize how much has been spoken and written ineptly about the Moonlight Sonata during the past century and a half, and how the one Frederic Chopin had something enlightening to say that was in accordance with its musical actualities, then we know what Robert Schumann meant when, in a mood of resignation or after a bitter experience, he said: "Vielleicht versteht nur der Genius den Genius ganz."—"Perhaps only the genius fully understands the genius."

The Dramatic Character of the *Egmont Overture*

ERNST OSTER

Richard Wagner, in addition to being a revolutionary composer and innovator, also had a profound influence on the esthetics of music. Because of his influence, Beethoven's "dramatic" overtures—*Coriolan, Egmont, Leonore Nos. 2 and 3*—were considered for a long time as forerunners of Liszt's symphonic poems, if not true symphonic poems themselves. Wagner even went so far as to consider that the *Coriolan Overture* depicts only one scene of the drama, the scene involving Coriolanus, his mother, and his wife in the military camp at the gates of his native town. However, this interpretation, interesting as it may seem, is not necessarily binding. And, what is more significant, Wagner's commentary fails to explain any purely musical fact in the composition, for example the tremendous opening of the recapitulation in F minor rather than C minor.

Today there exists a general aversion to Wagner's kind of approach to Beethoven's music, although this aversion seems to be more instinctive than based on reasoning. Perhaps it is felt that minor composers too wrote music that seems to be just as dramatic as Beethoven's overtures or as descriptive as the "thunderstorm" from the Pastoral Symphony. And yet these minor composers wrote weaker compositions. Consequently the difference between their and Beethoven's compositions must be elsewhere than in their descriptiveness. The determining factor in the greatness of Beethoven's overtures lies in how, from a purely musical standpoint, he wrote compositions of a dramatic nature.

On the other hand, one cannot go so far as to deny completely the possibility or the existence of descriptive features in music. If, for example, Beethoven, in one of his sketches to "Clärchen's Death," writes: "Death might be expressed by a rest," [a] he obviously thought this to be possible from an esthetic point of view. Even Bach's innumerable tone paintings in his Chorale Preludes for organ, which are of the same kind as those in his vocal music, have always been considered absolute music. We come closer to the true meaning of these phenomena if we do not consider them to be descriptive details, but ascribe to them symbolic sig-

[a] Gustav Nottebohm, "Ein Skizzenheft aus dem Jahre 1810," *Zweite Beethoveniana,* Leipzig: J. Rieter-Biedermann, 1887, p. 277n.

nificance. For the symbol plays an important role in the other arts, most obviously in the architecture of Bach's time, and accordingly in the music as well. And there is no doubt that Beethoven's "dramatic" overtures possess a highly forceful vigor and a narrative quality which is inescapable. But what is the reason for their dramatic strength if they are not descriptive music, nor symphonic poems? The problem is extremely complex, and to solve it in its entirety would be almost impossible.

In the *Egmont Overture* the problem is a little easier to solve because at least we know the "meaning" of its concluding F major section: Beethoven uses it, detached from the rest of the overture, as the "Victory Symphony" at the conclusion of the Incidental Music. Here it points toward the final triumph over death and oppression. However, for the introduction and the main section, the Allegro, there exist no similar clues, and whatever we feel while listening to them is our own personal response, which may be entirely different from that of our neighbor. At the most, we can say that the introduction has an oppressive, tragic character, that the Allegro is rather passionate, and that at the end of this Allegro a dramatic climax, which resembles the "catastrophe" in the classical drama, is reached. But we certainly would go too far if we considered that this sudden breaking-off depicted Egmont's execution. If it did, it would mean that the listener knew the plot of the drama which he is not yet supposed to have seen. And if we said that the second theme described Egmont's love for Clärchen or Clärchen herself, we would become lost in unfounded speculation. "Explanations" such as these are so problematical that they are uninteresting in a serious exploration of the facts.

If we want to find out the exact impression the overture creates in us we must strictly follow the work itself. This may sound trivial, but just the simplicity of this principle will prevent us from repeating Wagner's mistake, which was to transform prematurely into feelings and pictures what he heard in the music. We must try rather to delve as deeply as possible into the musical course of events to see where this method of procedure will lead us. However, the music theory commonly employed is not sufficient for our purpose. As in the article on Chopin's *Fantaisie-Impromptu*,[1] we will instead use the approach of Heinrich Schenker, the eminent musician and musicologist whose ideas have found an ever-increasing number of followers.

The kind of sketches used here, specifically examples 4, 5, and 7, shows with sufficient clearness to what extent Schenker's conception of

1. Ernst Oster, "The *Fantaisie-Impromptu*: A Tribute to Beethoven," *Musicology* 1, pp. 407–429.

music deviates from and far surpasses any other theory of music. Music as an art occurring in time cannot be understood in terms of static harmonies, motives, and themes. We must try to perceive the flow of music, how it develops, how one thought grows from the other, and how it all hangs together.

It is an opinion sometimes expressed that Schenker permits us to explain and see only the "technical" side of the musical work of art. On the contrary: Just because Schenker enables us to throw light into the utmost depths of a composition, we reach the point where matter and spirit blend. Actually, of course, they are inseparable; one is inconceivable without the other. But no shortcut exists to arrive at that point—no approach *à la* Wagner will lead us there. Only the most thorough "technical" analysis will help us to reach this goal, and we are much indebted to Schenker for giving us the means of fathoming musical works of art in a manner hitherto unknown.

Before going into a detailed analysis of the introduction, some facts regarding the whole Overture are pertinent. Really, did no one ever notice that the new motif of the D-flat major section in the introduction (example 1, part a), which also opens the Allegro (b), appears inverted later on in the Victory Symphony (c), again inverted and enlarged in the basses (d)—Beethoven writes *marcato* at this place!—and shortly afterward in the violins (e)? From the last four tones is derived the whistling motif of the piccolo in the very last measures, which, as we shall see, has particular significance.

Example 1

Even the second subject of the Allegro section is based on the same motif, but it is somewhat more concealed and less easily detected [see example 2]:

Example 2

How homogeneous the work appears to us now, and how the great master Beethoven uses his material with artistic economy! But beyond this technical explanation, quite definite emotional effects are produced by the inversion of the motif in the final section and its enlargement and extension to the second theme. And it is certain that no one can feel these effects in the right way if he does not hear accurately what is going on in the tonal matter. It would lead us too far astray to explain at this point what particular effects are produced by these musical occurrences. Rather, this would be the task of musical esthetics or even of psychology. It is the task of the musician to uncover musical relationships and facts which until now have been unknown.

It is surprising that even such a great musician as Wagner did not understand the second theme. He quotes it in his essay, *Ueber das Dirigieren.*[b] [See example 3.]

Example 3

This quotation shows clearly that he felt the relatively unimportant quarter notes of the last measure are more significant than the dotted half note c^2 which finishes the motif. It is said very often that the performing musician need not know such musical facts and that in performance the musical instinct is sufficient to present them in a manner appropriate to a particular composition. Wagner's quotation of the second theme is a striking refutation of this contention. If Wagner's instinct had felt the tone c^2 to be important, he would doubtless have written it as a dotted half note and as the continuation of the notes stemmed upward, not as a quarter note with the stem drawn downward. Furthermore, the way he writes the fourth measure shows that even in his interpretation he laid greater stress on the notes stemmed upward than on the c^2, and that his instinct—the instinct of a Richard Wagner!—misled him.

This second theme also shows us that in order really to understand Beethoven we must listen not only to what we usually call the "melody" (in the second theme the quarter notes), but the lengthy drawn-out connections and more elusive details as well.

[b] Richard Wagner, "Ueber das Dirigiren," *Gesammelte Schriften und Dichtungen*, Leipzig: E. W. Fritzsch, 1871-1880, Band 8.

In analyzing the introduction of the overture in detail, we shall discover even more surprising facts than those brought to light so far. Actually, what goes on in the introduction is of a much more complicated nature than the first four measures of the second theme, which are comparatively simple. Therefore, only those details which are essential to our specific investigation will be dealt with. Details regarding the harmony and the bass line will be discussed only insofar as is absolutely necessary.

There is another composition that, like the *Egmont Overture*, begins with a long drawn-out unison: Schubert's *Impromptu in C minor*, Op. 90, No. 1. A comparison of the two openings is extremely interesting. The unison of Schubert sounds, figuratively speaking, like a trumpet blare before the opening of a drama, or like a great "Hear ye." It is as if the stage were being set for the drama. After this, the play, or the narration, starts, and for quite a while there is no connection between the unison G and what it precedes. We can even experiment and abandon this first measure—the meaning of what follows will not be distorted.

In the *Egmont Overture* this experiment is not feasible: Although the unison (F) at first creates the same effect as Schubert's does, it is so closely connected with what follows that it is impossible to cut it off. In other words, it opens the drama in the sense that it leads directly into it, that it is itself part of the action, whereas in the Schubert *Impromptu* it was only a preparation of the drama to follow. In the *Impromptu* it was like the proclamation of a herald, after which the curtain rose; in the overture it is like the first outcry of one of the characters the moment after the curtain is raised and the drama has begun.

This impression originates from the simple fact that in the Beethoven the initial f^1 continues in the upper voice to $e^{\flat 1}$ in measure 4, both tones therefore being inseparably connected (example 4). Later on we will see that the step f^1–$e^{\flat 1}$ is only the beginning of a widely stretched-out line that is of the greatest importance for the composition as a whole.

For the present let us follow the progression f^1–$e^{\flat 1}$ further. $e^{\flat 1}$ is part of a $\frac{6}{4}$ chord on G, and therefore we expect it to go on to d^1 and thence to c^1. c^1 appears, but not so d^1; we find it only in the lower octave, as a middle voice in the viola. But since it logically ought to appear in the higher octave, which is where we *expect* it, we hear at this point the breaking off of a line which should be f^1–$e^{\flat 1}$–$d^{\natural 1}$–c^1. We therefore write d^1 in our sketch, but in parentheses only. What we *really* hear is f^1–$e^{\flat 1}$, and then c^1, *piano*. Underlying the music is the idea of a line running without interruption from f^1 to c^1.

Since this passage will be repeated later on in a similar way, it is necessary to mention briefly measures 2 to 4. The tone $e^{\flat 1}$ is "fetched" from below, from $a^{\flat}$, and in such a way that the step-progression from $a^{\flat}$ to $e^{\flat 1}$ is subdivided at c^1, as is easily heard. This is indicated by the two slurs in the sketch.

In the oboe solo (measures 5 to 7) the main tones are without doubt f^2 and $e^{\flat 2}$. Thus this new melody proves to be a kind of altered repetition of the two tones f^1 and $e^{\flat 1}$ in measures 1 and 4. The violins repeat the same tone-pattern in measures 7 and 8, but this time as f^1–$e^{\natural 1}$, which leads us back to f^1 (measure 9). Later we will explain the first four quarter notes of the oboe part. At this point we will mention only that the initial c^2–b^1 takes up the conclusion of the violins (b–c^1) in measure 5.

So far the bass line is simple: Basically, it proceeds from F at the beginning via G in measure 4 to the dominant, C, which remains until F re-enters in measure 9.

It will be easier to understand the following measures (9–15) if we are at first clear in our mind about the bass line. Again we start from F and move to A$^{\flat}$, exactly as in measure 3 (see parts (a) and (b) of example 5). This A$^{\flat}$ is continued — the two neighbor notes b and g in measure 13 do not alter this fact — until it leads us to D$^{\flat}$, of which it proves to be the dominant, in measure 15. On a large scale we thus went only from F to D$^{\flat}$. At the end of the introduction this D$^{\flat}$ leads to C, the dominant of F minor, and thus is actually nothing but the upper neighbor note of C ("NN" in the sketch). The D$^{\flat}$ is extended and seemingly establishes D-flat major as an independent key.

It is far more difficult to understand the top voice in measures 9 to 15. Measures 9–11 are a repetition of measures 1–3, the only difference being that the full orchestra participates. But the repetition of measure 4, which we now expect, fails to materialize.

Example 4

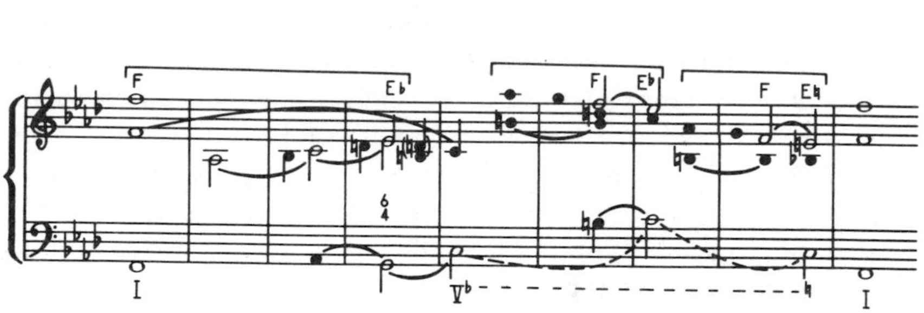

Example 5

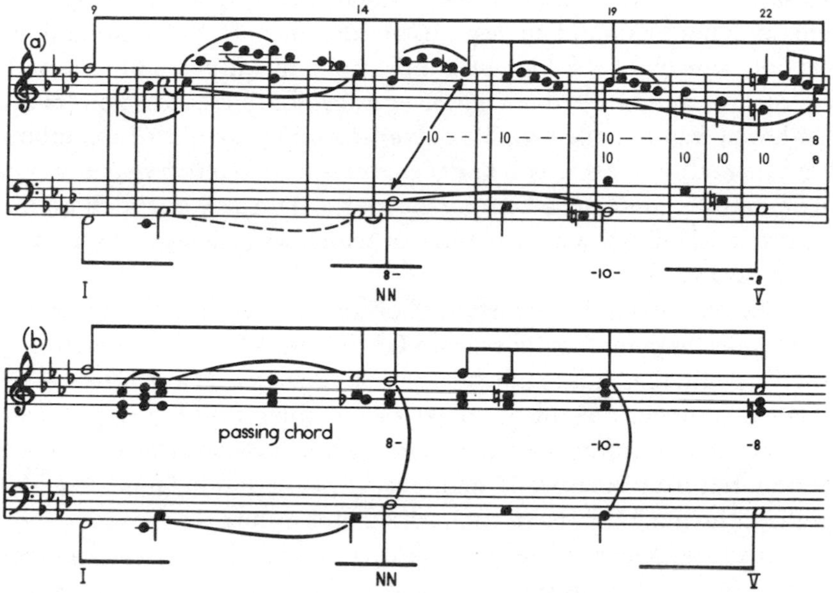

Level (b) is a further reduction of (a), showing the harmonic progressions omitted there for the sake of clarity.

Let us recall what the function of measure 4 was. We said that f^1 continues to $e^{\flat 1}$. Between these two tones we skip down to $a^{\flat}$ (measure 2) in order to "fetch" $e^{\flat 1}$ from below. In measure 10 Beethoven starts again in the same manner, and therefore we again expect an $e^{\flat}$ with which to continue the F of measure 9. This $e^{\flat 2}$ actually does appear at the end of measure 14, although in an entirely different way than in measure 4 and under altered circumstances. I do not intend to comment on all the details of measures 12 to 14; instead the reader is referred to the sketches in example 5, which are almost self-explanatory. The general idea is as follows: $e^{\flat 2}$, which in measure 14 is part of the seventh chord on $A^{\flat}$, leads to $d^{\flat 2}$ simultaneously with the resolution of this chord to the $D^{\flat}$ chord. In other words: $f^{2\,(1)}$ (measure 9)–$e^{\flat 2}$–$d^{\flat 2}$ is the main progression; subordinate to it is the motion from $a^{\flat 1}$ in measure 10 over c^2 in measure 11 to the $e^{\flat 2}$ in measure 14. But what happens in measures 12 to 14? As in measures 3–4, c^2 proceeds to $e^{\flat 2}$ by a passing tone, which this time is not $d^{\natural 1}$ but $d^{\flat 2}$ (measures 12–13); the chord beneath $d^{\flat 2}$ is a passing $^6_4$ chord. What a stroke of genius to use the idea of the woodwinds of measures 5 to 7 to elaborate this section from c^2 to $e^{\flat 2}$, thus combining simultaneously the idea of measures 3-4 (c, d, $e^{\flat}$) with the one of measures 5 to 7! What a light this passage throws on Beethoven's art in general. That he should conceive of an idea such as this combination is certainly worthy of the highest admiration. But it probably has to be regarded as an even higher sign of extraordinary creative powers that Beethoven was actually capable of transforming his idea of a combination into reality, especially if one recognizes how heterogeneous, almost incompatible, are its two component parts. To carry out such an idea requires an ability to write, the like of which was possessed by only the very great masters.

The remainder of the introduction requires but little comment. As our sketch shows the bass goes from $D^{\flat}$ through C to $B^{\flat}$ in measure 19, and this $B^{\flat}$ finally leads to C in measure 22. Between $B^{\flat}$ and C Beethoven descends by means of thirds, $B^{\flat}$-(G-E)-C, inverting the step upward $B^{\flat}$-C into a descending seventh. If we now take a look at the upper voice, we find that from measure 15 on it progresses in parallel tenths with the bass (see the marking 10-10-10 in the sketch); the f^2 in the top voice in measure 15 is clearly more important than $a^{\flat 2}$, since Beethoven continues it to $e^{\flat 2}$, whereas the $a^{\flat 2}$ fails to lead anywhere. (The new motive in measure 15—see (a) in example 1—is quite obviously derived from measures 13 to 14.) In measure 19 we have arrived again at $d^{\flat 2}$, now above $B^{\flat}$ in the bass. It then continues to c^2 (measure 22), always in parallel motion with the bass, $d^{\flat 2}$-($b^{\flat}$-g-e)-c^2. And thus we have arrived at the end of the introduction.

The bass note $B^{\flat}$ (measure 19) has a purely contrapuntal meaning. Basically, the $D^{\flat}$ of measure 15 proceeds directly to C in measure 22. Since, however, the upper voice also moves from $d^{\flat 2}$ to c^2, $B^{\flat}$ in the bass has been inserted to do away with the octaves (see the marking 8-10-8 in the sketch at level (b)).

What does all this add up to? We have seen the main progression of the top voice, f^2-$e^{\flat 2}$-$d^{\flat 2}$-c^2, in measures 9, 14, 15, and 22. In measure 15, after having reached $d^{\flat 2}$, Beethoven starts once again: f^2-$e^{\flat 2}$-$d^{\flat 2}$ (measures 15, 17, 19), whereupon this $d^{\flat 2}$ joins the chief $d^{\flat 2}$ and proceeds with it to the final c^2. Here, at the final c^2, the oboe once again states f^2-$e^{\natural 2}$-$d^{\flat 2}$-c^2. Thus we see before us the same motif in three different dimensions encased in one another. The *espressivo* for the woodwinds in measure 22 indicates the significance of the motif and of this measure in which all three motives are dovetailed. But the word *espressivo* reveals even more to us. For if we take a glance at the Allegro, we soon find (in measures 36–37) a < > mark, which is a special form of *espressivo*. And here we find the motif, three times in succession. [See example 6.]

Example 6

This surprising "citation" of the motif of the introduction makes it clear beyond doubt how conscious Beethoven must have been of all this while writing the overture. The line f–$e^{\flat}$–$d^{\flat}$–c with its bass not only provided a kind of skeleton for the introduction (see example 7), thus making it a coherent whole, but, as the citation shows, it was for Beethoven a musical idea, a real "motif." Although this becomes apparent with numerous repetitions *within* the introduction, it becomes even clearer through the quotation of the motif (which represents the entire introduction) *outside* it, in the Allegro.

Example 7

The psychological effect of the quotation in the Allegro may be described in the following way. The introduction was dominated by the slowly and heavily descending motif of a fourth. The remainder of the motivic material and everything else took place within its frame. That is why the introduction makes such a motionless, undramatic impression; it is as if it depicted only a state of affairs, only a situation. But now the Allegro, which has an entirely different character and meaning, appears—it picks up and quotes the motif. The entire content of the introduction was subservient to this motif. The Allegro, however, frees itself from its bonds and actively takes the motif into its own hands, molds it, and later on even transforms it.

The significance of the foregoing in relation to the drama *Egmont* is best left to the judgment of the individual. It will not be too difficult to recognize the analogies.

Let us return to the introduction. If we look at the first four measures with what we now know about the motif of a fourth, we are finally able to recognize their true meaning. We are witnessing how the motif of a fourth is born and develops, until it reaches its final state of maturity. As previously explained, the underlying idea of measures 1 to 5 was the uninterrupted line f^1-$e^{\flat 1}$-d^1-c^1, which appeared incomplete without d^1. And what other meaning do $a^{\flat 2}$ and g^2 (oboe, measure 5) have but that they, together with the main tones f^2 and $e^{\flat 2}$, make possible the four-tone idea which appears here really for the first time? [See example 8.]

Example 8

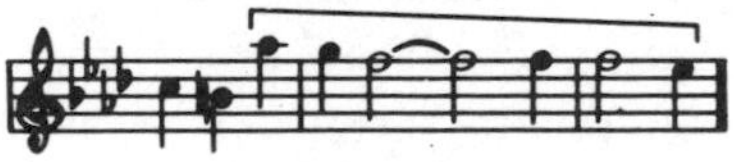

See brackets in example 4.

Of course this idea is also contained in the new motif of measure 15 (example 1, part a) which Beethoven later uses as the beginning of the Allegro (part b). We have previously mentioned that the first four measures of the second theme are based on an enlargement of this motif (example 2). Additionally, the four-tone motive is again present in measures 2–4 of the second theme, and, what is particularly astonishing, it even appears in the same position as in the introduction (f-e♭-d♭-c), not transposed to A-flat major. Its meaning of course is completely changed, since now f^1 has become the neighbor note of $e^{\flat 1}$ and is no longer one of the tones establishing the main harmony. And yet it is not merely coincidental that the tones are identical, as could easily be assumed; there exists a very subtle connection between this point and measure 37 (example 6). Unfortunately, to describe the nature of this connection would require lengthy discussion. It must suffice to mention the fact of its existence.

However, it whould be noted that the *Egmont Overture* is not singular in its literal use of part of the first theme in the second subject. Beethoven, in his Piano Sonata, Op. 111, bases his second theme partly on a repetition of the eighth notes of the first theme (a♭-g-f-e♭-d-(c)), after having repeated even the beginning of the first theme, though freely altered. In this respect the first movement of Mozart's Sonata in D major (K. 576) comes still closer to the *Egmont Overture*, because the four notes $c^{\sharp 2}$-d^2-e^2-$f^{\sharp 2}$ recur constantly, until they finally assume different meaning in the A major section and in the measures marked *dolce*.

The motif of a fourth contained in the second subject of the *Egmont Overture* lends it a kind of somber undertone, despite the brisk beginning of the theme. Of course the skip into the higher octave and the change from the strings to the woodwinds somewhat counteract this impression, since they almost split the first four measures and their underlying motif into two parts. It is absolutely necessary, therefore, for the conductor to be conscious of the motif and to connect closely these two groups, in order to keep them from falling apart.

The importance of the knowledge of these and similar facts for the interpretation cannot be emphasized too much. A conductor who is conscious of the significance of the motif in measure 37 (example 6) will bring it out with more passion and fervor, since he feels the whole introduction compressed into it and expressed by it. And if he is aware of the fact that f^2 in measure 9 will eventually move on to $e^{\flat 2}$ and $d^{\flat 2}$ in measures 14 and 15, he will resist the temptation of dwelling with too great devotion on the woodwind episode between these points. Lyrical as it is, he will feel that it is only a transient phase in the larger plot of the introduction. By keeping $e^{\flat 2}$ and $d^{\flat 2}$, the goal, in mind, he will make the woodwind part recede and thereby maintain the secondary importance of this minor episode.

The compass of this study precludes a comprehensive analysis of the second theme. However, it should be pointed out that in measure 92, in the woodwinds, we hear the four-tone motif ascending: e-f♯-g♯-a. Obviously the A major chord must be read as a $B^{\flat\flat}$ chord, and consequently e♮, with which the motive starts, as $f^{\flat}$. Thus it becomes clear that the ascending motif starting from $f^{\flat}$ (e♮) in measure 92 replaces the descending motif of measures 83–85, which started from $f^{\natural 1}$ and which we also expect in measure 91, perhaps as shown in example 9.

Example 9

Earlier, in measure 66, we find a similar kind of replacement of the descending version by the ascending one. After the first theme of the Allegro has been repeated *fortissimo* we expect the motif to appear as in measure 37 (example 6). Instead it appears in the reverse direction.

Measures 68–70 are a contraction of [example 10], so that the motif even appears in the same position as in measure 37, only inverted. In other words, Beethoven introduces the inversion both times at just the places where the motif is expected in its original direction. This is an ingenious use of artistic means to achieve a dramatic effect. The contrast between the expected descending motif and the more active ascending one makes the inversion all the more striking.

Example 10

Let us proceed to the concluding part of the overture, the Victory Symphony. We mentioned previously that the motif opening this section (example 1, part c) is an inversion of the "D-flat major" motif of the introduction (measure 15) and of the beginning of the Allegro. We must add that it also contains the motif of a fourth in the ascending direction.

In measure 307 (measure 21 of the Victory Symphony) something extraordinary happens. We have, in a way, arrived at the end of the composition, and what follows has the character of a coda. The horns, and the *sforzati* in the other instruments, repeat f^1–g^1, f^1–g^1, which are the concluding tones of the brass instruments in measures 306–307. If we detach the tone g^1 in the new idea of the 'celli, the result is f^1–$e^{\flat 1}$–$d^{\natural 1}$–$d^{\flat 1}$–c^1, again the motif, introduced by the eighth notes in the two preceding measures. [See example 11.]

Example 11

At the coda, that is at the beginning of the end of the entire composition, we look back, one last time, to the starting point, the introduction. But, since we now find ourselves in F major, the motif appears as a combination of F minor and F major; $e^{\flat 1}$ and $d^{\flat 1}$ are part of the original minor version, yet $d^{\natural 1}$ confirms the fact that F minor has been decisively overcome. For $d^{\natural 1}$, owing to its rhythmic position, is considerably stronger than $e^{\flat 1}$ and especially $d^{\flat 1}$, which now sounds almost like a chromatic passing tone. This is the last time that we encounter the motif in the descending direction. After two measures the violins join with a counterpart that contains the ascending motif, triumphantly effacing the descending version. In measure 315 the basses take over this counterpart and continue with the enlargement of the motif (example 1, part d). The same motif is also contained in the eighth notes beginning in measure 341 (shortly before the end)—see example 1, part e; the last four notes of this gesture are identical with the motif of the fourth. And the motif of the fourth is all that remains in the last measures: The piccolo states it inverted in major, in the uttermost diminution, high above the full orchestra.[2] [See example 12.]

Example 12

Who would suspect, in a less thorough examination of the overture than ours, that this little motif, which sounds like an almost meaningless whistling in a military band, is so closely related to the introduction in its full extension? What a contrast between the beginning and end of the overture! There the motif is present in minor, here in major; there descending, here ascending; there slowly sinking down in gigantic, heavy steps and embracing all the secondary ideas (even the brighter D-flat major episode), here a short military whistling. How different this whistling sounds to our ears if we remember its musical origin, how fraught it is with the deepest meaning! It is a victory symphony in the literal sense of the word, and we are witness to that struggle and ultimate triumph. We hear the drama of a motif as it frees itself from tragic somberness, as it undergoes various transformations and finally emerges victoriously. We see in this work what the full implication of a title such as "Victory Symphony" is to a composer like Beethoven. For Beethoven did not depict the "victory" in an external way, for example, only by means of the orchestration; rather the title has a much deeper meaning than one at first would be inclined to believe.

2. In the Sonata in C major for violoncello, Op. 102, No. 1, Beethoven inverts a motif of a fourth, though much more obviously than in the *Egmont Overture*.

To be sure, this drama takes place in a different sphere from that of everyday reality—it is a drama in the world of tone. We cannot say that it follows Goethe's drama step by step, nor that it is shaped exactly after it. But then, is Egmont, the Egmont in Goethe's play, an imitation of the real, historic Egmont, and is he not also purely the "idea" of Egmont? No, it is never the task of art to imitate reality and to create the illusion of the real world before our eyes. For only if art transforms reality into a free play of our spirit will it raise us above our physical life and make us free. In order to make this transformation possible it must "stylize" reality, adapt it to the laws of art, and therefore it no longer shows us reality itself, but a symbol of reality.

Just as the drama cannot imitate actual life, so music cannot imitate drama. What we hear in music, as for example the drama of the motif in the *Egmont Overture*, are occurrences of symbolic nature, and as such they assume in our mind a relationship with the happenings in Goethe's tragedy. There exist certain analogies between them, and they make it possible to have the overture precede the drama Egmont. In each, the drama and the overture, the happenings are shaped in a way that conforms with the laws and necessities of their respective materials—the laws and necessities of the drama and those of music, which are fundamentally different. That is why a direct comparison of the *Egmont Overture* with Goethe's *Egmont*, in the manner in which Wagner compared the *Corolian Overture* with the drama *Coriolanus*, is impossible. Only by an unprejudiced examination of the two works of art, separately, can we recognize their true meaning, and thus also find the analogies that exist between them.